# THE PAN-INDUSTRIAL REVOLUTION

# THE
# PAN-INDUSTRIAL
# REVOLUTION

---

HOW NEW MANUFACTURING TITANS

WILL TRANSFORM THE WORLD

---

# RICHARD D'AVENI

HOUGHTON MIFFLIN HARCOURT
Boston   New York   2018

To my grandparents, Antonio and Rosa D'Aveni:
thank you for your bravery in coming to America.

And to my parents, Anthony and Marion D'Aveni:
thank you for all you did to make me a better person.

The four of you taught me the meaning of family.
I'll love you all for the rest of my days.
May you rest in peace.

---

Copyright © 2018 by Richard D'Aveni

For information about permission to reproduce selections from this book,
write to trade.permissions@hmhco.com or to Permissions,
Houghton Mifflin Harcourt Publishing Company,
3 Park Avenue, 19th Floor, New York, New York 10016.

hmhco.com

*Library of Congress Cataloging-in-Publication Data*
Names: D'Aveni, Richard A., author.
Title: The pan-industrial revolution : how new manufacturing
titans will transform the world / Richard D'Aveni.
Description: Boston : Houghton Mifflin Harcourt, 2018. |
Includes bibliographical references and index. | Description based on print version
record and CIP data provided by publisher; resource not viewed.
Identifiers: LCCN 2018012276 (print) | LCCN 2018013427 (ebook) |
ISBN 9781328955913 (ebook) | ISBN 9781328955906 (hardback)
ISBN 9781328606693 (international edition)
Subjects: LCSH: Manufacturing industries — Technological innovations. |
Three-dimensional printing — Economic aspects. | International trade. |
BISAC: BUSINESS & ECONOMICS / Commerce. | BUSINESS & ECONOMICS /
Industries / Manufacturing Industries.
Classification: LCC HD9720.5 (ebook) | LCC HD9720.5 .D38 2018 (print) |
DDC 338/.064 — dc23
LC record available at https://lccn.loc.gov/2018012276

Book design by Kelly Dubeau Smydra

Printed in the United States of America
DOC 10 9 8 7 6 5 4 3 2 1

# CONTENTS

# PROLOGUE

## Hidden Clues to a Coming Upheaval

As a professor at the Tuck Business School at Dartmouth College in Hanover, New Hampshire — the world's oldest graduate school of business and still one of its most prestigious — I'm not accustomed to playing the role of amateur sleuth. When I am engaged in researching an emerging business trend, I can generally call up any number of *Fortune* 500 CEOs and get a warm reception. And while these executives often ask me to keep some details of their businesses confidential, they are usually eager and proud to share with me their newest technological breakthroughs and cutting-edge strategies.

But for several years, as I worked to document and analyze what I've come to believe is the most important new strategic business development in the world, I suddenly ran up against a virtual stone wall of silence, evasion, and occasional misdirection from the corporate leaders who were most deeply involved. Of course, rather than discouraging me from pursuing the story, this unfamiliar secrecy only deepened my conviction that this trend is a real game-changer — the kind of epochal business shift that happens only once a century.

### Hidden in Plain Sight: How Additive Manufacturing Is Transforming the World of Business

It all started when I became intrigued about the new manufacturing technology known as 3D printing.

Of course, everyone has heard of 3D printing—one of the latest "cool" technologies to break through from geekdom into the popular consciousness. But many people still associate it with cute plastic trinkets or, at best, the design and production of small prototype products as models to be adapted for "real" manufacturing processes. They do not realize that 3D printing is just part of a broader range of revolutionary methods known collectively as *additive manufacturing* (AM); that AM is now being adapted to a wide range of materials, product types, and purposes; that many of the most important manufacturing businesses are beginning the transition to using AM as a major production method; and that big new industries are already being launched with AM as their primary foundation.

As someone who has long been fascinated by the impact of new technologies on markets, economies, and business strategy, I've spent the last several years closely following the development of AM. So you can imagine my excitement when in 2015 Meg Whitman, then the CEO of one of the companies that is driving the spread of AM, invited me to visit one of Hewlett Packard's major facilities in the beautiful Spanish city of Barcelona.

I'll never forget the day I spent "in the garage" with Scott Schiller, the leader of HP's research and development effort in the field of multi-jet fusion (MJF) printers. Scott took me to a large door with a 2D printed image of wood planks and metal hinges designed to resemble the garage door behind which the proverbial startup company would be launched. But behind this door was no ordinary garage, but rather a massive space where more than four hundred engineers with advanced degrees were working on breakthrough technologies for both 2D and 3D printers. Among other things, they were developing advances to perfect the consistency, durability, efficiency, and affordability of 3D printing technology—all in an effort to eliminate the last remaining quality gap between AM and older manufacturing methods.

For example, I visited a suite of four testing rooms where multi-jet fusion 3D printers were being put through their paces. One room, decorated with color images of tropical plants and animals, was artificially conditioned to simulate rainforest conditions of heat and high humidity; a second room was as hot, dry, and dusty as a desert landscape and decorated accordingly; and a third was frosty cold and lined with photos of Arctic icebergs. The printers in these rooms were being tested repeatedly to ensure consistent product quality no matter what the environmental conditions. In the fourth room, a giant robotic arm had been programmed to grab a printer and shake it violently, simulating the rough handling it might receive when being moved from one office to another, or during overseas shipping. Before and afterward, the printer's parts would be measured to see whether they'd shifted or bent even a micrometer, and the quality of products printed would also be tested.

During my tour, I also got to see new 3D printing technologies in development. I saw experimental printers being designed to print plastic parts that are rigid on one end, flexible on the other — ideal for eyeglass frames, for example. I saw other printers testing new methods to produce plastics that contain additives to enhance properties such as color, strength, rigidity, and porosity — essential when manufacturing tools or parts to be used in extreme conditions, for instance. And I saw other new processes in the works that I'm not yet free to divulge.

It's obvious that HP is determined to play a leading role in making 3D printing a major factor in the future of manufacturing. And industry experts aren't betting against them — even though there are already dozens of other companies, many of them armed with amazing new technologies, that are competing with HP for spots at the top of the AM world.

The fact is that Scott Schiller and the rest of the now spun-off HP, Inc., may be the *only* people in the world who have already successfully *digitized a pre-existing industry* — namely, traditional 2D printing, in which layers of ink or pigment are laid down on paper or other materials to form words or images. With that track record, it's not surprising that the engineers and executives at HP are confident that they will succeed in revolutionizing manufacturing in much the same way.

In truth, the process has already started. In 2016, HP launched its first generation of MJF industrial 3D printers, with pre-orders for hundreds of machines they expect to fulfill over the next two years. Within months, HP was expanding its manufacturing capacity to keep up with the burgeoning demand. In November 2017, the company introduced the MJF 4210, a second-generation model with even more remarkable capabilities. Among other benefits, the 4210 has enabled mind-boggling improvements in the speed and efficiency of 3D printing. For example, compare MJF printing with selective laser sintering (SLS), one of the most commonly used 3D printing methods. In the same time it takes to make 1,000 gears using SLS, an MJF printer can make 12,600 gears.

Improvements like this have raised the economic break-even point for large-scale 3D printing to 110,000 units. It's a milestone in the process of making 3D printing economically viable for manufacturing on a bigger scale than was previously possible. And HP has since announced further breakthroughs — including a new line of lower-priced printers that will feature the first high-quality, full-color 3D printing capabilities.

My visit to HP was an eye-opening introduction to the team behind these and other transformational developments. But when I asked my contacts at HP the obvious next questions — "Who is buying all these 3D printers? And what are they using them for?" — they became a lot more reticent. They were only able and willing to introduce me to a couple of their key customers.

One was Jabil, Inc., the world's third-largest contract manufacturer. (It trails two giant companies that are much better known, the Taiwan-based Foxconn and Flex Ltd., founded in Silicon Valley but now based in Singapore.) Headquartered in Florida, Jabil has 102 production facilities in 28 countries around the world. It makes printed circuit boards (PCB) and plastic and metal enclosures for PCB assemblies, as well as thousands of other machined parts for companies in industries from consumer electronics to aerospace, pharmaceuticals to home appliances.

As I'll be detailing later, what I learned about Jabil led me to conclude that it may be poised to become one of the world's most important companies in the next few years. It will be powered not just by the capabilities of AM but by Jabil's entire array of brilliantly innovative strategies. Jabil is now building one of the world's first *manufacturing platforms* — a system for using digital technology to connect scores of businesses around the world into a smoothly interconnected manufacturing powerhouse. Platforms like these will effectively turbocharge the unprecedented efficiencies of AM.

But beyond Jabil and one or two other names, there was a veil of secrecy over the identity of HP's customers. I repeatedly heard variations of "I'm sure you understand that for competitive reasons our clients insist on confidentiality about their purchases." It was obvious that AM was changing from a novelty into an important factor in the world of manufacturing. But how and why? What sort of companies were positioning themselves to take advantage of this breakthrough technology? And what did it all mean for the global economy of the twenty-first century?

To answer these questions, I had to become a kind of business detective.

## From Adult Diapers to Fighter Jets

I started my sleuthing by spending months studying every document, article, interview, and comment about AM that I could find on the Internet. I was helped by a number of my smartest B-school students, as well as several veteran engineers who were able to walk me through the complex story of this rapidly changing technology. We tracked down a handful of substantive stories identifying and detailing current users of 3D printing and other forms of AM . . . supplemented by plenty of tantalizing hints about the many emerging technologies and their potential uses.

I came across an article that referred to the fact that one company had been producing 3D printed antennas for cell phones. Who was the supplier, and which electronics company had manufactured these cell phones? Was this a true story or simply a rumor? A diligent search through Internet sources yielded almost nothing beyond hints that the supplier was based in China. Determined to put some flesh on these bones, I hired a couple of young Chinese-speaking students to scour the business sections of newspaper archives in their native language. After months of work and an investment of several thousand dollars, we were ultimately able to confirm the rumors indirectly — through chat room comments and Help Wanted ads, for example. We discovered that a supplier known as Lite-On had been using AM to build antennas for HTC, the Taiwan-based manufacturer of Android

and Windows-based smartphones. Armed with an array of 3D printers built by a New Mexico company called Optomec, which were specially equipped for producing electronics, Lite-On had been turning
out some *fifteen million* antennas per year.

This was a giant deal that had received no coverage in the mainstream business media. It also reflected the little-known fact that AM
is rapidly expanding beyond the spheres of design prototyping and
small runs of customized products and entering the world of mass
manufacturing . . . a world that even many experienced engineers remain convinced is off-limits to AM.

Some of the stories I tracked down showed that AM is also spreading into businesses far removed from high technology. For example,
I uncovered a number of references to so-called Cosyflex technology
— a breakthrough technique for making garments and nonwoven fabrics using 3D printers. The firm behind Cosyflex, a British company
named Tamicare, had received almost no publicity. All I could find was
a 2014 article in a local Manchester paper naming a husband-and-wife
team of Israeli inventors, Tamar and Ehud Giloh, as the duo behind
Tamicare and saying the company has garnered £10 million in investment capital.

With great difficulty, I tracked down Tamar Giloh. She is notori-
ously close-lipped and apparently grants few interviews. But I persuaded her to share some of her story with me. She pointed me to a
video showing her machines in action, producing (of all things) multi-
layered waterproof undergarments for adults with incontinence problems. The video showed a small glass-encased room outfitted with 3D
printers, robotic arms, and metal plates moving on a conveyor belt. I
watched the process with three engineers whom I'd hired to help me
interpret the video. We saw layers of various plastic polymers mixed
with different natural fibers being sprayed onto plates to form the basic garment; robotic arms placing absorbent pads and sealing the garments with heat; and the plates then bending and folding to prepare
the garment for final crimping and sealing.

I was told that a single Cosyflex machine can make a waterproof
undergarment every three seconds — up to three million undergarments per year. The cost? Somewhat higher than traditional manufacturing . . . but actually *lower* once you consider ancillary expenses. For

example, transportation costs can be reduced significantly by locating these machines close to the customers — which is made possible by using a compact, flexible, AM production system.

This was a typical pattern that I discovered through extended analysis of the economics of AM. Many engineers with extensive knowledge of traditional production methodologies still scoff at the potential of AM, declaring it "too expensive to replace the old systems." As I'll explain in more detail later, there are several holes in their logic. One of the biggest is their failure to consider the cost savings generated *around* the production process itself, in activities such as distribution, materials, warehousing, and marketing.

Clearly, the cost efficiencies enjoyed by Cosyflex hadn't been lost on the company whose video I watched. The video showed that the system was being used to produce thousands of cartons of undergarments. But when I pressed the Tamicare owner to divulge the name of her customer, she fell silent.

Once again, I had to go back into my amateur detective mode. I started asking everyone I knew for leads to big manufacturers that might be the mystery company that was using Cosyflex. Based on what I'd heard, I realized that the most probable major user of Cosyflex technology was a particular company that makes adult diapers, hospital bandages, and first-aid products. Later, I heard that Tamicare had signed a multimillion-dollar deal with an apparel company to mass-produce sports shoes and bras, and that a market test of adult incontinence undergarments produced by Cosyflex had been conducted in Israel. But further details behind both of these stories have proved elusive.

Meanwhile, someone gave me a fresh lead to an even more remarkable, innovative use of 3D printing. "I don't know any of the details," an acquaintance remarked, "but I hear that Lockheed Martin is applying 3D printing to aviation." I called people I knew at the company, but they refused my requests for an interview. So I devised an alternative strategy. I searched the database on the LinkedIn social media website for the names of professionals working at Lockheed Martin. I ended up making hundreds of phone calls in search of someone who would be willing to talk with me.

Eventually I got hold of a young Lockheed Martin engineer who was happy to discuss his work in confidence. He explained that Lockheed Martin had developed a new composite material that could be used to produce ultra-light, ultra-strong bodies for its F35 fighter jets using 3D printing. "We can print the entire jet body and interior in about three months using a process called BAAM — *big area additive manufacturing,*" he explained. "It's a huge improvement over the two to three years it takes to manufacture the same jet using traditional technologies. Now our goal is to get it down to three weeks."

These details that my young friend shared with me were mind-boggling. The F35 jet is more than fifty feet long, has a wingspan of thirty-five feet, and weighs (when empty) some twelve tons. The idea that it can be *printed* like a piece of plastic jewelry seems absurd. But apparently Lockheed Martin had found that the jet's body and interior panels could be built by an array of printers mounted and moving up, down, and sideways on scaffolds of metal tubes. The scaffolding is easy to fold and load into an ordinary shipping container. This is BAAM, and even a non-engineer can quickly see how it cleverly overcomes some of the apparent limitations of size and flexibility that might seem to minimize the potential of AM.

Even more impressive, Lockheed was using a business model no one had previously described or even named. After learning about it, I labeled it *mass modularization.* As practiced by Lockheed, mass modularization means that a standardized jet body and interior is built by BAAM with 3D-printed wiring embedded in its fuselage, wings, cockpit, and undercarriage. Spaces are left open for the insertion of modules — specialized communication systems, navigation systems, weapons systems, and others — each in a separate box, ready to be screwed into place. The modules automatically connect with the embedded wiring so that the jet is ready to go as soon as the modules are inserted and the missiles and engines are strapped on.

The ramifications of BAAM coupled with mass modularization are astounding. Cars, ships, harvesters, earth-moving equipment, and other complex machines can be produced this way. And the F35 jet itself can be retrofitted in seconds by replacing the modules with upgraded ones. Rather than having to return a fleet of aircraft back home to upgrade them, the modules can instead be flown to the battlefield, making it possible for the jets to be outfitted with new electronic capabilities or new countermeasures from one mission to the next.

Most impressive of all, an aircraft "factory" no longer needs to be a giant hangar built at a cost of hundreds of millions of dollars and easily visible to spy planes and satellites. Instead, the factory can be a small warehouse containing a few BAAM systems in shipping containers, quick to set up and easy to disassemble and move if needed. When a country can print an air force on the spot and just in time, as needed, the implications for geopolitical and military strategy are enormous.

Naturally, I asked for permission to visit the plant and watch these processes in action. "I'll get back to you," my Lockheed Martin friend told me. He never did, and my subsequent phone calls and emails went unanswered. But later, when I learned that BAAM was being developed in a joint venture by Cincinnati Incorporated and Oak Ridge National Labs, I verified that a BAAM system was being used by Lockheed Martin.

In 2016, Lockheed Martin finally filed a patent covering its process for additive manufacturing of jet airplanes — which is why I am now free to write about what I discovered through my amateur sleuthing.

As I delved further, I heard other reports about 3D printing innovations being pursued by several of the world's leading industrial firms — giant, highly respected companies such as the German-based Siemens, Japan's Sumitomo Heavy Industries, and the American firm United Technologies. One of the standard-bearers in this group was the venerable technology company General Electric. For a time, under the leadership of then CEO Jeff Immelt, GE made few public pronouncements about its efforts in AM. But a series of company acquisitions made GE's interest in the field clear. These included the 2012 purchase of Cincinnati-based Morris Technologies, a pioneer in 3D printing, and the 2016 acquisitions of two premier metal 3D printer manufacturers — Concept Laser and Arcam AB — for a total of $1.4 billion, the largest deals in the 3D printing business to date. Finally, in mid-2017, GE issued a series of announcements divulging its plans to become a major global force in the development and spread of additive manufacturing.

Less widely trumpeted but perhaps even more significant in

the long run, GE also announced its intention to become one of the world's top ten software providers within the next decade. One of the keys to the remarkable flexibility and power of AM is the fact that it completely *digitizes* the manufacturing process. And that means the ability to create world-class software for controlling digital manufacturing — from product design, prototyping, and testing to production, warehousing, and logistics — suddenly leaps to the forefront of valuable business skills.

Since then, GE has experienced some significant bumps in the road. Under pressure from Wall Street due to a period of lackluster earnings, the company replaced Immelt with John Flannery, a company veteran who had most recently run the GE Healthcare division. By the end of 2017, rumors were circulating that GE might be planning to divest itself of a number of underperforming businesses, and some outside analysts were calling for a breakup of the company. Yet at the same time, GE announced its commitment to spend a total of $2.1 billion on digital manufacturing technologies by the end of 2017, noted that orders for its industrial software had grown 24 percent in the first half of the year, and reaffirmed its intention to be "a major player" in the digitized manufacturing business, which it expected to reach $225 billion by 2020.

As of this writing (winter 2017–18), the future shape of GE is uncertain. But it seems likely that in some form, the company once famous for "bringing good things to life" will be a significant player in the continuing development and growth of AM.

This, then, is the story of the research project that led to the book you're now reading. It started with 3D printing, but it certainly didn't end there. It continued with countless conversations with engineers, scientists, production managers, R&D experts, and product designers, as well as the perusing of hundreds of articles, conference presentations, and research reports. The more I learned, the greater my fascination — and the deeper my conviction that the story I was uncovering was one of the most important business developments of our time.

Here is a brief preview of the story that my ongoing research has revealed — a kind of trailer of a few highlights from the film you're about to see.

3D printing is just one of the powerful new digital manufacturing technologies in which companies like GE are investing billions of dollars. Originally, 3D printing was merely 2D printing of layers of material, repeated over and over until a 3D object is built up. But new methods are now being developed that are far more sophisticated and powerful. They include innovative techniques with names like *monolithic printing* and *self-assembly,* as well as other forms of non-layering-based additive manufacturing. These AM techniques are being supplemented by new developments in other fields that are more familiar but that are also changing at breakneck speed — fields such as robotics, artificial intelligence, big data analytics, cloud computing, and the Internet of Things (which links millions of devices in homes and businesses in an electronic network that allows data sharing and data collection on a massive scale).

The crowning breakthrough will be the perfection and spread of additive manufacturing platforms like the ones now being built by companies like Jabil, GE, and Siemens, as well as infotech giants like IBM. Additive manufacturing platforms are poised to revolutionize the world economy in ways that most experts have failed to grasp. For example, a number of pundits have described a vision of the future under the rubric of Industry 4.0, in which traditional manufacturing methods are upgraded and modernized using tools such as automation and robotics. When AM is included in this vision, it is merely regarded as an adjunct to a fundamentally traditional manufacturing system — for example, by having a few 3D printers on hand to feed parts to workers on an assembly line.

In stark contrast, the emerging industrial platforms will be built around AM as the core of an entirely new way to create value. These AM-based platforms will help firms to manage complex and diverse operations by creating giant industrial networks that link and adroitly control hundreds of business processes, creating unprecedented efficiencies and opening up opportunities to create businesses with levels of flexibility, diversification, and size unheard of in the past.

I refer to these vast new businesses as *pan-industrials.* As I'll show, there's every reason to believe that the pan-industrials will come to dominate the global economy within the next two or three decades, driving unprecedented changes with an impact that will extend far beyond the world of manufacturing. This is a level of economic change far beyond the one envisioned by advocates of Industry 4.0.

Hence the title of this book — *The Pan-Industrial Revolution*. This phrase defines the transformation that today's emergent technologies will produce over the next twenty to thirty years. It's an era that will be marked by a series of logical yet dramatic economic shifts, including the following:

- *a shift toward dramatically greater efficiency* — from centralized, capital-intensive manufacturing facilities that are slow and costly to change, to much more efficient production units, coordinated by digital industrial platforms, that are less capital-intensive, as well as more decentralized and flexible;
- *a shift toward more intense real-time competition* — from long, complex supply chains that privilege low-cost producers to short, simpler supply chains that benefit from drastically reduced shipping costs and lead times, greater closeness to customers, and almost instantaneous responsiveness to changes in market needs, product designs, and competitors' moves;
- *a shift toward competition for spheres of influence in an economy without clear industry boundaries* — from defined market and industry segments separated by high entry barriers to converging industries linked by shared manufacturing materials and methods;
- *a shift toward digital business ecosystems* — from traditional supply chains to vast, interlocking, diversified businesses and collectives — the pan-industrials — that share digital, market-based information about supply and demand, manufacturing technology, trading and financial shifts, and consumer knowledge, generating powerful networked intelligence; and, ultimately,
- *a shift toward collective competition* — from competition between companies that specialize in particular products and markets to competition among a relatively handful of giant pan-industrials, each at the center of its own uniquely designed ecosystem.

Along the way, we can also expect to see a host of managerial, strategic, and social developments that very few people have anticipated — for example:

- *the death of the maker myth,* as small, independent, craftlike 3D printing shops producing items in tiny quantities give way to complex systems that combine many digital technologies to mass-produce goods with newfound quality controls, speed, and efficiency;
- *the emergence of new forms of vertical integration and conglomeratization,* as organizations use the powers of digitization to achieve synergies that the corporate giants of the past could never attain;
- *an era of what I call superconvergence,* which will be more sweeping in its effects than the industry convergence of the 1990s, in which boundaries between business functions, company divisions, corporations, industries, and markets will rapidly erode and even disappear;
- *a decline in the power of Wall Street,* as the pan-industrials amass stockpiles of capital and market power that make them practically independent of the lords of finance;
- *an era of material abundance with minimal environmental cost,* as the new manufacturing technologies dramatically reduce material waste, energy consumption, and market inefficiencies;
- *major shifts in the global balance of power,* including severe economic dislocations, such as rampant unemployment, within the developed nations, as well as a decline in the relative power of developing nations like China; and
- *a potentially devastating challenge to the system of free enterprise,* as the unprecedented economic and political power of the pan-industrials leads to clashes between government, citizens' groups, and the corporate titans who will dominate the new economy.

I've been analyzing business trends since the days when I wrote the best-selling strategy guide *Hypercompetition* in 1994. I'm convinced that the new changes we're about to experience are some of the biggest ever. It would be risky to try to predict the precise outcomes of these complicated, interconnected trends. But I think one thing is clear: Business will never be the same.

How will all of this come to pass? What must business leaders do to prepare themselves and their companies for the upheavals ahead? And how will these changes affect communities, nations, the global economy, and the lives of ordinary citizens? These are some of the questions I'll address in the pages of this book.

# PART ONE

# THE REVOLUTION IS HERE

Part 1 will describe the remarkable new technologies that are changing the way virtually everything is currently being made, giving manufacturers vastly greater flexibility, speed, efficiency, responsiveness, and power. It will also show how traditional assumptions about the physical limitations that constrain today's manufacturers are being upended by these technologies.

For example, the powers of 3D printers and other additive manufacturing tools will enable manufacturers for the first time to benefit from *economies of scope*. These are economic benefits that arise from the ability to make almost anything, anywhere, rather than being forced to specialize in one or a few products.

At the same time, the new manufacturing technologies are rapidly achieving the quality, speed, and efficiency they need to produce mass quantities of identical goods in certain vanguard industries, beating old-style plants based on the *economies of scale* from which giant companies have long benefited.

To enable companies to take full advantage of the economies of scope and scale that AM makes possible, new systems that use digital tools to monitor and control far-flung operations are now being developed. The emerging *industrial platforms* use the powers of big data, machine learning, and artificial intelligence to make manufacturing processes more efficient than ever before.

These changes are portents of even bigger transformations to come. The most dramatic change I anticipate: the rise of giant business combinations that I call *pan-industrials*. They'll superficially resemble the conglomerates of today, operating in many business sectors in locations around the world. But the pan-industrials will take advantage of the new manufacturing technologies to achieve unprecedented levels of synergies, diversification, efficiency, flexibility, profitability, and innovation that are beyond the reach of any conglomerate. A few of these pan-industrials will grow large, rich, and powerful enough to become titans that dominate the world economy.

# 1

# THE SHAPE OF THINGS TO COME

## *Birth of the Pan-Industrial Revolution*

**BACK IN 1983,** an obscure engineer named Chuck Hull, working on projects for a small company that made tough surface coatings for furniture, had gotten into the habit of staying up late to pursue his arcane experiments. One night, Chuck surprised his wife, Anntionette, with a phone call. "Get out of your pajamas," he told her, "get dressed, and come down to the lab. I've got something I want you to see."

"This better be good!" his sleepy spouse responded.

It was. Playing around with a variety of acrylic-based materials called photopolymers, Hull had invented an almost-magical way of turning liquid resins into hard, durable objects simply by exposing them to ultraviolet light. He called the new technique *stereolithography* . . . and through the months of development that followed, it became the basis of the technology we now call 3D printing.

Anntionette Hull recalls what happened next on that fateful night:

> He held this part in his hand and he said "I did it. The world as we know will never be the same." We laughed and we cried and we stayed up all night just imagining.
>
> I knew on that night that he had achieved something grand and that it would hold meaning, and I hold it dear to my heart.

Anntionette still owns that first 3D printed item—a nondescript blob of black plastic some two inches across. She carries it in her purse and will happily show it to you if you ask. One day, she says, she will donate it to the Smithsonian.

Her husband's brainchild, 3D printing, is a form of *additive manufacturing* (AM). The term refers to any kind of production in which materials are built up to create a product rather than cut, ground, drilled, or otherwise reduced into shape — techniques known as *subtractive manufacturing*. (Subtractive manufacturing, in turn, is one of several activities that constitute what is now being referred to as *traditional manufacturing*. Other techniques of traditional manufacturing, sometimes called *formative manufacturing*, include *injection molding, forming, joining, stamping,* and *assembly*.)

And while additive manufacturing is a relatively new term, the methodology itself is not. Ancient forms of additive manufacturing include lost wax casting (also known as investment casting), long used by artists to produce duplicates of existing sculptures or other objects. A more recent technique is inkjet printing, in which droplets of pigment are sprayed onto a surface to create an image. Hull's invention of stereolithography opened the door to an array of new forms of AM, many of which are loosely grouped under the name 3D printing.

Today, more than three decades after Hull's discovery, many people still associate 3D printing with the kind of small plastic desk accessory or toy you might pick up in a gift shop. But if you're one of the hundreds of thousands of Americans who has gotten a knee or hip replacement in recent years, you have probably had your life transformed by the genius of AM.

Stryker Orthopaedics is one of the most innovative U.S. companies few people have ever heard of. It was founded back in 1941 by Homer Stryker, a surgeon and prolific inventor with nearly five thousand patents to his credit. Today, the Kalamazoo-based firm has annual revenues of almost ten billion dollars and is responsible for some of the most notable breakthroughs in the world of orthopedic implants. Stryker builds titanium components for joint implants, many uniquely designed to fit the bone structure and musculature of an individual, freeing him or her from the agony of arthritis and providing years of blessedly pain-free movement.

And one of the things that few people realize is that many of those custom-made parts are manufactured by Stryker using 3D printers.

Among other advantages, Stryker's 3D-printed components can be implanted by surgeons without the need for cement, glue, and other clumsy, often ineffective methods once used to make the replacement joint adhere to nearby bones. Years ago, researchers discovered that living bone will grow naturally into an artificial implant if the texture and structure of the implant is just right — rough-edged and with a precise degree of internal porosity that provides spaces into which the bone can expand, in a process called biologic fixation.

An implant design that encourages biologic fixation was very hard to create using traditional manufacturing methods. But for a smartly programmed 3D printer, which is able to dole out precise amounts of titanium measured just a few molecules at a time, it's easy. No wonder 3D-printed joint implants have swept the market.

In 2016, Stryker announced plans to invest $400 million in building a new AM printing facility that will use a technique known as *selective laser melting* to make even better implants. At the same time, Stryker is working with hospitals on the next big breakthrough: developing small, specially programmed 3D printers that will create a custom implant right on the premises while the surgeon and the patient wait to receive it, saving time and money.

The Stryker story is one of many that make it abundantly clear that additive manufacturing has long outgrown its reputation as a tool for making cute plastic toys and simple trinkets.

## A Quiet Revolution Gains Momentum

Here's the oddity: Although additive manufacturing has been claiming an expanding place in the landscape of manufacturing, it has been doing so with relatively little fanfare, even in a world where technological developments are too often trumpeted with excessive hype.

There are a number of reasons for the relatively modest levels of hype and publicity surrounding this emerging manufacturing transformation. One has been the sheer number and high visibility of other technological developments, especially those associated with IT and communications, from smartphones, Internet-based business platforms, and driverless cars to machine learning and virtual reality.

These ultra-cool breakthroughs, along with the charismatic CEOs who have trumpeted them, have sucked up most of the media attention around technology in recent years, even though some of them (like those self-driving cars) have yet to be effectively implemented.

Some companies that are moving quickly to embrace AM have their own reasons for avoiding publicity. As I suggested in the Prologue, some want to avoid attracting attention from rival companies who might try to leapfrog ahead of them. Others may be concerned about triggering negative reactions from their employees ("What happens to my job if 3D printers take over?") or from consumers ("Are 3D printed parts really as strong and safe as traditional ones?"). Still others may be worried about intensified scrutiny from government regulators. For all these reasons, a number of big companies are pursuing AM strategies with a minimum of public fuss.

An additional reason for the relative lack of recognition of AM as a driving force of economic change has been the persistence of skepticism about the technology's true potential. Early versions of 3D printing technology had so many limitations and weaknesses that many people wrote it off prematurely. This skepticism — understandably — was particularly prevalent among engineers who'd spent lifetimes using and improving traditional manufacturing tools. It has taken the skeptics time to adopt the new ways of thinking required to fully grasp the possible benefits of the new manufacturing technologies. In the meantime, they spread their doubts to many non-techies in the business community — even as scientists and engineers experimenting with AM were finding ways to overcome the technology's initial limitations.

To this day, I still encounter some remnants of the old skepticism among many in the general public who still believe some of the persistent myths about additive manufacturing (see Table 1-1).

Because of the prevalence of these myths, most people — including many business leaders who are not directly involved in AM — still have only a vague sense of its incredible potential to transform countless industries, and of the rapidity with which that potential is now turning into reality.

In some cases, entire industries have already shifted to AM. I've already explained how the hip and knee implant industries have trav-

TABLE 1-1: MYTHS AND REALITIES OF ADDITIVE MANUFACTURING:
Why AM Is Poised to Be So Much Bigger Than You May Think

| MYTH | REALITY |
| --- | --- |
| AM is limited to plastic trinkets. | AM now employs materials ranging from stainless steel, gold, silver, and titanium to ceramics, wood, concrete . . . even food and stem cells. |
| AM is mainly for tiny items just a few inches across. | AM is now being used to build industrial products of increasing size and complexity, making this technology a viable replacement for many traditional forms of manufacturing. |
| AM is a hobby tool for individual "makers" in basement and garage workshops. | A growing number of industrial giants are converting all or part of their production systems to utilize AM. |
| AM can't match the consistent quality of traditional manufacturing methods. | AM technologies are rapidly improving, to the point where they are beginning to provide better quality at lower cost for many important product types. |
| AM's only real advantage lies in its ability to facilitate custom design of parts. | Customization is one big benefit of AM. But there are many others, including less material waste, lighter product weight, easier assembly, reduced capital costs, smaller manufacturing footprint, and more. |
| AM will be used largely to produce small quantities of specialized parts for high-end uses. | AM now offers such significant quality, efficiency, and cost advantages that it is increasingly being used for mass production of standardized products. |

eled far down this path. Another example is the hearing aid business, which seeks to serve the estimated 35 million Americans who suffer hearing loss, as well as the hundreds of millions more around the world.

The traditional method of manufacturing hearing aids included nine complex steps, including making cast molds of the exterior of the ear, converting them into ear impressions, and trimming the final shell. These tasks required the skills of trained artisans and more than a week's time from start to finish. Sometimes the finished product fit comfortably and securely, sometimes not. "They might fit in nicely within the ear or wriggle around due to loose fittings," says Jenna Franklin, an executive with a 3D printing firm.

The breakthrough to simplifying and improving this complicated process using digital technology began in 2000. In that year, the Swiss hearing aid maker Phonak collaborated with Materialise NV, a Belgian firm specializing in 3D printing and software, to make the first customized hearing aids using additive manufacturing.

Even then, the logic was obvious: No two ears are alike, so being able to make a hearing aid that fits your ear precisely is both complicated and extremely valuable. AM offered an ideal solution. Because a 3D printer builds a product in a precise shape as dictated by a sophisticated software program, it is easy to make an item fully customized to the needs of a particular user. Once Phonak demonstrated that 3D-printed hearing aid shells could be produced in large quantities, the new technology dominated the field.

The new, streamlined technique involves an audiologist who uses a 3D scanner equipped with lasers to create a digital ear impression. This is given to a modeler, who designs a customized shell for 3D printing and fitting with the appropriate electronic inserts — all generally completed within a day. By 2015, more than fifteen million customized hearing aids had been produced by 3D printers worldwide. Perhaps most remarkable, according to one CEO I interviewed, the entire U.S. industry converted from traditional manufacturing techniques to 3D printing within a year and a half — with a number of stragglers simply going out of business. It's a testimony to the speed with which an innovation can sweep an industry when conditions are right.

Another example is the manufacture of customized dental braces for straightening teeth. Zia Chishti is an American-born entrepreneur of Pakistani ancestry who discovered, while attending Stanford Business School, that his crooked teeth were marring his professional appearance. Unwilling to wear the kinds of conventional metal braces people associate with teenagers, he came up with the idea of creating transparent aligners to adjust the spacing of his teeth. That stimulated a business idea: Why not use the new technology of stereolithography (SLA) to create molds for customized dental braces? In 1997, Chishti founded Align Technology to test the concept.

Today, Align's proprietary software designs clear aligners for individual dental patients based on a digital model of the mouth captured by a 3D scanner. Each unique mold is then manufactured by an SLA printer at a facility run by printer manufacturer 3D Systems, which ships up to 80,000 aligners per day, sold under the brand name of Invisalign. Other companies, such as ClearCorrect and Orthoclear, have developed their own systems for designing and printing customized dental molds. These and other firms are competing with Align for shares of the vast global market for invisible orthodontics, estimated at six million cases per year. Since each case ultimately requires a dozen or more sets of aligners to gradually move the user's teeth into the proper position, it's a big business — and another industry in which additive manufacturing has quickly yet quietly claimed a dominant role.

Industries like these are already dispelling the myth that AM is useful only for product prototypes, low-quantity items, or specialized parts for niche markets.

## Nearing the Tipping Point

Then there are industries in which AM is not yet dominant but is making increasing inroads. Take the automobile business, for example. Some people still connect 3D printing with cars mainly through the stories told by the comedian and talk show host Jay Leno, who uses the technology to make replacement parts for his collection of vintage vehicles. Leno loves to tell his fellow auto enthusiasts about the way his 3D printer lets him create an exact duplicate of any damaged or missing part, from a piece of trim or a scrolled door handle to a complete radiator for a 1907 White Steamer.

That's cool, no doubt. And so, in a very different way, are the growing stories in the business press about the startup Local Motors. The company made headlines at the 2014 International Manufacturing Technology Show in Chicago when a live audience witnessed the production of a Local Motors Strati — the world's first 3D-printed car. (To be precise, about 75 percent of the Strati's components were 3D printed; items such as the rubber tires, brakes, battery, and electric engine were manufactured using conventional methods.) A small, curvy roadster that seats two and has a chassis and body made of carbon-fiber-reinforced plastic, the Strati takes about forty-four hours to fully print and consists of 50 individual parts, as compared to the 30,000 parts in a traditionally built car. About one-quarter of the Strati's components — the tires, as noted — are manufactured using traditional means; the engineers hope to reduce that fraction to 10 percent in the next couple of years. Depending on the features included, the estimated retail price for a 3D-printed Strati is between $18,000 and $30,000.

A critic from *Popular Mechanics* took the Strati for a test run in September 2015 and declared it "a blast to drive." And after analyzing the streamlined production methods used to build the Strati, the same writer concluded, "We currently take it for granted that cars are complicated and expensive. When you're driving the Strati, it's easy to imagine a day when we take it for granted that they're not."

The Strati is just one of a series of pioneering 3D-printed vehicles that Local Motors has developed. First unveiled in 2015, the LM3D Swim is a four-seater that, like the Strati, runs on electric power. The car's design was created by Kevin Lo and won a competition judged by a panel that included Jay Leno. At the moment, the Strati and other cars designed by Local Motors are classified as "neighborhood electric vehicles" (comparable to golf carts), which limits their use on streets and highways. But once these regulatory hurdles are overcome, Local Motors hopes to build the cars in its small factory in Knoxville, Tennessee.

Today, the company's central focus is on Olli, an autonomous (that is, self-driving) electric bus originally designed for the Berlin 2030 Urban Mobility Challenge competition (Figure 1-1). It seats twelve and can be used to take school or community groups on outings, to provide public transportation on regular routes, or to offer customized service when hailed using a mobile app. Olli's self-driving capabilities are provided by artificial intelligence using IBM Watson technology — the first time Watson has been so used. Olli has been demonstrated live and is being readied for production at the Local Motors factory in Chandler, Arizona. Interest in putting the vehicles to work in urban

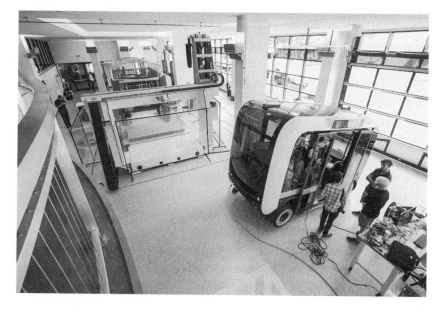

FIGURE 1-1: A demonstration model of the Olli at Local Motors' lab in National Harbor, MD. On the top left, we can see the large 3D printer used to print the shell of the bus. On the right, the Olli is being assembled, including the electronics and other internal components. © THE VERGE, JUNE 17, 2016. PHOTO BY AMELIA KRALES/VOX MEDIA, INC.

settings has been expressed by cities from Las Vegas, Nevada, to Ves-thimmerland, a municipality in northern Denmark. The planned uses for Olli — for example, as a shuttle bus used by visitors inside a theme park — would not be subject to the same on-road regulatory restrictions that currently limit the availability of the Strati. In 2018, Local Motors lined up over a billion dollars in financing for customers who wish to lease Ollis, and had already booked orders for more than four hundred of the vehicles.

All of Local Motors' vehicle designs are unique and trailblazing. The company is also taking advantage of the flexibility of its production facilities to allow customers to engage in "co-creation" of their products. The first product ever developed by Local Motors was the Rally Fighter, an off-road vehicle designed for adventurous outings in the desert or other backcountry locations. Launched in 2010 after just twelve months in development — a speed that is close to miraculous by usual auto industry standards — it was designed by members of the then-new Local Motors community using crowdsourcing techniques.

The Strati design emerged from a similar collaborative process. Today the online Local Motors community has grown to include more than 70,000 contributors — "designers, engineers, and gearheads," as one writer calls them — who earn royalties when their vehicle design concepts are used.

Justin Fishkin, Local Motors' chief strategy officer, explains the approach this way:

> Rather than having a million copies of one car made in one place and shipped around world, why not allow regional actors to design, produce and upgrade application-specific vehicles compatible with local technologies, infrastructure and energy ecosystems? . . . It's economy of scope vs. economy of scale. We can make smaller lots of more differentiated products at higher margins. By connecting a digital thread between design and flexible production we've reduced the minimum efficient scale for producing new vehicles and deploying new technologies. This is enabling communities to define their own mobility futures.

Local Motors views its co-creation and micro-manufacturing model as applicable to many other industries — and leaders at other companies agree. Hence the creation of Launch Forth by LM, a division of Local Motors that is selling its systems in the form of software-as-a-service. It has also announced a project called Fuse in partnership with GE, which will provide the same kinds of expertise and guidance to business people, engineers, entrepreneurs, and students both online and in micro-factory facilities around the country, starting with one based at the mHub on the west side of Chicago.

Of course, Local Motors is far from having achieved dominance in the world of auto manufacturing. As of mid-2018, the traditional giants still rule the industry, with Toyota, Renault-Nissan, Volkswagen, and General Motors holding the top four spots in the revenue rankings. But now traditional carmakers — not just startups like Local Motors — are beginning the inevitable shift toward additive manufacturing as a major part of their production processes.

At the high end of the auto industry, the power of AM to easily customize parts to a purchaser's specifications is being used by companies such as Porsche, BMW, Bentley, and Ferrari to add unique personal touches to a "bespoke" vehicle — for example, a dashboard clock with a face modeled after the driver's favorite wristwatch, available on some models from Rolls-Royce. Industry experts say these enhancements have significantly boosted sales of particular car models, generating profits far in excess of costs.

But these small-scale innovations, while intriguing, are relatively trivial in comparison to some of the big changes that additive manufacturing is beginning to bring to carmakers. By 2014, 3D printing was already widely used throughout the auto industry for the design, prototyping, and testing of new models. Now the technology is finding its way into daily manufacturing and operations. Audi, for example, has drastically simplified its supply chain by shifting to 3D printing replacement parts on demand rather than warehousing and shipping them.

In the next few years, additive manufacturing is expected to take over more and more of the auto production process. The demand for lighter, stronger cars that are more fuel efficient while remaining crash-resistant is stimulating interest in AM parts made from ultra-strong composite materials containing carbon and glass fibers. Companies like Honda have already exhibited experimental vehicles in which the body panels and a majority of other parts are produced via AM. Analysts say AM revenues in the auto industry reached $600 million by the end of 2016 and will grow to some $2.3 billion as soon as 2021.

Some of the world's leading auto companies are even making major strategic choices that reflect their commitment to the coming revolution in manufacturing. They are opening additive manufacturing labs, forging partnerships with AM companies, and investing in startups that own promising new technologies.

They are also hiring talent with a deep understanding of the new methodologies. In May 2017, for example, Ford surprised many industry observers by choosing Jim Hackett as its new CEO and president upon the retirement of Mark Fields. Hackett had formerly headed Ford Smart Mobility, a division dedicated to exploring the high-tech future of the car business — in the company's words, through investments in "connectivity, mobility, autonomous vehicles, the customer experience and data and analytics." But more intriguing is that Hackett had previously been CEO of Steelcase, the furniture and design company that had already plunged into the AM world through a much-ballyhooed creative collaboration with MIT. Thus, Hackett has direct experience in several technology areas that will be crucial to the future of AM, including both design for 3D printing and the use of networked data and analytics to enhance the development and creation of products.

Hackett is expected to invest major resources in projects like Ford's trial use of large-scale 3D printers from a firm called Stratasys to manufacture car interior modules. Within weeks of Hackett's elevation, Ford also announced details of a new partnership with Carbon (formerly known as Carbon3D), developers of the new AM technology called CLIP, which can produce parts much faster than older 3D printing methods (see Table 1-2, page 20). In the words of Ellen Lee, leader of Ford's additive manufacturing research, "If we can shave months off of production time and get a new model onto the market earlier, we can save millions."

A century ago, under the leadership of its legendary founder, Ford pioneered the modern assembly line and helped lead one of the great transformations of the manufacturing world. Today, under a new leader with strong ties to the world of high-tech design and manufacturing, Ford appears poised to help lead a second such transformation — one that may end forever the dominance of the Fordist assembly-line system that once defined mass manufacturing.

Another industry that seems to be ready to join the AM revolution is traditional building construction. It's a huge industry worldwide, accounting for $9 trillion in revenues and 6 percent of global GDP. But it has also been a technology laggard, with productivity barely rising over the past few decades. Even with blueprint design software and other digital tools, builders still put up buildings pretty much as they did a century ago — one brick, timber, or girder at a time.

AM has the potential to digitize the construction process. Among other benefits, everything is reduced to precise measurements, so owners and architects can make buildings just the way they want them, without the quality compromises and errors that inevitably arise from analog work and traditional manual labor. That's one reason why builders are excited by the potential of 3D printing. The flexibility of the technology also promises to vastly accelerate the construction process with no loss of strength, durability, beauty, or safety.

Of course, scaling up AM to work on projects the size of homes — let alone office buildings or skyscrapers — is no small feat. But demonstration projects scattered around the world have made it clear that AM techniques for building construction have now reached levels of reliability and economy that make big building projects feasible. Construction firms experimenting with AM have produced buildings with traditional styling that meet all normal standards for strength and cost.

For example, in June 2016, the Chinese company HuaShang Tengda unveiled a 4,300-square-foot "luxury villa" it had 3D printed using very strong, C30-grade concrete applied around a steel frame (built elsewhere and transported to the site). The villa has walls that are 250 millimeters (almost ten inches) thick and capable of withstanding an earthquake that measures 8 on the Richter scale — a great earthquake of the kind that demolishes cities and occurs only once a year, on average, anywhere in the world. Time required to build the villa? Forty-five days, about half the time that would be typical using traditional construction methods.

Additive manufacturing offers construction companies new and better ways to produce buildings much like those that are already familiar sights in our towns and cities. But it also creates new possibilities few have previously imagined. For example, we'll be able to make buildings in shapes that haven't been economical to produce up to now. Instead of the rectilinear forms that dominate our streetscapes and skylines, we'll get the kind of curves you see in nature. That's not just good for fans of *The Hobbit* and the iconoclastic Spanish architect Antoni Gaudi. It also makes for stronger, lighter structures with the flexibility to conform to human needs as well as the limits of artistic creativity. To see what I mean, check out the futuristic design of the office buildings that a Chinese company named Winsun printed in Dubai in 2017 (Figure 1-2). Their dramatic, curvilinear styling was likened by one journalist to the midcentury modern "House of the Fu-

FIGURE 1-2: The organically curved buildings make up an "Office of the Future," 3D printed in Dubai by Chinese construction firm Winsun and officially unveiled in May 2016. AP PHOTO/KAMRAN JEBREILI

ture" unveiled by Monsanto at Disneyland in 1957 — a vision of space-age architecture that never really came to pass, until now.

The new AM buildings will also be a lot cheaper to construct than most traditionally built houses. Because the whole process is digitally controlled, builders will be able to rely on robot printers to do much of the work. Already the Institute for Advanced Architecture in Gaudi's hometown of Barcelona has developed "minibuilders." These are small-scale robots, positioned via sensors, linked via software, and equipped with AM capabilities, that swarm around and put up a building in less time and at lower cost than human workers could do. The process also generates a lot less waste. And this isn't just about making concrete structures. The robots also work with composites of wood, plastic, and metal.

That's for building on-site, but if you prefabricate the structures and assemble them at the construction site, you get even greater savings. Prefabrication has been around for a while, but 3D printing allows for such precision that the assembly process is literally a snap.

Saudi Arabia, the population of which is exploding, is talking with Winsun about printing as many as 1.5 million partially prefabricated, 3D-printed housing units over the next five years. Winsun thinks this technology could eventually go a long way toward solving the global scourges of homelessness and substandard housing.

## The Growing Benefits of Additive Manufacturing

As you're beginning to see, AM technologies provide manufacturers with a number of advantages that traditional production techniques can't match. In addition to the benefits I've already explained, including inexpensive customization and greater speed to market, they include the following:

- *Greater design complexity.* The ability to create objects layer by layer makes it possible to build products with more complex internal architectures than ever before. Geometries formerly too fine to mill can now be 3D printed a few molecules at a time, if necessary, making more labor-intensive and costly production processes needless. As Avi Reichental, former president and CEO of 3D Systems, once famously remarked, "With 3D printing, complexity is free. The printer doesn't care if it makes the most rudimentary shape or the most complex shape, and that is completely turning design and manufacturing on its head as we know it." Reichental's dictum, though still frequently quoted, is not literally true. Complex items can take a bit more time to 3D print, and they sometimes consume additional materials, so complexity does bear a meaningful cost. However, that cost is usually significantly less than with traditional manufacturing. So complexity is not "free" — but it is remarkably affordable.
- *One-step production.* In some applications, pieces that must be made separately and then assembled when traditional manufacturing methods are used can be produced in a single step using 3D printing. (This is why the number of parts in a Strati is just a fraction of those in a conventional car.) As a result, assembly costs are dramatically re-

duced or eliminated altogether, along with opportunities for human error during the assembly stage.

- *Lighter, stronger, simpler products.* Single-piece 3D parts and products are often both lighter and stronger than the multipiece traditionally built equivalents, which offers cost savings through lower shipping costs and longer product life. As Ric Fulop, CEO and cofounder of Desktop Metal, explained to me during a visit to his company's factory, the ability to combine a variety of internal honeycombs makes it possible to achieve a near-perfect balance between weight, strength, material usage, impact resistance, and cost. Fulop also noted the benefit of *de-contenting* — the ability to easily remove extraneous features of a product that customers neither need nor want. It's another way AM is simply better than traditional manufacturing.

- *Multiplying materials options.* More and more materials are being adopted to 3D printing technology. Enhanced plastics strengthened with carbon fibers or nanotubes for high-end uses and extreme environments are already widely in use. So are metals and metal composites for heavy industry, electronics, and consumer durables. Now 3D printing techniques for glass, ceramics, stone, wood, Kevlar, and many other materials are being developed for mass production. And new technologies are allowing two or more materials to be printed in the same step, increasing manufacturing flexibility even more and cutting production times and costs further.

Here's one simple, remarkable example of how these new capabilities are playing out in practical reality. Cessna Denali turboprop engines, manufactured by GE through a joint venture with the aircraft manufacturer, have been redesigned for production via 3D printing. The newly designed engines produce 10 percent more power than similar engines while burning up to 20 percent less fuel. Even more amazing are the gains in manufacturing efficiency. The engines used to contain 845 separate parts, all requiring individual assembly. In the new design, they contain just *eleven* 3D-printed steel and titanium components. Imagine the resulting savings in time, labor, money — not to mention the hundreds of opportunities for a simple yet costly, even dangerous, assembly error eliminated.

## One, Two, Three, Many Technologies

As the industry examples I've presented illustrate, the idea that AM can be used mainly to create desk knickknacks and Christmas ornaments is long past its sell-by date. Attracted by its powerful economic and business benefits, some of the world's biggest industries are already in the process of converting to AM.

Another widespread misunderstanding is the assumption that additive manufacturing is a *single* technology. In fact, there is an amazing number of varieties of AM, and new techniques are continually being developed (see Table 1-2). In this book, I'll be discussing a wide range of innovative AM techniques as applied to many industries. Because my central focus is on the business, strategic, economic, and managerial impacts of these manufacturing innovations rather than their technical underpinnings, I'll often lump all these methodologies together under the general heading of AM, referring to the technical differences among them only when relevant. However, it's important to remember that, in fact, AM is not one technology but rather a family of technologies that is continually being expanded and improved.

The spread of AM into more and more industries is being driven, in part, by a stream of new breakthroughs in specific technologies. Five that are particularly worth watching in the next two or three years are *Multi-jet fusion printing,* rapidly spreading under the auspices of the 3D printing giant HP; *continuous liquid interface production* (CLIP), as pioneered by the printer company Carbon; *bidirectional single-pass jetting,* a new technique developed by Desktop Metal that is as much as a hundred times faster than older, laser-based systems; *aerosol jet printing,* being developed by Optomec, to print entire electro-mechanical devices in a single run; and *3D inkjet printing,* which companies such as Kateeva are using for mass production of OLED display screens at costs up to 50 percent lower than traditional methods. During 2016–17, all five of these technologies achieved remarkable new levels of speed, accuracy, and affordability — which means they are ready to transform new industries that previously have not been affected by the AM revolution.

One category of technological breakthrough that deserves to be

## TABLE 1-2: SELECTED VARIETIES OF 3D PRINTING

| PROCESS | NOTABLE TECHNOLOGIES WITH DATE INVENTED | DESCRIPTION |
| --- | --- | --- |
| Extruded Layers | Fused Filament Fabrication (FFF) (1989) and Big Area Additive Manufacturing (BAAM) (2014) | Nozzles extrude material to print out plastic parts. |
| Photo-Hardened Layers | Stereolithography (SLA) (1986), Continuous Liquid Interface Production (CLIP) (2014), and Direct Light Processing (DLP) (1987) | Light sources solidify liquid resins in a vat to build an object. |
| Powder-Bed Fused Layers | Selective Laser Sintering (SLS) (1986), Selective Laser Melting (1995), and Multi-Jet Fusion (MJF) (2014) | A laser or infra-red light beam fuses, melts, or welds powdered plastic, ceramic, or metal layer by layer to create a solid structure. |
| Material Jetted Layers | 3d Inkjet Printing (1998) | A hollow needle lays down dots of liquid resin that are bonded by an ultraviolet laser to form an object. |
| Aerosol Sprayed Layers | Aerosol Jet Manufacturing (AJM) (2004) | A mist generator breaks down source material (polymers) into a fine stream that is precisely laid down by a deposition head. |
| Direct Energy Deposited Layers | Laser Engineered Net Shape (LENS) (1997) and Electron Beam Additive Manufacturing (EBAM) (2009) | Metal powder or wire is melted or welded together using heat from a laser, electron beam, or other sources. |
| Cladded Layers | Laser Cladding, also called Laser Metal Deposition (1974) | A laser melts powdered or wire feedstock materials to cover a surface with a thin layer of metal. |
| Adhered Layers | Binder Jetting (1993) and Single-Pass Jetting (2015) | A roller or print head lays down a layer of powder that is then bonded using a bonding agent or a sintering process. |
| Laminated Layers | Selective Deposition Lamination (2003) | Heat, pressure, or binders are selectively applied to adhere layers of material together to form an object. |

| TYPICAL USES | COMPANIES |
|---|---|
| Prototyping, plastic end-use parts for automotive and aerospace industries, and making large objects such as car structures and submarine hulls | Ford, Jabil, Lowe's, Mattel, Boeing, Local Motors, Oak Ridge National Lab |
| Prototyping and production of parts for the dental, jewelry, footwear, and automotive industries | Sony, GM, Ford, GE, Tesla, Disney, New Balance, Adidas, Boeing, Novartis |
| Manufacturing of functional components with complex geometries for many industries | Boeing, Airbus, Nike, New Balance, GE, 3M, NASA, Stryker, Johnson & Johnson, Siemens, Autodesk |
| Manufacturing of OLED screens and embedded electronics including multi-layer printed circuit boards | LG, Samsung |
| Manufacture of fine-feature circuitry and embedded electronic components, including antennas and sensors | GE, NASA, Lockheed Martin, US Air Force, Lite-On, Bosch |
| Repair of metal structures or adding material to existing components; low-quantity manufacturing of large-scale, high-value parts in the aerospace, defense, and medical industries | GE, NASA, Autodesk, TE Connectivity, Airbus, Lockheed Martin |
| Applying high-performance corrosion-resistant materials to pipe interiors or turbine blades | Toshiba, GE, United Technologies |
| Production of sand molds, cores and parts for aerospace, automotive, and heavy industries | US Navy, BMW, Ford, Caterpillar, BMW, Lowe's, Google, Caterpillar |
| Full-color parts for industries including education, architecture, and medicine | Staples, Honda, NASA, Boeing, Nike, MIT |

specially highlighted is *monolithic printing*. This refers to a number of techniques that create products without joints or seams — in one continuous process — without reliance on layering methods. Carbon's CLIP technology is one example. Monolithic processes are much faster than layering processes, providing increased capacity, faster turnaround times, and access to complex geometries that are otherwise impossible. As of late 2017, monolithic processes with these capabilities are still under development. However, they will eventually eliminate the need for human interaction with printers, leading to a completely autonomous factory setting.

Another factor that is driving the accelerating spread of AM is the emergence of open materials, product design, and software systems for controlling 3D printers and other machines. Closed systems generally discourage adoption and tend to slow the development and spread of innovations, while open systems invite the world to participate in producing and sharing new applications. The world became familiar with this dynamic by following the lengthy battle between Apple's once-closed software system and the open systems championed by Microsoft and Linux. Eventually, Apple's belated launch of its app store paved the way for thousands of outside companies to create applications for the iPhone and other Apple devices.

For years, 3D printer companies used closed systems to run their machines. As of 2017, however, there is a growing trend toward open systems. For example, the giant HP now offers a materials development kit to third parties who want to test the compatibility of new materials with HP's Multi Jet Fusion printers. HP has also launched partnerships with a host of chemical and materials companies, with whom it is co-developing new materials for use in 3D printing. These trends are opening up the field and encouraging creativity. Unfortunately, open systems also increase the vulnerability of AM to malicious hacking, a problem that I believe will have the long-term effect of giving an advantage to big companies that are rich and powerful enough to develop and implement strong security systems.

In addition, we're now seeing the emergence of a number of remarkable offshoot technologies in which AM is applied in unique ways for specialized purposes. Some of these have startling implications for the future.

One such offshoot is *4D printing*, in which Einstein's fourth dimension — time — plays a critical role in shaping the product and maximizing its usefulness. In 4D printing, 3D-printed structures take on a new, permanent form when conditions such as heat or moisture are applied. 4D printing is closely related to *self-assembly*, an experimental new technology that enables multipart devices to reshape themselves over time. The Self-Assembly Lab at MIT, a hotbed of experimentation in these areas, has developed innovations like the so-called Active Auxetic material — a fabric that automatically contracts in cold weather, thereby providing extra warmth for a user wearing an Auxetic garment. The lab is also working on technologies to enable automated self-assembly of devices as complex as smartphones. Once perfected, these technologies could drastically reduce manufacturing costs for a wide range of electronic and other products, putting more powerful tools into the hands of millions more people, with profound and far-reaching economic effects.

In the Prologue to this book, I mentioned the use of *big area additive manufacturing (BAAM)* by Lockheed Martin. This is a technique that enables the use of 3D printing to build very large objects. Picture an array of 3D printers mounted on scaffolding and actually *moving* in space to generate 3D parts larger than the printer itself. The objects built in this way often include bays into which specialized, separately made modules can be fitted — a process I've dubbed *mass modularization*. This approach is now beginning to be applied to products from cars and airplanes to houses, saving time, money, materials, and other resources. It also makes possible a new degree of flexibility, with production of large-scale objects moving from giant factories to on-site locations that can be moved from place to place quickly and easily as market changes demand.

Yet another remarkable AM innovation is *nanoprinting*, used to print objects at scales of between 1 and 100 billionths of a meter. (A typical protein molecule, for example, might be around 10 nanometers across.) Nanoprinting is currently being used in research work, particularly in medicine — for example, to test the feasibility of using 3D-printed nanobots to deliver medicines to specific locations in a patient's body or to perform cleanups of toxic or cancerous regions within the body. Eventually, it's likely to enable an array of therapeutic techniques that physicians and biologists are only beginning to imagine. Breakthroughs in nanoprinting will also make it possible to use AM to produce precision-formed objects that are incredibly small — for example, batteries tinier than a grain of sand that could serve as energy sources for nanorobots assisting in ultradelicate medical procedures.

One more area of innovation — and maybe the most mind-boggling of them all — is *bioprinting*, a form of AM that uses so-called bioinks to create structures that mimic the functioning of naturally created living tissues. These bioinks are generally composed of a mixture of two kinds of substances: living cells, and the "extracellular matrix," a combination of biological materials and chemicals that provides structural and chemical support to the cells. Experimenters with bioprinting are working to create functional blood vessels made from endothelial cells, which make up the inner lining of natural blood vessels. The availability of AM-produced blood vessels could be a big step forward in making organ transplants easier and safer, since the lack of blood vessels is a major stumbling block in such transplants. Bioprinting is already being used to create tissues for use in drug testing and pathology experiments, skin cells for use in grafts and repairs, and living materials for other applications.

In all its variations, AM is poised to open up many incredible new technological, scientific, and commercial opportunities in the future. Some will involve arenas of human activity you might be startled to associate with digital manufacturing. Take food, for example. Companies such as Hershey, Nestlé, and Barilla (an Italian pasta maker) have already been using AM techniques to make food items with unique shapes, textures, and forms. It's a natural application of the slow, precisely controlled additive layering process that AM enables. Now scientists and researchers have been experimenting with more unusual food-related AM applications, including the possibility of converting proteins from algae, beet leaves, and even insects into flour, which is then used to make healthy, tasty, and edible pastes for use in 3D printers. NASA is even testing AM as a method for producing foods in space — printing pizzas in the International Space Station, for example.

The unique capabilities of AM are also being applied to a serious environmental challenge below the seas — the deterioration of the world's coral reefs due to climate change, water pollution, and overfishing. Fabien Cousteau, grandson of the famous underwater explorer Jacques Cousteau, is working with his own nonprofit organization, the Ocean Learning Center, to test the use of AM to create artificial coral reefs that closely mimic the shapes and textures of natural reefs. The goal is to attract young coral polyps to nest in the nooks and crannies of the printed reefs, creating a growing structure that will eventually provide a home for many other forms of sea life. No other technology is capable of producing structures so similar to those found in natural reefs. Cousteau is using the technique in Bonaire in the Caribbean, hoping to revive a local reef that is suffering from bleaching and a loss of biological diversity. If it works, the same approach could be used worldwide, from the Persian Gulf to Australia's Great Barrier Reef.

Perhaps you're beginning to sense what close observers of the world of technology have realized — that 3D printing and other forms of additive manufacturing have the potential to play a transformative role in practically every field of human endeavor.

## Systems Within Systems: AM as a Crucial Link in a Chain of World-Changing Technologies

The remarkable, still-evolving array of new technologies that constitutes additive manufacturing is interesting and significant in itself. More important is the long-range impact these technologies are poised to have on the world economy. In the years ahead, additive manufacturing is likely to transform the way practically everything is made. The changes will affect the nature, size, organization, and location of manufacturing facilities; the scale and structure of employment in the manufacturing sector; the ways goods are marketed, sold, warehoused, and distributed; the ways R&D, innovation, and product development are conducted; the internal and external structures of companies and the interrelationships among them; the nature of competition; the structure of entire industries; and even the global balance of power among countries in the developed and developing worlds.

These changes will take time, of course. But all will be the ultimate outcomes of the playing-out of trends launched with the invention, spread, and development of additive manufacturing.

If it seems far-fetched to imagine that a single breakthrough could have this kind of impact, consider the long-term effects of James Watt's 1781 development of the first steam engine capable of producing continuous rotary motion — the core technology underlying the first industrial revolution. Or the ultimate impact of Claude Shannon's 1948 article "A Mathematical Theory of Communication," which established the intellectual basis for the digitization of information, and therefore, in turn, for the computer revolution.

Of course, these individual breakthroughs required many supporting elements before they could transform the world. But history suggests that once the crucial core technology is in place, the other pieces of the puzzle generally follow. That's what happened with the steam revolution and with the computing revolution . . . and the same process is well under way with the manufacturing revolution of the twenty-first century.

In the first stage, already happening in many industries, additive manufacturing technologies are being combined with more familiar, traditional manufacturing techniques — such as the assembly line pioneered by early-twentieth-century innovators like Henry Ford. In many factories around the world, 3D printers are being installed in spare corners, where they are used to turn out parts or tools on demand. The items thus produced help to feed the conventional manufacturing process, often obviating the need to pre-order and warehouse little-used parts and thereby saving time and money.

These systems in which AM tools serve merely as accessories or adjuncts to traditional production methods are just the first stage in the emerging manufacturing revolution. Before long, we'll consider them relatively primitive. The next stage is already beginning. In this stage, the new AM techniques will increasingly be combined with other high-tech tools that are themselves undergoing rapid development and advancement — tools like robotics, lasers, cloud computing, artificial intelligence, machine learning, and the Internet of Things.

All these tools are made possible through the power of digitization, which makes the entire system more flexible, efficient, and versatile, since it is controlled by software systems that can quickly and easily be revised, updated, and enhanced as circumstances require. Their impact will expand several-fold when combined with the power of the industrial platforms that many companies are now developing. These platforms will use the connective tissue of the Internet and the data storage and analysis capabilities of the Cloud to link hundreds of companies, thousands of 3D printers and other AM machines, and millions of suppliers and customers into networks that can respond instantly to shifts in demand, supply fluctuations, economic trends, and other changes.

Over the next two to three decades, this array of developments — the various forms of AM, the ancillary digital tools that help make AM even more efficient, and the industrial platforms that combine all these technologies into vast, ultrapowerful, and hyperefficient manufacturing systems — will add up to what I'm calling the pan-industrial revolution. It will generate upheavals that will transform not just the world of manufacturing but the entire global economy.

# 2

# EXPANDED SCOPE

## *Making (Almost) Anything, Anywhere*

MASS MANUFACTURING AS DEVELOPED in the late nineteenth and early twentieth centuries was a remarkable technological and economic achievement. By developing methods of unprecedented efficiency for making standardized products by the millions, mass manufacturers drove down the price of goods and made them available for the first time to vast numbers of newly middle-class consumers around the world. But that efficiency came at a cost. Typical mass manufacturing methods are both highly capital-intensive and very inflexible. Setting up the machines to produce and assemble a particular product is expensive and time-consuming, and changeovers from one design to another lead to additional costs and loss of productivity. Factor in unpredictable problems like mechanical breakdowns, power outages, raw material shortages, and operator errors, and you come up with a total downtime rate that varies between 3 and 6 percent — all of it representing hours when money is being spent without generating a dollar in revenue.

The inflexibility of traditional manufacturing methods drastically reduces the scope of what a factory can do. For maximum efficiency, a company is forced to restrict the range of products made at a given facility and avoid frequent changes in design, materials used, and other variations. The result is a rigid system with painfully limited ability to respond to ever-changing consumer demands.

If only there were a better way . . .

## Making So Much More: Additive Manufacturing
## Expands the Scope of the Factory

Manufacturing experts have long wrestled with the challenges of bringing greater flexibility, efficiency, and scope to factory operations. For decades, they've worked on problems like the cost of changeovers, the complexity of setup processes, and the losses caused by machine breakdowns, and they've achieved incremental improvements in all these areas. Beginning in the 1990s, the *lean manufacturing* movement, inspired by the success of Toyota and other Japanese manufacturers at the forefront of the quality movement, has tackled many of these challenges, with fair success. But the fundamental problem of relying on dedicated machines that are designed, set up, and programmed to perform just a single production function — and that must be completely overhauled or replaced whenever a change in product or product design takes place — has remained unsolved.

Today, thanks to entirely new methods of making things, a better way is finally emerging. Companies around the world are implementing AM technologies that make production facilities more efficient, flexible, and productive than ever before.

One example is NextGenAM, a "factory of the future" being built in Varel, Germany, by a consortium of three firms — the 3D printer manufacturer EOS, the Airbus subsidiary Premium Aerotech, and the automaker Daimler AG. In this giant automated plant, machines will be arranged in banks for each stage of the production process: 3D printing, milling, heat treatment, laser texturing, assembly by robotic arms, and inspection. Each bank is connected to the next by a fleet of moving machines that collect and transport parts or materials to the next bank. The goal: to build a variety of metal parts for cars, aircraft, and potentially other products using additive manufacturing more quickly and efficiently than is now possible. In particular, the NextGenAM system is expected to trim the expense and time requirements associated with the postprocessing of 3D-printed parts, which now makes up close to 70 percent of the total cost of AM.

Another example is an AM facility opened in 2017 by the U.S. engineering giant Emerson on its manufacturing campus in Singapore. This is Emerson's second facility with AM capabilities; the first was opened in Marshalltown, Iowa, in 2014. The Singapore plant is especially targeting Emerson's customers in the Asia-Pacific region, which produce some 22 percent of the company's revenues. In addition to handling pilot production projects, the Singapore facility is focusing on manufacturing parts that are impossible to build using traditional manufacturing methods — for instance, advanced industrial control valves, which are highly complex devices that can be built more quickly and inexpensively, and with less extraneous weight, using 3D printing. The Singapore plant will provide similar customized parts for power plants, refineries, and other business sectors, including precision engineering and aerospace.

Then there is the TechCenter AM facility in Mulheim an der Ruhr, Germany, opened by the engineering firm ThyssenKrupp in September 2017. Equipped with machinery for 3D printing in both plastics and metals, the factory manufactures customized products for several of Thyssenkrupp's customers across a range of industries, including engineering, automotive, naval shipbuilding, and aerospace. A number of the items manufactured at the center would be impossible to produce using traditional manufacturing methods — for example, a probe for taking gas samples from furnaces that includes integrated cooling channels, making it extraordinarily heat-resistant.

GE's factory in Pune, India, offers yet another example of this rapidly growing trend. Like the other facilities I've described, this "multimodal" factory uses AM to produce parts and products for a variety of industries. The Pune facility illustrates what GE calls its "Brilliant Factory" strategy — a new approach to production management that combines 3D printing and other forms of additive manufacturing with robotics, digital sensors to gather data, powerful analytic software, and distributed controls integrated into the Internet of Things. GE executives claim this array of technologies has already reduced machine downtimes in its Brilliant Factories to *less than 1 percent*. Compare this with typical rates of 3 to 6 percent, and you can quickly imagine the many millions of dollars in cost savings that GE is realizing.

The innovations being implemented at factories like these are the first steps toward a future in which companies can efficiently manufacture almost anything, almost anywhere — and shift production from one product to another, and even from one industry sector to another, whenever market changes require it.

That's the power of vastly expanded scope. It's something new in the world of business.

## Economies of Scope: A Set of Newly Available Strategic Tools

Every business student is familiar with the term *economies of scale*. These are the cost benefits that companies enjoy when they are able to serve a large market with goods and services produced in mass quantities. They include the lower cost of raw materials purchased in bulk; the ability to spread fixed costs for administration, sales, marketing, and other functions over a larger revenue base; and the competitive advantages often enjoyed by companies with large-scale operations.

Economies of scope, however, are quite different — and much less familiar. They arise when a company is capable of producing a wide range of products and product categories, thereby serving a broad array of markets, spanning customer types and geographies. This kind of broad-scope business model can produce enormous cost savings. When you can market, sell, and distribute a huge portfolio of goods while operating as a single business platform, the ratio of your overhead expenses to overall revenues becomes much smaller, greatly enhancing your profitability. When you can also manufacture a wide array of goods by processing a relatively simple array of raw materials in a single factory equipped with a few highly versatile machines, additional cost savings materialize, driving profits higher still.

Not so long ago, such economies of scope were very difficult or even impossible to obtain. A few businesses could generate some of them. For example, when the online retailer Amazon expanded from a bookseller into "the everything store," it realized economies of scope that few retailers have enjoyed since the decline of the once-mighty department store empires. But most companies have found that practical limitations — especially the sheer complexity of trying to successfully manage a business that addresses multiple markets with a vast array of varied goods — put economies of scope out of reach.

This explains why the conglomerate business model, so popular in the 1960s, fell out of favor. It's the reason the legendary investment guru Peter Lynch coined the term "diworsification" to describe the results obtained by most corporations that expanded beyond their scope of competence. It's why such businesses tend to command share prices *below* the value of their combined assets — the so-called conglomerate discount. And it's also why industrial giants such as General Electric and Honeywell are under pressure to "deconglomerate" — to sell off disparate divisions in an effort to become more focused operations.

The advent of additive manufacturing has the potential to change all that.

3D printing and other AM technologies enable companies to vastly expand their scope of operations *without* suffering any of the disadvantages such breadth formerly entailed. The managers of a multimodal manufacturing plant don't have to focus narrowly on a single industry in order to be efficient. The versatility of AM means they can operate simultaneously in several industries, producing a wide range of products and parts on the same machines and often using the same raw materials (such as standardized metal powders).

AM also involves much simpler, faster, and cheaper setup costs than other forms of production. Expensive dies, molds, tools, and other devices aren't needed; instead, a relatively easy swapping-out of a digital design file enables the same basic machine to produce any desired product or part. And this flexibility means that the factory as a whole — as well as every individual machine in the factory — will experience much less downtime, leading to huge savings for the company.

### Why Additive Manufacturing Is the Best Way to Achieve Economies of Scope

The economies of scope made possible by additive manufacturing come in other forms as well. Because the same equipment can be used to make a wide range of products, the cost of capital equipment is spread out over a much bigger sales base, effectively making the machinery cheaper to buy, install, maintain, and upgrade. In the same way, other costs associated with running the business — administrative costs, IT costs, and the cost of developing and managing the complex computer software and data analysis systems that control the additive manufacturing system—can be spread out over a bigger base, making them a smaller fraction of the total.

Something similar happens with the cost of raw materials. Imagine a factory equipped with a number of the new AM machines that can print a wide variety of tools, parts, and devices from the same kind of metal powder. It's a form of highly flexible manufacturing that the latest methods of 3D printing have made possible. The managers of such a factory can buy vast amounts of that powder, thereby qualifying for bulk purchase discounts. Traditional manufacturers who need to buy raw materials in more specialized forms and in smaller quantities— sheet metal for some parts, plate metal for others, rods or bars for still others—aren't usually eligible to obtain such discounts.

Of course, I'm not arguing that AM enables companies to manufacture literally anything. Differences in materials, customer needs, marketing methods, and financial requirements will still encourage manufacturers to specialize to a degree. For example, in the near future, we can expect to see AM-based manufacturing companies that focus on products made with metals, or more specifically on heavy metal equipment sold to businesses. Other AM companies might focus on plastic consumer goods. Thus, manufacturers will continue to choose to limit the products they make, focusing on a collection of related goods they can market and sell to a reasonably coherent set of customers.

Still, it's clear that a factory that can make a wide array of products can operate much more efficiently than a traditional, limited-scope factory, leading almost inevitably to a vastly enhanced economic picture—and a much rosier bottom line.

Notice that these benefits are quite different from those promised by Industry 4.0, an alternative vision of the future of manufacturing —and much more transformational. Turbocharging the traditional factory by equipping it with robots, lasers, and other forms of new equipment (as prescribed by Industry 4.0) can certainly produce improvements in production speed, waste reduction, and other efficiencies. It may even make a plant more flexible. But it can't generate the vastly expanded scope that AM makes possible—or the economies of scope that emerge as a natural consequence.

Other ways additive manufacturing can achieve economies of scope include the following:

*Ability to adjust the company's product scope as needed.* A flexible AM factory can widen or narrow its product scope much more quickly and easily than a traditional manufacturing facility. This means that when market demand for one product falls while demand for a new product increases, the company can shift gears swiftly. And if a company finds itself with an unexpected megahit on its hands, it can rapidly convert an entire string of factories to producing huge quantities of the hot product — thereby avoiding the frustrating problem of leaving money on the table due to the inability to satisfy demand.

*Ability to adjust the company's geographic scope as needed.* AM factories making a given product mix can be located almost anywhere in the world. They can vary in size, be positioned close to customers, and can be moved closer to sources of raw materials, expanded, or shrunk more easily than traditional facilities. Thus, the reallocation of production across geographies is easier. When changes in the supply chain become desirable — for example, when transportation costs, tariffs, and duties are increased to protect a country or trade bloc, or when a natural disaster cuts off the supply of an essential raw material in another region — the parent company can make rapid, inexpensive adjustments. As a result, the efficiency and production level of a company can be stabilized or optimized, and supply chains can be, more than ever, driven by smart management choices rather than forced by practical limitations, making greatly expanded scope far easier to achieve.

*Access to a wider scope of information.* Expanded scope gives a company the opportunity to establish a foothold in many industries — which means the ability to learn from designers, engineers, technology experts, and marketers from a wide range of industries. As AM companies develop expertise in a wide assortment of industries, great ideas will spread more rapidly, accelerating the pace of innovation. And production coordination will be easier.

*Preferential treatment by suppliers, retailers, and others in the value chain.* Companies such as Procter & Gamble and Colgate-Palmolive get most-favored-nation treatment from supermarkets because of the huge assortment of consumer goods they make. In a similar way, when a given company uses the expanded scope provided by AM to broaden its array of product offerings, it will gradually become a one-stop shop for selected customers, and will increase its relative standing among other companies in the value chain — materials suppliers, service providers, retailers, distributors, and more.

*Enormous cost savings by spreading expenses over a broader market base.* Every organization has significant costs that can't be attributed directly to a single product — backroom expenses, warehousing and shipping facilities, R&D budgets, administrative expenses, and more. A company that takes advantage of the expanded scope AM makes possible will be able to draw upon wider, deeper, and more numerous revenue streams in defraying these costs, thereby boosting profit margins across the board.

*Improving the scope to innovate within current or new markets quickly and easily.* The flexibility of AM processes means companies can make changes in product designs far more frequently than in the past. The stages of product design, prototyping, testing, and manufacturing that traditionally have taken months or years can now be reduced to weeks or even days thanks to digital systems that streamline every step. Thus, when new product ideas surface or customer preferences shift, companies that use AM methods can respond quickly, and their boundaries become amorphous. This wider scope to innovate includes the following:

*Increased opportunity to find and fill white spaces in between products.* Historically, one of the biggest sources of growth for companies has been the ability to identify and fill unfilled market niches. For example, a company can design and produce products that are a little bigger, more complex, and highly featured than those wanted by Customer A but smaller, simpler, and easier to use than those wanted by Customer C. The result can be a product that turns out to be perfect for Customer B — a person never before recognized or catered to. The unmatched speed and flexibility of innovation that AM makes possible will enable companies to experiment with white-space product launches more creatively and aggressively than ever before.

*Increased opportunity to occupy red spaces in markets through richer product assortments.* Companies that take advantage of the expanded scope made possible by AM will be able to produce more goods, in greater variety, to satisfy the needs of existing customers even more fully. They'll develop variant products that can be used more frequently, on different occasions, in different settings, and to meet different consumer objectives. This type of creativity generates the ability to sell many more products to a particular set of customers, thereby maximizing the bang from every buck spent on marketing, selling, and advertising efforts aimed at that market segment.

*Increased opportunity to discover and claim blue spaces in untapped, previously unimagined market territories.* AM is already making possible the design and production of entirely new kinds of products, from microscale and nanoscale medical and scientific devices to artificial coral reefs and, someday, 3D-printed human organs. It's impossible to predict the variety of new markets that AM-driven companies will create in the decades to come, but it's likely that some will help to spawn the giant growth industries of the future, occupying blue spaces no one today has defined.

*Ability to meet almost all the needs of particular customers, thereby simplifying their purchasing choices, reducing their costs, and becoming even more important to them.* The best-run AM companies will use the broader scope they enjoy to produce goods that meet an ever-growing share of the needs of a given set of companies. For example, a business-to-business (B2B) supplier may find it can grow from making 25 percent of the parts used by a particular customer to making 35 percent, then to 50 percent and more. This will tend to generate a positive cycle of effects, since the customer will find it easier and more convenient to coordinate purchasing, delivery, payment, and other processes with one big supplier than with a host of smaller ones.

These are just a few examples of the wide variety of ways that AM enables the creation of economies of scope. In the years to come, the expanded scope of AM will give leading-edge manufacturing firms huge advantages their less-advanced rivals can scarcely hope to match.

## The Next Frontier: Economies of Integration

As I've explained, AM creates the potential to vastly expand the scope of manufacturing companies through the unprecedented flexibility it provides. In this new world, the same factory equipped with the same machinery can be used to produce parts for sports cars, lawn mowers, minivans, golf carts, and railroad carriages — just by downloading new design files to the printers. Companies will have a broad range of new options as to what to produce, where to produce it, and which markets to serve.

Some companies will choose to orchestrate a new overarching strategy around a particular set of technological options. For example, it would be possible to build an industrial empire around the technology of 3D printing in metal. Such a company could be the "go-to corporation" for any firm that wants to employ flexible digital technologies for building a wide array of metal-based products. Similarly, other companies could choose to specialize in AM with plastics, ceramics, concrete, bioinks, or other materials, thereby carving out spheres of expertise that would span industries and open up vast areas for long-term growth.

Over time, 3D printing and the other new additive manufacturing techniques will be combined with the whole range of emerging digital technologies, thereby producing even greater capabilities. The ability to electronically link and coordinate the work of many factories in locations around the globe will enable the creation of multiproduct, multimarket manufacturing empires with flexibility, speed, and nimbleness that the old conglomerates could only dream of.

This new flexibility will lead to the most powerful set of economies of scope: a series of benefits referred to as *economies of integration,* which will be the steppingstones to the eventual rise of pan-industrials.

Economies of integration are a special type of economies of scope. They arise when an organization is able to manage a complex set of interrelated, mutually supporting activities with extreme efficiency. We can identify several categories of economies of integration. Here are three of the most important:

- *Product integration* — this can occur through combining parts during the design process so the product is simplified, eliminating assembly and reducing the need for human labor. It can also occur through combining two or more products into one, making it easier to meet multiple customer needs through a single purchase. AM is already making product integration possible for the first time in many cases, as when a complex machine part is 3D printed in a single process rather than having to be assembled from several separately manufactured components.

- *Production stage integration* — combining or coordinating two or more stages of production, thereby simplifying the manufacturing process; reducing the need for special tools, assembly lines, and other facilities; and reducing reliance on outside suppliers. When production stage integration is complete, a single array of AM machines will be able to carry out the entire production process, starting with raw materials, then creating parts, subassemblies, and the complete finished product in one continuous process.

- *Functional integration* — combining processes that have traditionally been separated within companies. For example, the co-creation system Local Motors uses to generate and develop ideas for new vehicles serves to combine the R&D, design, and market testing processes into a single activity. Similarly, when business customers can use 3D printers located at their own facilities to quickly manufacture parts or tools designed by outside suppliers, the manufacturing and inbound logistics processes have been collapsed into a single, integrated function.

You may be familiar with economies of integration from the old "vertically integrated" companies that once benefited from controlling the entire value chain associated with a particular product, service, or market. For example, early automakers once owned and managed every stage in the automotive value chain, from mining raw materials and forging steel to manufacturing car parts, assembling vehicles, and selling them in company-owned dealerships.

During the twentieth century, many vertically integrated businesses disappeared. The main reason was that despite the advantages of integration, they suffered from a variety of economic ills. The two greatest problems were *agency costs* and *bureaucracy costs*.

Agency costs arise when managers who provide goods or services to other divisions of the same company become complacent or inefficient because they're not subject to the pressures of competition found in the open market. As a result, they produce inferior or higher-priced goods.

Bureaucracy costs exist in every organization, simply because planning, organizing, managing, and monitoring activities demand time, energy, and both physical and human resources. In a vertically integrated company, the complexity of the activities being managed is particularly great, leading to exceptionally high bureaucracy costs.

The combination of high agency costs and high bureaucracy costs exerted a serious downward drag on profitability. Considering these problems, executives gradually realized that — in the conditions then current — it was more efficient to break apart the old integrated empires into separate companies that coordinated their activities only through marketplace interactions. As a result, carmakers, for example, came to rely on networks of suppliers for raw materials and parts, and even for activities like design, assembly, marketing, and sales over which they once kept tight internal control. This was a rational change in strategy, reflecting the fact that the existing bureaucratic systems for information management, communication, planning, and coordination were simply too slow and too limited in their capacities. It wasn't possible then to operate a giant, vertically integrated business empire efficiently.

Thanks to AM, this is beginning to change. Consider, for example, the way the economic benefits of production stage integration are starting to emerge through the development of *hybrid fabrication systems*. These systems complement advanced AM techniques with other technologies, such as robotics, electronic sensors, and powerful software systems that are capable of using machine learning and artificial intelligence to continually improve their operations.

An example is the Cosyflex system I described in the Prologue. It starts by combining raw materials to make textiles (rather than requiring workers to specify, select, purchase, ship, store, and deliver textiles to the production facility as needed). It then manufactures the components of the diapers in layers and assembles the parts into a finished garment. Along the way, it uses automated sensors and robotic arms to precisely position, manipulate, and fold the garments as they are produced by the 3D printers.

Another example is the Form Cell, an automated production system introduced in 2017 by a Massachusetts-based 3D printer company called Formlabs. The Form Cell includes a scalable array of Form 2 SLA 3D printers, which can be stacked on shelves; an industrial robotic gantry system; and Form Wash and Form Cure units, which automate the postprinting steps. Smart software handles print job scheduling, error detection, remote monitoring, and part and serial number printing. The entire production system is coordinated by a computer program, allowing production with little or no supervision, making possible, in the words of Formlabs, "the lights-out, 24-hour digital factory."

Thus, the Form Cell integrates 3D printing of parts or products with postprocessing steps, then passes the output to a conveyer belt that delivers it to an assembly line or to a different 3D printer for add-ons (Figure 2-1).

FIGURE 2-1: The Formlabs Form Cell is an automated 3D printing production system powered by a series of Form 2 SLA printers. The enclosed, fully automated system handles printing, postprocessing, and part pick-and-place using robotic arms and smart software controls. COURTESY OF FORMLABS

The hybrid fabrication systems being designed and tested today will be used in a variety of ways. In some factories, a series of 3D printers and other AM machines will be coordinated to produce a multipart product. In others, AM machines will be combined with traditional manufacturing machines or integrated into a traditional assembly line through automated mechanisms for transferring products from one location to another.

Over time, hybrid fabrication systems will become increasingly sophisticated, and able to build large, complicated objects and even combine many kinds of materials — metals, plastics, ceramics, fabrics, and more — in a single pass through the system. As artificial intelligence and machine learning are improved and integrated into the software systems that control the machinery, the result will be tremendously powerful, flexible fabrication systems that actually *learn from experience*. Both agency costs and bureaucracy costs will be drastically reduced as smart machines increasingly replace humans who may be slow, inefficient, and poorly motivated.

The impact of the increasing synergies between additive manufacturing and artificial intelligence has been well described by Peter Zelinski, an astute observer of technological developments. Zelinski notes that AM is inherently more complex than traditional manufacturing, involving "more variables and more combinations of variables affecting the form and properties of the part than we have yet recognized, let alone mastered." Historically, such complexity surrounding a new technology would have meant that learning to take full advantage of that technology would be a long, slow process. But we live in a new era, one in which "machine learning will enable the speed of AM's advance . . . A billion different relationships among many inputs and outputs can be explored rapidly through computation, whereas just a fraction of the same exploration might take human beings working on their own something like a century to carry out." Thanks to the combination of AM and AI, Zelinski writes, "It is simply the speed of discovery that will change, but this change will be profound, and we will even see it accelerate."

In the years to come, the potential for efficient integration of functions thanks to these new manufacturing technologies will expand rapidly. One by one, an array of additional business functions will become closely integrated with manufacturing. In the new world that will exist when the AM transition is complete, it will be possible to organize, manage, and coordinate activities along an entire value chain with much greater efficiency than ever before. Corporations will now discover new advantages to owning and operating entire business ecosystems — a strategy that will be especially valuable in immature markets and emerging economies. Thus, a corporation introducing a new product like electric cars in sub-Saharan Africa may choose to use the new manufacturing, information management, and communications technologies to create and run an entire network of related businesses that will do everything from building and marketing the cars to providing charging stations in convenient locations, servicing the vehicles, and managing car-sharing and ride-hailing services.

Economies of integration will add a powerful new dimension to the economies of scope that AM makes possible. In the near future, a growing number of manufacturing companies will not only be able to make (almost) anything, anywhere; they will also be able to *do* (almost) anything, anywhere. They won't just produce goods but also market them, sell them, deliver them, maintain them, and provide a host of ancillary support services for them, adding untold value to the offerings they provide to customers.

Remarkable, yes — but a natural long-term outcome of the changes now being launched by additive manufacturing and the related technologies now sweeping the planet. This is where we're now headed with AM and the inevitable rise of the pan-industrials.

# 3

# BOUNDLESS SCALE
*Making More, Faster and Cheaper*

WE'VE EXPLAINED HOW ADDITIVE manufacturing — especially in combination with other new technologies — is on the verge of creating new economies of *scope* that have generally eluded traditional companies. But an even bigger surprise may be the way new manufacturing technologies are achieving breakthroughs of *scale* as well.

Economies of scale result when making larger quantities causes the marginal costs of production to go down. Thus, for example, when the same assembly line with a total cost of $100 million is used to produce 100,000 cars rather than 10,000, the cost of all that production equipment is spread out over a much larger number of vehicles — a classic economy of scale. Another example is the way the cost of raw materials often falls when larger quantities are purchased, thanks to the special price discounts that a big customer may qualify for. And yet another example — one that's slightly more subtle — is the economy of scale that may be associated with transportation costs, since producing a large quantity of goods makes it easier to pack trucks to the brim rather than sending them off half empty. The result of this improved efficiency: a lower shipping rate per pound of product.

Economies of scale can have a huge impact on the finances of traditional manufacturing. This is one reason for the dominance of giant companies serving national and even global markets during the nineteenth and twentieth centuries. When it comes to traditional manufacturing, more is virtually always cheaper — and cheaper means more profitable.

Does the same apply to additive manufacturing? The answer is far from obvious. That's especially true because, traditionally, scale and scope have generally been in tension. Historically, a company seeking economies of scale usually had to sacrifice scope — logically enough, since most of the benefits of producing large numbers of a product materialize only when the items produced are identical, or nearly so. That's why Henry Ford used to tell customers considering a Model T, "You can have any color as long as it's black." Customizing cars to meet individual preferences would have slowed Ford's assembly line and mitigated the benefits of scale.

Of course, over time, production methods became more sophisticated, making a modest degree of customization relatively simple and affordable. New car buyers now have several colors to choose from, as well as a variety of other options. But the push and pull between scale and scope remains powerful; traditional mass manufacturing is most efficient only when scope is limited. Therefore, since AM makes possible an unusual array of economies of scope, it might seem logical to conclude that economies of scale are absent when AM is employed. Is that the case?

### The Conventional Wisdom on AM and Economies of Scale

Conventional wisdom says there are no economies of scale with AM. According to this view, the cost of the first item printed is the same as the cost for the one thousandth item printed. But the fact is that some economies of scale do kick in when AM is involved. For example, lower shipping costs will happen when trucks are full rather than half empty, no matter what production method is used in creating the products.

It is true that when AM is employed, some other economies of scale are less significant. For example, 3D printing machines are relatively cheap compared to the kinds of machines found in most traditional factories. (As of spring 2018, many industrial 3D printers carry prices in the $150,000 to $500,000 range, while the machines incorporated in traditional manufacturing systems are routinely priced in the millions.) Since the capital costs associated with AM are much lower than in traditional manufacturing, the ability to spread the cost of production equipment over a large quantity of products will have a smaller impact on the economics of the business. The economies of scale still exist, but their value is more modest.

The relatively smaller role played by certain economies of scale in AM has been a driving force behind some of the lingering skepticism concerning the future of AM. The logic usually goes: "Economies of scale play a major role in making traditional mass production affordable and profitable. AM lacks economies of scale. Therefore, mass production using AM will never be affordable and profitable."

Thus, in a 2015 article, a respected Oxford professor of operations management named Matthias Holweg, after conceding the cost advantages AM enjoys when it comes to customized items, commented, "However, we also know that 99% of all manufactured parts are standard and do not require customization. In these cases, 3D printing has to compete with scale-driven manufacturing processes and rather efficient logistics operations." This led Holweg to conclude, "Contrary to what some say, 3D printing is *not* going to revolutionize the manufacturing sector, rendering traditional factories obsolete. The simple fact of the matter is the economics of 3D printing now and for the foreseeable future make it an unfeasible way to produce the vast majority of parts manufactured today."

In one sense, the objection raised by skeptics like Professor Holweg had some validity . . . for a time. In the earliest systems for 3D printing, unlike in many traditional manufacturing methods, one item was indeed made at a time. This tended to make AM relatively slow, and therefore relatively costly, in comparison with traditional manufacturing. Furthermore, the same one-at-a-time methodology meant that every item produced cost practically the same as any other, in comparison to the sharply reduced unit costs enjoyed whenever a mass manufacturer could increase production quantities.

In effect, the skeptics believed that the comparative cost efficiencies of *traditional manufacturing* and *additive manufacturing* could be depicted in a graph like the one shown in Figure 3-1.

Based on this supposed absence of economies of scale, skeptics often declared that AM would always remain a niche technology with limited impact on the business world. A few still make this claim. But

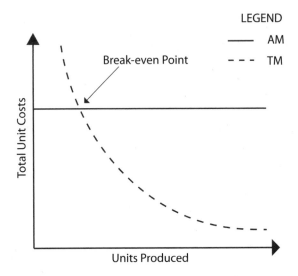

FIGURE 3-1: The conventional view of additive manufacturing efficiency, which assumes that there are no economies of scale associated with AM. In this view, traditional manufacturing (TM), which does enjoy economies of scale, becomes more cost-efficient than AM at a relatively low break-even point. However, advances in AM technology mean that this view is no longer valid.

most of the skeptics are now retreating in the face of certain crucial, changing realities.

## The New Wisdom on Economies of Scale and AM

Today, additive manufacturing is achieving economies of scale in a variety of ways — and doing so without sacrificing economies of scope. As a result, we are now seeing the increasing application of AM to the making of standardized products in mass quantities. No longer limited to product prototypes, customized one-offs, or specialized items made in small quantities, AM is now beginning to take over the kinds of mass manufacturing that have long dominated the industrial economy.

It has taken time for this to happen. As with any complex technology, the process of development and adoption has not been a matter of simple upward progress but rather a mixture of reversals, dead ends, and remarkable breakthroughs.

Several new AM technologies are enabling rapid production of mass quantities of products. They include multi-jet fusion for plastics, single-pass jetting for metals, aerosol jet spraying for electronics, printoptical for glass, inkjet printing for digital electronics screens, and SLA printing for dental braces. New tools like these are steadily making additive manufacturing faster and lowering the unit cost of the items so produced.

A notable source of improved production speed and reduced cost has been the increased size of the build chamber, resin vat, or powder bed in new AM devices. The larger the build area, the more copies of the same product that can be made in a given time. Other sources include faster, more precise ways to deposit and harden materials layer by layer.

Another big breakthrough in mass additive manufacturing has come about through improvements in production quality. For example, in the early days of 3D printing, the layering processes commonly used created striations on the surface of products. Removing these defects often required postprocessing steps involving machines for smoothing and polishing surfaces or time-consuming hand craftsmanship. These problems have now largely been solved thanks to better printing processes, automated postprocessing systems, and digital technologies for monitoring and managing product quality. Thus, the yield rate of AM is getting better, making large-volume production more affordable.

Still another breakthrough has been the development, spread, and multiplication of hybrid fabrication systems like the ones I described in Chapter 2. Such systems are now on the cusp of producing high-quantity efficiencies equal to those that traditional manufacturers enjoy.

Consider, for example, the growing number of companies that are developing sophisticated robotic systems to "tend" 3D printer farms — collecting finished objects as they emerge from the printers, placing them on racks for drying or finishing as needed, and inserting new "build plates" into the printers to start the processing of creating a new object. A single robotic arm, cleverly programmed, can tend a cluster of printers untiringly, handling these menial but essential tasks with near-perfect accuracy, and permitting 3D printing facilities to run continually.

Jonathan Schwartz, chief product officer for Brooklyn-based Voo-doo Manufacturing, describes an experiment with a system of this type (Figure 3-2). The system features a robotic arm tending nine 3D printers with a conveyor belt to transport objects as they are finished:

> Seeing it fully operational for the first time was amazing. We ran it unmanned overnight, and in the morning it had been producing parts for 14 hours straight! We're now excited to deploy it at scale and increase our factory's capacity by close to 400% . . . This is how we're going to scale the company of the future from 160 printers to-day, to ten thousand 3D printers tomorrow.

3-2: Voodoo Manufacturing's "Project Skywalker," which uses a robotic arm, 3D printers mounted on server racks, and an automated "plate hopper" that feeds new tasks to the printers as needed. It's a small-scale version of the kind of hybrid fabrication systems that are bringing unprecedented speed and efficiency to additive manufacturing. COURTESY OF VOODOO MANUFACTURING

The Form Cell system I described in Chapter 2 is another exam-ple of a fabrication system. Unlike the Voodoo system, Form Cell adds postprocessing among the production steps that can be managed au-tomatically. Note, however, that both the Voodoo system and the Form

Cell system allow manufacturers to increase production speed and quantity simply by adding more printers. As a result of breakthroughs like these, additive manufacturing operations can now begin to build products not by the tens or even by the hundreds but rather by the thousands, the tens of thousands, and ultimately the millions. This means that manufacturing-based economies of scale based on sharply reduced unit costs are beginning to emerge, making true mass market additive manufacturing a possibility for the first time.

## How Additive Manufacturing Enables Economies of Scale in Adjacent Functions

You've seen how the latest AM technologies are making it possible for companies to achieve economies of scale through increasingly efficient production of large quantities of products. Equally impressive is the fact that these new, more efficient AM technologies enable cost savings *in adjacent business functions*. These are economic efficiencies centered in activities that are *not* part of the manufacturing process itself but still highly relevant to the overall costs incurred by the business. Here are some examples of the business processes that are benefiting from the indirect cost savings made possible by improvements in additive manufacturing:

- *Outbound logistics and distribution.* AM facilities can be smaller and more flexible than the giant plants built to house long assembly lines. Thus, rather than building a huge factory to produce goods for an entire continent, a company can create a series of small, localized production facilities. If production quantity is great enough to justify building many AM factories, many of these facilities can be placed closer to customers. This has the effect of reducing outbound shipping costs, the inventory carrying costs of finished goods, and the need for large warehouses. It will also shorten lead times. Each of these changes trims expenses and benefits the bottom line.
- *Purchasing costs.* When a firm produces more copies of the same item, it needs to purchase more raw materials. This often qualifies the firm for lower bulk purchase rates. In addition, when a firm uses

more of the same material for many copies of the same item, there is more unused material left over from the earlier print jobs. This material can be recycled, again reducing the unit cost of the items printed later in the run. This means that the savings enjoyed when materials are purchased in bulk are now becoming possible with AM — as vividly illustrated by Carbon's 2017 announcement of a "production-scale materials program" slated to reduce the cost of resin by more than 50 percent in the next few years.

- *Marketing, sales, and distribution costs.* When a company produces more of a given product, the per-unit cost for advertising, branding, promotion, access to shelf space, and other selling and marketing expenses goes down. The net effect is an economy of scale.

- *Overhead costs.* As the volume of a product that is printed goes up, the cost per unit for overhead allocation is decreased. For example, the costs of IT infrastructure, software, human resources management, headquarters, taxes, insurance, interest payments, and rent are all spread out over more units.

Taken together, these indirect economies of scale provide the newest AM systems with cost advantages that slower, low-volume 3D printers couldn't match.

The failure to recognize the existence of these indirect economies of scale is another problem with the conventional analysis of AM efficiencies of scale as presented by skeptics like Matthias Holweg. For example, in Professor Holweg's 2015 paper, which I had the opportunity to discuss with him, he ignored ancillary economic benefits made possible by AM, such as reduced inventory carrying costs, discounts on raw materials thanks to the use of bulk powders, and reduced transportation costs.

In that sense, Holweg's paper was a typical illustration of what might be called "the engineer's blind spot." Holweg meticulously calculated the costs of AM that are direct, obvious, and easily measurable . . . while ignoring more substantial costs that are indirect, subtle, and often difficult to measure. In addition, he made another mistake in his logic. He chose an older AM technology (selective laser melting) that was not designed for large-volume production, and hence tautologically found no evidence of lower costs from volume production.

Experience is now revealing economies of scale associated with AM that did not exist when the technology was largely restricted to low-volume 3D printing. In effect, the traditional view of AM cost per unit shown in Figure 3-1 needs to be replaced with a new, more accurate image — one in which the AM cost line is curved to reflect lower costs and higher volumes. The new graph, seen in Figure 3-3, reflects that AM actually enjoys its own economies of scale, though ones that are different from those produced by traditional manufacturing.

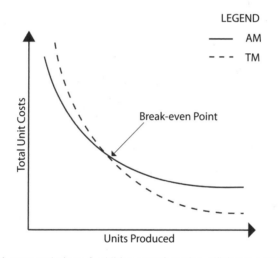

FIGURE 3-3: A corrected view of additive manufacturing efficiency, which reflects the economies of scale associated with AM. These economies of scale drive down the cost of producing goods using AM as the number of units manufactured increases—hence, the curved line shown for additive manufacturing cost per unit (replacing the straight line assumed in Figure 3-1). At the present time (mid-2018), in many industries there is still a relatively low break-even point at which traditional manufacturing becomes more cost-effective than AM.

A more inclusive, big-picture analysis reveals the emerging reality. Rather than being in tension, scale and scope can now be combined. This represents a huge win for manufacturers, as the costly tradeoffs demanded by traditional manufacturing are no longer necessary.

## Non-Economies-of-Scale-Based Cost Savings in AM

Other big shifts in AM costs help to explain why AM is rapidly becoming a replacement for traditional manufacturing methods. Production
experts have gradually come to recognize the nonscale advantages
that AM can offer — that is, cost reductions equally available at all volumes of 3D printing.

Consider, for example, the 2015 report on the present and near-term
prospects for 3D printing in which the consulting and research firm
A. T. Kearney concluded that "traditional manufacturing will have
cost advantages in large-scale production settings for the foreseeable future." In other words, while 3D printing was already more cost-
effective than traditional subtractive manufacturing for small quantities of products back in 2015 — and in some cases even cheaper at high
quantities — traditional manufacturing won out in most cases. The report concluded that 3D printing was still five to seven years away from
rivaling traditional manufacturing for most high-quantity applications. To that extent, the Kearney report reinforced what was then the
conventional wisdom.

However, the same report also listed a series of predictable improvements in 3D printing technology, together with the cost impacts
these could be expected to have. These included a reduction in raw
material prices by 35 percent (which would improve the break-even
level for additive manufacturing), reduction in setup times almost
to zero (yielding another 5 percent improvement in overall costs),
and acceleration of material application rates — that is, the speed at
which 3D printers can deposit material (providing an improvement
of 82 percent in production speed at any volume of input). A. T. Kearney predicted that these would reduce costs so greatly that the break-
even point — that is, the maximum of number of units that can be 3D
printed at or below the unit cost of traditional manufacturing — would
rapidly increase.

Today we can look back at this report and take stock of the current situation. When we do, we discover that *all* of the predicted improvements have come to pass in the three years since the report was

issued. At the same time, other cost reductions not based on econo-mies of scale are rapidly emerging, including reduced waste during production, reduced material usage from more efficient designs, and reduced assembly by combining parts — all of which reduce the unit cost whether you make ten or ten thousand of a given item.

The impact of this economic trend is depicted in Figure 3-4, which shows how the AM cost curve is lowered across the board, moving the

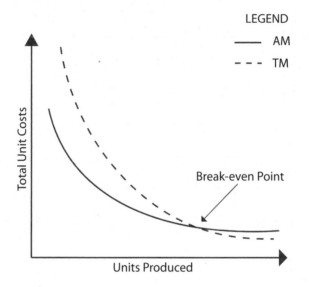

FIGURE 3-4: In the near future, as the economies of scale associated with AM increase, the cost of producing goods using AM will continue to fall, driving the break-even point for traditional manufacturing higher. Thus, in a growing number of industries, AM will soon become more cost-efficient than traditional manufacturing even at large production quan-tities.

break-even point even further to the right.

Reality is outstripping A. T. Kearney's five- to seven-year predic-tion. While results vary by industry, the economics of additive manu-facturing are catching up to those of traditional manufacturing *more quickly* than the experts forecast. As AM technology continues to ad-vance, there will be further movement of the break-even point to the right, allowing AM methods to take over more and more of the manu-facturing sector.

## Other Benefits of Boundless Scale

As businesses take advantage of the emerging economies of scale provided by AM, they will grow to rival traditional manufacturers in size. As they do, more economic benefits made possible by scale will begin to fall into their laps.

As I've noted, one driver of scale-based benefits is preferential access to suppliers, distributors, marketers, and other participants in the value chain. Big companies have always enjoyed advantages when negotiating deals with partner companies, and the same will apply to the emerging giants of AM.

Another benefit is the greater financial stability enjoyed by giant companies; because such businesses have a lower risk of bankruptcy or default than smaller firms, they enjoy a lower cost of capital, which makes it cheaper and easier for them to expand, modernize, and grow even larger than their rivals.

Still another benefit is the enormous political influence and power that big companies inherently enjoy, which can enable them to help shape government regulations and policies on issues like taxation and antitrust enforcement in their favor.

Perhaps the most important benefit of scale is the learning curve — the new knowledge and methodology innovations that are gained by companies as their experience expands. Bigger companies with greater experience and deeper market exposure naturally have opportunities to learn more — and the more they learn, the more they can improve their operating methods. The learning curve is particularly dramatic in the case of AM because it is a revolutionary new technology still in its infancy. So much is now being learned about how to manage AM operations that dramatic breakthroughs are happening and are likely to continue for years to come. It's the same phenomenon we've seen with other emerging technologies, such as solar power, nanotechnology, and batteries.

Most exciting of all is that, in the near future, the learning curve benefits generated by advances in AM are likely to be greatly enhanced by new tools such as machine learning, artificial intelligence, and digital networking. As the transition to AM progresses, bear in mind that it won't just be human engineers and managers who are learning from experience — thanks to AI, the production systems *themselves* will be learning and improving their operations as a result.

For these and other reasons, the emerging economies of scale enjoyed by companies that use AM are a big deal. As AM-powered businesses take advantage of economies of scale to outcompete and outgrow the competition, they will begin to reap additional benefits that will help them grow even bigger and faster. A gradual, self-reinforcing, virtuous cycle of expanding wealth and power will be set in motion. Once the cycle starts, it will be very difficult to stop. The natural result of this cycle of growth will be the emergence of the pan-industrials — manufacturing corporations that combine the economics of scope with the economics of scale to be gigantic in size, highly diverse in their product offerings, and enormously profitable.

## Why Some Companies Still Fail to Recognize the Scale Advantages of AM

Not everyone in the manufacturing world has yet grasped the new realities about AM. The recognition of the existence of economies of scale in AM has been slowed by the fact that many of the manufacturers who have been quickest to embrace AM are relatively small firms, including a number of startups. It's not surprising that smaller companies are among today's AM pioneers. History shows that it is often easier for small companies that do not have long histories of success, big investments in traditional technologies, or top-heavy, conservative bureaucratic establishments to make the leap to new business models. (Of course, there are some exceptional big companies, like GE and Siemens, that show how long-established firms can pursue innovation as aggressively as any startup.)

The fact that small businesses have been among the most enthusiastic early adopters of AM technology means that makers of 3D printers and other AM systems have tended to focus their sales, marketing, and publicity efforts on the needs of small companies. This means that economies of scale — which by definition are experienced only by big companies — have so far received fairly short shrift in the business media. When more giant companies — automakers, appliance manufacturers, electronics companies, and the like — convert their core production facilities to AM, the media coverage of economies of scale made possible by additive manufacturing will expand naturally.

The cultural biases of technology professionals have also slowed the recognition of the growing advantages of AM. Manufacturing engineers, who are the gatekeepers of the technology used in factories, are mostly highly skilled and very experienced at performing precise calculations regarding direct production costs. They can determine to the penny how the cost of producing a given widget by additive manufacturing will compare to the cost of producing the same widget using a traditional technology such as injection molding. However, neither their training nor their professional culture has prepared them to think more broadly about the costs and benefits of alternative production methods — which means that they habitually tend to shortchange additive manufacturing.

The result has been a bifurcated response to AM and other manufacturing innovations. Companies in which managers are comfortable with the status quo have been slower to adopt the new methodologies. Some have installed 3D printers in their R&D labs for use in making prototypes and small-scale models, yet have been reluctant even to experiment with more ambitious applications. Meanwhile, other companies, in which a spirit of innovation, risk-taking, and outside-the-box thinking is more widespread, have been leading the charge to develop new uses for additive manufacturing. As a result, they are not only enjoying the benefits of the current advantages of AM but also pioneering the discovery of new applications . . . thereby widening the already sizable knowledge gap between themselves and their more conservative industry rivals.

In the long run, virtually every manufacturing company will have to come to terms with the implications of the current technological revolution. But in the short run, there will be some big winners and big losers.

## Breaking the Tradeoff Between Scope and Scale:
## Six Models of Mass Additive Manufacturing

Economies of scale are becoming more significant in additive manufacturing as the technology expands into more and more mass production applications. As this occurs, a number of distinct models for mass AM are emerging. To understand these models, you need to understand how and where additive manufacturing is superior to traditional production techniques. AM offers six kinds of advantages, which can be understood along a spectrum from uniquely customized products to standardized goods. The first three described below exploit AM's superiority in product variation relative to traditional manufacturing; the fourth and fifth make the most of its benefits in complexity; and the sixth takes advantage of certain superior efficiencies that AM offers. These models apply to both B2B and B2C businesses. Some of these models are farther along in practice than others, but altogether they show the current range of possibilities that AM provides.

Note that the very existence of such a spectrum represents a noteworthy breakthrough made possible by AM. No longer are scale and scope opposing poles between which companies are forced to choose.

It used to be assumed that to enjoy economies of scale, you needed complex, specialized equipment with high switchover costs ... making economies of scope impossible. By contrast, to enjoy economies of scope, it was assumed that you needed a job shop using high-skilled workers equipped with general tools to make many different items in small quantities ... making economies of scale impossible.

AM abolishes this tradeoff. In the world of AM, manufacturers can fine-tune the combination of scale and scope they choose to pursue. Thus, they can take advantage of both economies of scale and economies of scope in proportions ideally calibrated to the needs of particular customers and the demands of specific markets.

Here are brief descriptions of the six emerging models of mass AM.

*Mass customization.* AM technology facilitates making fine adjustments to products, including alterations that would be impossible or prohibitively expensive to produce using traditional subtractive methods. This is why the manufacturers of hearing aids switched over to additive manufacturing for producing the shells that fit into the ear, and why a similar adaptation of 3D printing is now happening in other industries in which customer personalization is critical. This mass customization approach works for any sizable market in which customers are dissatisfied with standardized products and in which it's easy to collect information about individual needs or preferences.

These products may or may not become as cheap as those that need no customization, but AM brings them within reach of many more customers. The main competitive challenge is developing a quick, simple, and affordable system for gathering individual customer information — for example, the laser measurement technique used in analyzing ear shape variations for hearing aids.

*Mass variety.* In cases where it is not necessary to personalize each unit to the customer, manufacturers can alternatively produce products in a great variety of styles, thereby increasing the odds that nearly every buyer will find something they like. Mass variety manufacturers could still produce items according to specific orders, but they wouldn't have to collect personal information on customers.

Jewelers, for example, can use AM to make many varieties of a basic form to appeal to many different customers — hundreds of slightly different versions of the traditional diamond solitaire engagement ring, for example. Jewelry makers are, in fact, already applying this strategy. They are taking advantage of the flexibility of AM to produce model designs for rings, bracelets, earrings, and other items using plastics and similar materials. These models can be used as samples for customers to choose from — and because the samples are much lighter and less expensive than samples made with solid gold, silver, or platinum, the sample cases are easier to transport and don't attract would-be thieves.

Like mass customization, mass variety offers manufacturers a way to outcompete both traditional manufacturers of standardized goods and high-cost handicraft producers. Mass variety offers a greater array of goods than the former while keeping prices lower than the latter.

*Mass segmentation.* This model goes after preferences that are more limited still than in mass variety. Traditional manufacturers put out standardized products to get economies of scale, and many customers must either live with the required compromises or adjust the items themselves at some cost. With AM, a manufacturer can easily offer a variety of options to suit different customer segments, taking advantage of the ability of AM to run smaller batches more efficiently than traditional manufacturers can. It can make a batch of one version of a product, then immediately switch over to a batch of a slightly different version, all at a still-affordable price. Even in AM, batch production is still cheaper than the individual production required in mass customization and variety. So mass segmentation will beat out mass variety as long as it offers enough variety to satisfy a large number of customer segments.

Mass segmentation is a good model for manufacturers in trendy consumer industries, or in seasonal, cyclical, or short-term fad markets. They can quickly adjust production according to emerging consumer desires, while traditional manufacturers have to bet ahead of time on what consumers will want several months in the future. Consider, for example, the way clothing manufacturers are now experimenting with using AM to embed sensors in garments, as companies ranging from Samsung and Alphabet to Ralph Lauren and Tamicare are doing. Depending on customer response, clothing with built-in biometric sensors to monitor fitness and health measures may soon become widely available.

Batch production may not generate the scale economies of TM, but it more than makes up for it by producing far fewer goods that are unwanted and so must be sold at a heavy discount. The main competitive advantages with this model are AM's ability to change over quickly without retooling costs, and to engage in experimentation with product batches to see what sells. The model works as long as the total demand for the product is large and the range of preferences is segmented in a way that justifies batches rather than individual production.

*Mass modularization.* This approach allows for flexibility within well-defined parameters. Conventional manufacturers have long achieved a degree of flexibility by combining printed product bodies with a variety of insertable modules that fit inside. Customers can switch modules in and out to configure their product. But AM does this better because of its increased flexibility.

For example, an electronics manufacturer using the AM technique of aerosol jetting can print electronic wiring directly on the plastic shells of the devices it builds, which makes for better integration of the modules that contain specific capabilities — radios, cameras, and the like. Modularization is less expensive than customization, so it's the better model for high-quantity markets where customers are simply looking for greater choice rather than complete personalization.

This, too, is a strategy around which businesses are already being designed. Modular cell phones and other consumer electronic devices are now in development, attracting the attention of some interesting and surprising companies. For example, in September 2016, Facebook boosted its growing hardware presence by purchasing Nascent Objects, which uses additive manufacturing to build modular electronics that incorporate cameras, sensors, batteries, and other components.

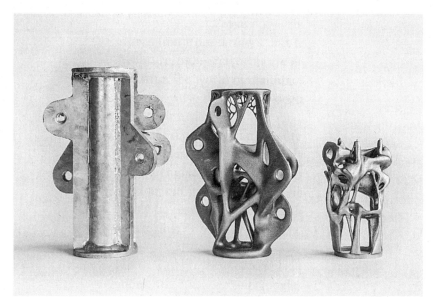

FIGURE 3-5: Three stainless steel parts designed to connect support cables for an outdoor lighting system. The part on the left was designed and made using traditional manufacturing processes. The part in the middle, built using computerized tools and AM production, keeps the cable connection points in roughly the same locations and weighs 40 percent less. The part on the right was more flexibly designed and weighs 75 percent less than the original part. All three meet similar standards for strength and durability. COURTESY OF ARUP. PHOTO ©DAVIDFOTOGRAFIE

*Mass complexity.* This model takes full advantage of AM's unique quality capabilities. As I've observed, AM machines can generate complex geometries that are impossible with subtractive manufacturing. For example, Boeing has found that honeycombed support girders for aircraft are easy to print, and they are both lighter and stronger than anything that can be produced using traditional production methods. Adidas is using Carbon's CLIP printers to produce midsoles of running shoes with designs that were formerly considered impossible. Similar improvements are now being made in a wide range of products using AM technologies (see Figure 3-5).

The goal is not complexity for its own sake; it's about boosting product quality with the kind of complex design improvements that subtractive manufacturing can't achieve even at a much higher price. These complex, higher-quality products often wouldn't attract mass markets, or would be somewhat variable, so they'd be made in batches, in a kind of mass segmentation rather than in mass production *per se.*

Thanks to emerging software capabilities, this model may soon expand beyond high-performance industries. Autodesk, Dassault Systèmes, and other providers are now developing software tools that will enable *generative design* — an approach that allows engineers and product developers to specify desired attributes, then let the software generate a design that optimizes product performance and cost. In many cases, only AM methods will be able to produce the complex designs that result. In the years to come, generative design may prove to be the "killer app" that convinces many manufacturers to take the plunge into AM.

*Mass standardization.* This model involves products in mass markets with simple structures that traditional subtractive manufacturing can easily produce. As we've explained, conventional wisdom formerly held that AM would never be able to compete with the enormous economies of scale available to subtractive manufacturing. But this is changing, as AM is becoming more economical and efficient, and as manufacturers realize that AM can lower costs in other ways. For example, the electronics maker LG discovered that traditional methods of manufacturing OLED video screens wasted a great deal of expensive electrochemical material. In response, they built a pilot factory to use the YIELDjet system developed by the California-based Kateeva to make these screens. LG hopes to produce tens of thousands of units using this AM technology. And in early 2018, a consortium known as JOLED announced that it had begun shipping inkjet-printed OLED screens for use as medical monitors to an unnamed customer, which industry observers believe to be Sony.

Over time, AM will become increasingly competitive for standardized products thanks to the indirect cost advantages it provides — shorter supply chains, reduced transportation costs, lower inventory carrying costs, a smaller factory footprint, and so on.

The lines separating these six models are not sharp. In fact, they will shade into one another as technology improves. We'll eventually see convergence as consumers seek both customization and complexity. A complex product could become the new standard in a mass market. And as manufacturers move along the learning curve, the savings described in all six models will increase and spread.

Companies can also explore multiple models at the same time, if market demand warrants. This analysis assumes customers are homogeneous, but companies may be able to segment their customers. The vast majority of buyers in a given category might prefer standardized products, while a subset may demand some degree of product variation. That select group may be numerous enough, and willing to pay enough of a premium, to make the modularization or customization model work.

### Project Ara: AM's Zigzagging Path to the Mass Market

At long last, the conventional wisdom that AM simply doesn't lend itself to mass production has begun to change. We've seen the increasing application of AM to the making of standardized products in mass quantities. No longer limited to product prototypes, customized one-offs, or specialized items made in small quantities, AM is now beginning to take over the kinds of mass manufacturing that have long dominated the industrial economy.

It has taken time for this to happen. As with any complex technology, the process of adoption has not been a matter of simple upward progress but rather a mixture of reversals, dead ends, and remarkable breakthroughs.

An exemplary story that illustrates how rapidly technologies are emerging in the world of manufacturing — and upending expectations in the process — is that of Project Ara. It originated in 2013 as a widely publicized plan by the digital giant Google to build modular smart-phones — gadgets that would allow users to swap out the separate units that control the screen, the battery, the camera, the phone, and other components. All this would be contained within a sturdy, long-lasting frame that itself would be variable depending on the color and style choices of the consumer. Thus, an Ara phone would be infinitely cus-tomizable and upgradeable at the whim of its owner. It would be a fine example of the business model I've dubbed mass modularization — and it would have the potential to transform the smartphone market.

A key element in the Project Ara plan was the idea that the phones would be made with bodies produced using a revolutionary high-speed 3D printing system capable of turning out units fifty times faster than then-current machines. The South Carolina–based 3D Systems was working on the new system, which included a racetrack-like car-ousel on which printing pallets would be mounted like trains on a rail. As the items being printed moved along this circuit, many production stages could occur simultaneously, eliminating the long wait times re-quired when machines and materials need to heat up, cool, and cure. Techies were excited over the prospect that Project Ara, sponsored by the super-ambitious Google, might revolutionize both smartphones and AM.

But those hopes seemed to be dashed in late 2014 when 3D Sys-tems pulled out of the project. It turned out that the technology simply wasn't up to the challenge; product quality was inconsistent, the pre-cision timing required in controlling the movements of the carousel was elusive, and the available printing materials weren't adequate. By September 2016, Google had canceled Project Ara altogether.

It was a setback for the additive manufacturing industry. But, char-acteristically, it proved to be a temporary one. Within days, Dan Ma-koski, the Google executive who'd headed Project Ara, resurfaced in a new position with Nexpaq, a Hong Kong–based startup that has revived the concept using technologies it has already incorporated into customized, modular phone cases. And a European consortium headed by the Dutch research firm TNO has announced that it has achieved a series of breakthroughs in designing a high-speed 3D printing carousel that remedies the problems that plagued 3D Systems' version.

TNO's PrintValley Hyproline system incorporates an inline inspection module that uses a fast laser scanner to examine each product as it passes by, as well as an innovative new "pick & place" robot made by Codian Robotics that is capable of moving and replacing project pallets on carousels moving up to two meters per second. TNO also added better motion controls and printers capable of working with different materials. Thus, a product containing multiple materials or an array of products made with varying materials could be printed at the same time. In fact, company data says that about 100 different products can be made on the Hyproline system simultaneously (Figure 3-6).

FIGURE 3-6: TNO's fully automated, racetrack-style 3D printing production system, called the PrintValley Hyproline. It combines multiple 3D printers: the extruder heads remain stationary while the bottom plates move around, as in an assembly line, manufacturing the part completely. © AMSYSTEMS CENTER. PHOTO BY BART VAN OVERBEEKE.

Now it appears to be only a matter of time before the ambitious dreams once attached to Project Ara turn into realities.

This is the same pattern we've seen in one subspecialty of additive manufacturing after another: the ambitious (perhaps overambitious) initial announcement triggering high expectations; the emergence of complex technical challenges leading to missed deadlines and product delays; the sense of disappointment; the quiet, behind-the-scenes race to meet the technical challenges; and then the series of breakthroughs leading to an ultimate success that justifies the original excitement.

The Project Ara story also illustrates how hybrid systems, which incorporate 3D printing into manufacturing solutions that include other technologies, will play a crucial role in the next stage of the industry's evolution.

### One by One, Large-Scale Industries Convert to Additive Manufacturing

Here's the coming reality: As production prices fall and quality standards rise, many mass production industries are adopting similar methods.

One of the industries making the switch is the athletic shoe business. In 2016, Adidas used AM and robotics to make limited numbers of its 3D Runner and Ultraboost Parley training shoes. Rarity and the coolness factor quickly made those shoes into collectors' items; by January 2017, 3D Runners that originally retailed for $333 were selling on eBay for prices upward of $3,000. Encouraged by the results of these experiments, in 2017 Adidas opened a new facility it calls the Speedfactory in Ansbach, Germany, where it plans to make up to 500,000 pairs of customized shoes per year. The word *speed* doesn't refer only to the boost runners will get from the shoes: Ben Herath, Adidas's vice president of design, reports that the digitization of the design and production processes will reduce the time from sketch to finished product from eighteen months to "days, and even hours." A second Speedfactory in Atlanta began operating later in 2017, with similar facilities in Western Europe to follow.

AM is also gradually taking over the mass production of electronic antennas for smartphones. As I explained in the Prologue, I came across this story during my initial research into the growing power of AM. Optomec, a privately held company supported in part by an investment from GE Ventures, has developed a number of advanced AM technologies, including laser-engineered net shaping (LENS), which can 3D repair metal components with remarkable accuracy, speed, and economy, and high-density aerosol jet printing, for integrating sensors, chips, antennas, and other functional electronics into printed devices that require minimal assembly. Now aerosol jet printers from Optomec are turning out millions of antennas for Lite-On Mobile Mechanical SBG, a contract manufacturer that builds electronic products for some of the best-known brands in the world. The benefits to Lite-On includes not just speed and affordability but a less obvious third advantage — reduced environmental impact, since AM of electronics eliminates the need for plating, minimizes the use of toxic chemicals, and reduces waste.

Another industry that appears to be on the verge of conversion to AM is that of OLED displays. An organic light-emitting diode (OLED) is an LED with a film of organic compound that emits light in response to an electric current. OLEDs are used to create digital displays in devices such as television screens, computer monitors, mobile phones, and handheld game consoles. Because an OLED display works without a backlight, it can display deep black levels while being thinner and lighter than a liquid crystal display (LCD). In January 2013, Panasonic unveiled the first 3D-printed OLED display on a 56-inch television at the annual electronics show in Las Vegas. Today, LG, Samsung, and other companies are all working on AM of OLED displays, with mass production just over the horizon.

Another intriguing story of AM moving into the mass production sphere — in this case, through the business model we call mass segmentation — involves the jet engine industry.

The LEAP engine fuel nozzle was one of the first mass-produced devices to be made via 3D printing. Jet engine fuel nozzles are extremely complex, as befits the importance and delicacy of the work they do: they spray fuel into the engine's combustor and play a major role in determining the efficiency of the engine. As traditionally made, the insides of these nozzles had more than twenty separate parts to be separately integrated — including, for example, parts made from a nickel alloy that needed to be brazed together (that is, soldered at a high temperature with foils made of gold or other metals, an especially difficult and expensive process). Engineers at GE and other manufacturers had long wrestled with the challenge of producing these crucial devices more affordably and efficiently.

At the request of GE, the AM pioneer Morris Technologies took on the challenge. Sworn to secrecy, the engineers in a Morris workshop spent several days figuring out how to convert the complex multipart design into a single piece, eliminating the welding and brazing steps. What's more, it weighed 25 percent less than an ordinary nozzle and was more than five times as durable. GE ended up purchasing Morris Technologies. By February 2017, they'd received orders for 12,200 of the newly configured engines, valued at $170 billion.

Now GE is pressing forward to use AM in even bigger aircraft engine applications. For example, the company is in the process of building a new AM factory, scheduled to open in 2022 outside of Prague in the Czech Republic, that will produce turboprop engines for the next-generation Cessna Denali, a jet built by the conglomerate Textron.

Many other large-scale industries are now on the cusp of being revolutionized by additive manufacturing methods.

One example is the optical lens industry, involved in manufacturing not just eyeglasses and contact lenses but a host of other products, from medical equipment to camera gear. The use of AM in making optical lenses had long seemed impossible due to technical limitations such as the layer-by-layer processing common to many 3D printing techniques — the interface between layers inevitably introduced tiny imperfections that scattered or distorted light, a disastrous problem in a lens.

A Belgian company known as Luxexcel set out to solve the problem. They developed a unique process involving droplets of fluid that obviates the need for layering. In February 2017, Luxexcel announced that it had earned certification from the International Organization for Standardization (ISO) for the quality of its 3D-printed ophthalmic lenses. This creates the real possibility that the global optical industry may be now poised for the same kind of transformation that jet engines are already experiencing.

### Goodbye, Henry Ford

The fact that AM is now achieving levels of quality and cost efficiency suitable not just for small quantities of customized or high-end products but for mass quantities of standardized goods means we are on the verge of true revolution in manufacturing. This revolution will accelerate a long-term historical transition that is already under way — the decline and ultimately the death of the Fordist assembly-line model that dominated manufacturing for a century. In this phase of the manufacturing revolution, Fordist methods will be gradually replaced by lower-cost, high-quantity additive manufacturing techniques, making the inflexible, capital-intensive factories of the past increasingly obsolete.

Like most revolutions, this one will have both winners and losers. Companies that are slow to adapt will be stuck with giant Fordist plants that have been "souped up" by the addition of a few 3D printers, robotic assembly units, or other innovative gadgets. But because they have failed to maximize the advantage provided by completely redesigning their products and operations around AM technologies, they will be fighting a losing battle, much like the U.S. automakers who were tardy or half-hearted in their adoption of innovative Japanese manufacturing processes. By contrast, rival firms that have been quick to make the leap to the new, lower-friction production model will enjoy huge economic advantages.

The next logical step in this manufacturing revolution? Pan-industrial companies that combine the benefits of scope with the benefits of scale provided by large-volume production. They'll be able to produce many widely varied items in their ultraflexible facilities, switching nimbly from product to product as quickly as market requirements change. And they'll be able to do so more efficiently and faster than the best mass manufacturers of the Fordist era, thanks to savings from reduced inventory carrying costs, transportation cost, material waste, assembly costs, and changeover costs.

Henry Ford would be amazed. He might even be rolling over in his grave!

# 4

# THE POWER OF INDUSTRIAL PLATFORMS

*The Emerging Digital Business Ecosystems*

**IN APRIL 2016, I** was invited to visit the Blue Sky Center in San Jose, California, a research and development center and showcase operated by Jabil, Inc. I toured the company with John Dulchinos, then Jabil's vice president of global automation and 3D printing (he has since been promoted to vice president of digital manufacturing). It was the first in a series of eye-opening conversations I've had with managers at this unusual company — one that I've discovered is at the forefront of some of today's most consequential business developments.

You may not be familiar with Jabil. It's an Electronics Manufacturing Services (EMS) company, headquartered in Florida, that enjoys annual revenues of $19 billion, employs 180,000 workers, and manages over 100 facilities in 29 countries. Jabil manufactures goods, packaging, electronic devices, industrial tools, and much more for thousands of global companies. Many have names you recognize, from Apple, GE, and Cisco to Tesla, Johnson & Johnson, and Disney. The media has given more coverage to two other contract suppliers, Flex Ltd. and especially Foxconn. But Jabil is becoming one of the most remarkable companies in the world as it develops breakthrough uses of 3D printing, industrial platforms, and other advanced production technologies. These innovations are poised to place Jabil at the forefront of the emerging manufacturing revolution.

Since its founding in 1966, Jabil has steadily built its core competence in traditional manufacturing methods, new product design, and supply chain management. A series of acquisitions expanded Jabil's

expertise in fields like materials and electronics (with its 2007 purchase of the Taiwanese manufacturer Green Point), design and innovation (with its 2013 purchase of consulting firm Radius), and injection
molding (with its 2013 purchase of the precision plastics maker Nypro).

Another historical expertise of Jabil has been miniaturization. The
company helped to shrink the DVR video streaming system into a
two-inch dongle like Google's popular Chromecast device. It reduced
a video camera to three millimeters across — about the length of a nee-
dle's eye — for use at the end of a feeding tube by the medical device
maker Covidien. And it created finger rings for monitoring and tracking a user's activity level and health status just as a Fitbit wristband
would do. From its original roots in the electronics industry, Jabil has
expanded into sectors such as automobiles, pharmaceuticals, aerospace, and defense. It is also supporting clients in activities from late-
stage R&D and product design to packaging and retail distribution.

Little by little, Jabil has basically been teaching itself how to make
practically anything for anybody using traditional manufacturing
methods. Now Jabil is beginning to combine additive manufacturing
methods with innovative digital tools — a crucial next step for a company that aspires to be a leader in a new industrial era.

Up to this point in time, Jabil has built its network of plants by ded-
icating each plant to a single traditional manufacturing process, part,
or product. At the heart of Jabil's network of plants is its Jabil InCon-
trol™ system for monitoring, controlling, connecting, and optimizing
the company's manufacturing systems around the world. Using In-
Control's unique networking software and its eighteen core applications, Jabil managers can track the production of any of the hundreds
of thousands of unique parts that Jabil makes or provides through its
network of plants and 17,000 active suppliers. Responding to information provided by the software, the managers can reroute parts and
modify processes as needed. They can even reprogram individual machines in response to shifts in demand.

Here's a small but telling example of how the InControl system
works. In April 2016, an earthquake struck Kyushu Island in Japan,
disrupting local communications, travel, energy supplies, and other
systems. The InControl system, investigating on behalf of a Jabil client, immediately identified a Kyushu-based parts supplier that had

lost power. Within hours, InControl had found an alternative supplier and alerted Jabil managers to make arrangements so that Jabil's client would receive sufficient stock of parts to keep operating without interruption.

Contrast this with the disruptions caused by similar disasters in the past. The 2011 Tohoku earthquake and tsunami caused almost 16,000 deaths in eastern Japan. It also led to the devastating meltdowns at the Fukushima Daiichi nuclear power plant complex. Less tragically, it also produced major economic and business problems. Chuck Conley, Jabil's Director of Product Marketing for Digital Supply Chain Solutions, told me about how many of Jabil's client firms found their operations disrupted for weeks afterward. Some underreacted, allowing plant shutdowns and transportation problems to shut off supply chains; that led to millions of dollars in revenue losses. Others overreacted, making panic-driven purchases of supplies from alternative sources that ultimately proved to be needless and wasteful. "It was a wake-up call for Jabil," Conley says. The company's decision to create a global supply chain management network, powered by the Internet, was driven in part by the Tohoku disaster — and InControl is the result.

Under the guidance of John Dulchinos, InControl no longer simply reacts to supply disruptions like earthquakes, valuable as that service is. It also *anticipates* potential sources of risk to a company's supply chain, from natural disasters to political upheaval to economic instability. Jabil's managers can scan for risks as they manage the company's Electronics Manufacturing Services company operations. And client managers who have leased or licensed access to InControl for their own operations can use the InControl dashboard to view a detailed map of their own supply chains (Figure 4-1). The dashboard shows far-flung nodes (factories, assembly plants, warehouses) and the real-time flows of parts and products among them.

The "end-to-end visibility" into the supply chain provided by the dashboard requires integration of the data systems used by many different first-, second-, and third-tier suppliers. These systems are often incompatible — a tricky software-design challenge that the Jabil team had to solve. Now their clients can use the dashboard to get quick, clear answers to such basic questions as "Where's my stuff?" "What's

FIGURE 4-1: Jabil's InControl dashboard includes a wall-sized array of video screens show-ing plants, Jabil customers, and suppliers all over the world. Plant locations are color-coded to reflect ratings for risk, quality, and efficiency, while graphs track performance over time. The dashboard can monitor and display these and other characteristics for a single product, a product division, or an entire manufacturing system. COURTESY OF JABIL, INC.

holding up deliveries?" and "How can I make my supply chain more efficient?"

Potential danger spots can also be identified, making it possible for managers to take anticipatory steps that will prevent trouble before it arises. InControl analyzes more than seven million different kinds of raw materials and equipment parts using a constantly changing list of risk attributes that are weighted differently depending on the char-acteristics of the client company. For example, a product design team can be alerted to the fact that some of the parts they are planning to use in a new device may be available only from a single source or from a supplier located in a high-risk region — a port susceptible to flood-ing, for example, or a country currently threatened by worker unrest.

InControl's risk analysis apps can quantify the risks and identify bottlenecks and redundancies in a firm's network. And it can offer higher-rated alternatives. In response, the product designers may de-cide to substitute slightly more expensive parts, trading increased cost for greater peace of mind. Or they may choose to alter their supply chain, selecting producers with lower risk of disruption. Jabil's "design for supply chain" app walks companies through the process of product design with supply chain factors in mind. The software helps firms make smart design choices that greatly reduce the vulnerability of their manufacturing processes to disruption by external problems.

The InControl software also monitors less obvious strategic challenges to a client's business plans. For example, it keeps tabs on the financial viability of supplier companies, so that clients can avoid sourcing an essential part from a firm that is in danger of going bankrupt. It can even track and analyze Twitter comments and customer reviews about a company's products. In at least one case, it persuaded a client to reduce production quantities in time to prevent a costly overstock situation on a product that was about to take an unanticipated nosedive in popularity.

InControl can be used by manufacturing managers to conduct "what if" analyses. What if we reallocate work to a different plant or supplier? What if we switch from traditional manufacturing to additive manufacturing for some of our product parts? What if we change our product mix? What if Walmart sends us a huge rush order a few weeks before Christmas? Jabil's dashboard can display the impact of contingencies like these and help managers choose the optimal production path for efficient workflow, logistics optimization, and other profit-enhancing measures.

InControl wouldn't have been possible a decade ago. Advances in cloud computing, mobile connectivity, big data analytics, and artificial intelligence have all contributed to the system's remarkable speed and power. But what Jabil has accomplished so far represents just the first stage of an even more astounding evolutionary process.

Over time, as Jabil's artificial intelligence capabilities continue to expand, the manufacturing control operations that InControl oversees will become increasingly automated. This will soon make it possible for Jabil and its clients to react effectively to marketplace changes with a degree of speed and efficiency once undreamed of—for example, by shifting production among alternative suppliers within moments after a price arbitrage opportunity arises, with no need for intervention by a human decision-maker.

At the same time, Jabil is continuing to enhance and develop its own production capabilities, using all of the same tools its clients enjoy. In the coming months, Jabil's manufacturing facilities, including all-purpose printer farms scattered around the world, will be able to combine additive and traditional manufacturing processes when making parts and assembling products. Thanks to InControl, Jabil will be able to manage the flow of information from an engineer's computer-aided design (CAD) files all the way to the printer array that builds the specific product, no matter where in the world the operations may be located. In the words of John Dulchinos:

> Today, Jabil has over 100 factories throughout the world. Ten years from now, it's conceivable that we might have 1,000 factories — or 5,000 factories — all smaller, and each in a location that is closer to where our end-markets are and where people buy. This allows us to more fully produce products on demand, which ultimately is the most compelling aspect of 3D printing's value proposition.

The flexibility and responsiveness these systems make possible will be truly mind-boggling. For example, Jabil has already tested the economics of switching among different printer technologies. In a particular instance — let's say, to manufacture 100,000 shells to accommodate a new smartphone design that is ready to go to market — a Jabil manager can choose among three alternatives:

- mass production via a few highly expensive, very fast multi-jet fusion (MJF) printers;
- use of 1,000 inexpensive Dutch-made, desktop Ultimakers to print parts on a staggered schedule that would achieve a continuous stream of parts or products; or
- use of batch processes on a small number of superfast, high-cost stereolithography printers.

Each of these alternatives offers a variety of advantages and disadvantages in terms of cost, quality, delivery time, and other factors. Using traditional methods of analysis, choosing among them would be difficult, and shifting from one process to another would be complicated and costly. The InControl system simplifies these challenges. The apps can calculate which recipe, production processes, locations, and additive or traditional technologies are more cost-effective at a particular time. And at any given moment, as shifts in market demand require, it can switch production from one printer farm to another with unprecedented ease and efficiency. In this way, Jabil will capture some of the same economies of scope that companies like Siemens, Emerson, and GE are starting to realize through their "factories of the future"—but potentially at much higher quantities.

This means tomorrow's diversified firms will be organized very differently. While today's diversified firms often employ distinct, separate product divisions, AM and platforms, such as InControl, will enable the consolidation of several product divisions into a single division with more blurry boundaries, scope economies, and operational synergies. Over time, as Jabil's analytic capabilities continue to grow, its partnerships with consultants may expand—or many of the same capabilities may end up being automated and included among the benefits that Jabil clients routinely enjoy.

In the years to come, Jabil's ownership or control over the network and its access to the vast quantities of market data that network generates will become increasingly valuable—and powerful. With this new technology, Jabil will become much more than a wide-ranging Electronics Manufacturing Services company. Because Jabil will have its finger on the pulse of supply and demand conditions in almost every industry, it will be capable of instantly entering and exiting markets not only for clients but for its own account. Conversely, it could ultimately choose to exit manufacturing altogether and focus on selling or licensing its digital manufacturing software platform to many companies (though this option is not currently under consideration by Jabil's executive leadership).

In any case, Jabil's digital connection with suppliers and markets around the globe will potentially make it one of the most information-rich and powerful companies anywhere—a kind of Google for the transition to fully digital manufacturing with the flexibility of AM.

## How Platforms Work

What makes Jabil so potentially important for the future of industry is the fact that it is building one of the first great *industrial platforms*. But what exactly is a platform? And what makes it different from traditional business models?

A platform uses digital information tools, instantaneous communication, and the networking capabilities of the Internet to connect customers with suppliers of goods and services anywhere in the world. Platforms of various kinds have revolutionized many markets and created some entirely new ones. Familiar examples from the business-to-consumer (B2C) and consumer-to-consumer (C2C) markets include these:

- Amazon, which was conceived as an online bookseller but has rapidly grown into "the everything store," connecting thousands of manufacturers, distributors, and retailers in virtually every product category with millions of customers — as well as using its vast networking and data analysis capabilities to provide other services such as cloud computing, information storage, and a growing array of bricks-and-mortar retailing outlets, from bookstores to supermarkets.
- eBay, which originated as an online auction site and has expanded into a platform connecting millions of retailers and sellers of all kinds of goods with millions of buyers around the world, offering not only reliable product descriptions and delivery services but also a guarantee of safe payment through its PayPal subsidiary.
- Facebook, which was launched as a social interaction platform for individuals and has gradually grown into a platform that hosts countless other activities — gaming, political activism, media engagement, and above all consumer marketing.
- Google, which began life as a search engine that enabled users of the Internet to find specific sources of information and ideas but which has morphed into a provider of many kinds of information-based services powered by billions of global links.
- Apple's iPhone, which has evolved from a simple communications tool into a hub for connections among thousands of providers of

data, entertainment, and services, from publishers and music companies to movie studios, game makers, and app designers of every kind.

- More specialized platforms, such as Uber and Lyft, which are transforming the urban transport industry through their vast platform-based networks of ride providers; Airbnb, which has captured a growing share of the hospitality business from hoteliers through its platform linking homeowners to travelers; and an endless array of other service platforms, from Angie's List and Trivago to TripAdvisor, that link customers to countless service providers in exchange for a share of the revenues generated.

At first glance, what all these platforms have in common — other than their reliance on the Internet for their business infrastructures — may not be obvious. But all of them have as their core competence not just the ability to produce goods or to deliver services directly to customers but rather to *make connections* between those who do produce goods or deliver services and consumers who want them. They make these connections through their ability to attract, amass, analyze, and exploit *vast quantities of data* — richly detailed and minutely organized catalogs of company offerings; huge storehouses of information about customer needs, interests, and preferences; constantly changing arrays of data about pricing, logistics, shipping, product availability, service quality, and much more.

The usefulness of this data illustrates another key characteristic of platforms — their reliance on *network effects* to generate much of their value.

Network effects, also known as network economies, arise from the sheer number of participants in a given platform. The greater the number, the more attractive the platform, and the greater the economic value created both for users of the platform and for the company that owns and manages it. Shoppers are attracted to Amazon largely because of the huge number and variety of retailers who peddle their wares on the platform — and of course the retailers are attracted, in turn, by the enormous number of shoppers who frequent the site. The Facebook platform attracts hundreds of millions of participants simply because almost everyone else is already available on Facebook —

and this huge collection of "eyeballs" generates vast advertising revenues for the company, as well as a share of the income generated from sales of games, apps, and other items to Facebook members.

As these examples illustrate, network effects tend to be self-reinforcing. Once a platform attains a given critical mass, it can enter a virtuous cycle of growth in which the value generated by the large number of participants continues to expand almost without limit. Network effects help to explain why some of the platforms we've listed here are among the fastest-growing companies in the world.

Platform businesses have revolutionized one consumer marketplace after another. But until recently, they haven't made much of a dent in the industrial arena.

It's not for lack of trying. A number of efforts have been launched to create business-to-business (B2B) platforms that could serve as online marketplaces for industrial suppliers and customers. None has gained much traction, for a variety of reasons. Some attempted to adopt platform designs borrowed wholesale from B2C or C2C models like Amazon or eBay. They failed mainly because the demands of manufacturing customers are so much more complex than those of ordinary consumers. (Buying a music CD or a book online is one thing. Contracting for production of parts for a million self-driving passenger vehicles — sophisticated, high-tech creations with ultraprecise tolerances on which the safety of people may depend — is something else again.)

Other attempts to build industrial platforms foundered because they failed to keep up with changes in digital technology. For example, some continued to promote first-generation e-commerce websites after the majority of business purchasing agents had begun relying on apps, tablets, smartphones, and other mobile devices for most of their online activity. And in still other cases, experimental industrial platforms failed because the organizations that launched them did so only half-heartedly, worrying as much about the risk of cannibalizing their traditional sales outlets as about building a big, robust online community for online commerce.

But the reality is that the rise of Jabil is one sign among many indicating that the age of the industrial platform is finally here.

## Industrial Platforms — A New Breed of Business

Today, the failure of platform businesses to make inroads into the industrial sphere is finally beginning to change. Improved understanding of online commerce and better software design are part of the reason. But the biggest reason is the digitization of manufacturing. In a world of AM and other digital technologies for automating production, industrial platforms can have incredible power to increase the speed, accuracy, efficiency, and flexibility of manufacturing.

Industrial platforms will be quite different from the now-familiar consumer platforms. Their structure and functions will be more complex, and they'll operate within an ecosystem and a marketplace that is very different from the consumer arena that today's most successful platforms occupy.

The industrial platform, in turn, will serve a large, complicated business ecosystem that will embrace at least four different types of users, including these:

- *Direct users of the platform:* the platform owner, along with an array of companies that make use of various elements of the platform — manufacturers, suppliers, logistics companies, wholesale dealers, retailers, design firms, marketing consultants, and other service suppliers.
- *Indirect users of the platform:* organizations that interact with the platform and with direct users of the platform, including regulators, tax authorities, and other government agencies; private and university-affiliated research labs; and firms providing financial, legal, accounting, and other professional services.
- *Communications networks:* internal systems provided by the platform owner to the platform users, including Wi-Fi, near field communication, Bluetooth, wireless routers, range extenders, and repeaters, as well as external communication networks, such as telecoms, Internet backbone providers, ISPs, content distribution networks, and independent IoT networks.
- *End product users connected to the platform:* customers of the plat-

form owner and user companies, for whom the communication network monitors or upgrades the performance of the manufacturing network or its products.

As you can see, the business ecosystem around an industrial platform will typically involve hundreds or thousands of organizations and potentially millions of individual participants at different levels in the managerial hierarchy of their organizations. This is a world that is significantly different — and much more complicated — than the world in which today's consumer platforms operate.

Industrial platforms will also differ from consumer platforms in a number of other specific ways.

*Industrial platforms will bridge the B2B and B2C arenas.* Industrial platforms will connect participants of many kinds, including both businesses and the consumers who are customers of those businesses. Thus, the industrial platform will engage in B2B interactions while also engaging in B2C interactions like those that consumer platforms perform.

For example, picture an industrial platform with a strong presence in the market for electronic equipment — computers, tablets, phones, televisions, routers, cameras, and so on. This platform will connect with businesses that are engaged in designing, manufacturing, marketing, shipping, and servicing the equipment, including makers of smartphones, producers of corporate-level networking gear, companies specializing in industrial design, home electronics retailers, and many others. It will support these companies in various ways — helping them manage their supply chains, control flows of inventory, develop improved product designs, and so on. All of these interactions will fall into the B2B category.

However, the same platform will also connect with consumers who are the end users of the electronic equipment — smartphone buyers, students who use laptops to do their schoolwork, sports lovers who install giant LED screens in their living rooms. It will enhance their enjoyment of the electronic products in a variety of ways — for example, by monitoring the equipment via the Internet of Things and alerting users when a repair or software update may be needed, or by offering value-added deals like unique content streaming services. These interactions will fall into the B2C category.

If the platform is to create the greatest amount of value, it will need to be designed to be equally effective at both B2B and B2C activities.

*Industrial platforms will engage in more complicated user interactions.* Partly as a result of their combining B2C and B2B dynamics, industrial platforms will engage in much more complex interactions than consumer platforms.

Most consumer platforms concentrate mainly on simple matching functions. Facebook and LinkedIn match individuals with others who share specific interests; Lyft and Airbnb match travelers to service providers; Amazon and eBay match shoppers to sellers and products.

Industrial platforms, too, will provide some simple matching functions. For example, a manufacturing company seeking distribution of its products in South Asia might use an industrial platform to find a retailer interested in providing that service. But an industrial platform will also perform a wide range of activities aimed at *ecosystem optimization.* They'll help user companies improve their operations, maximize and allocate resources, develop and refine their strategies, manage risk, and much more. These activities will require information, insights, and processes that are much more complex than those engaged in by the typical consumer platform.

*Industrial platforms will create complex network effects involving both businesses and consumers.* The network effects that industrial platforms will create will also be quite different — and potentially much more powerful — than those produced by consumer platforms. And these network effects will help pave the way for the emergence of pan-industrial companies. Here's how we can expect the process to unfold.

The owners of an industrial platform will want to be able to build sizeable communities on both the business side and the consumer side. This will enable them to enjoy the full range of benefits that network effects can provide — including the benefits that grow from interactions between the business network and the consumer network. A large and growing network on the business side can offer a broad array of information, goods, and services that will attract more consumers. And a large and growing network on the consumer side will attract even more businesses with an interest in selling their wares to a big population of customers.

Growth on either side of the platform can feed growth on the opposite side in other ways, too. For example, when a new electronics retailer joins a particular industrial platform, it will "bring along" all of its consumer customers, who will be able to receive messages and offers from the platform. They will become targets for sales of ancillary products, service contracts, replacement parts, and upgrades, thereby stabilizing the revenue volatility that may hit an industry dependent solely on new-product sales. They will also give the platform access to additional sources of data about consumer preferences, shopping habits, and browsing patterns, making it easier for the platform's business users to develop offers and target new customers effectively.

Thus, the self-reinforcing benefits of network effects work across the aisle, helping to make the platform even bigger and more powerful. That means the managers of an industrial platform will have a strong incentive to master the skills involved in building and maintaining large networks on both the business side and the consumer side. This "double vision" is more challenging than the simpler task facing the managers of a consumer-only platform — but it's also potentially much more rewarding.

Business users will have the ability to create network effects that are particularly valuable to other participants in an industrial platform. For example, consider the depths of expertise that business users will bring to the table. Many will be experienced product designers; some will be gifted with engineering, scientific, or technical know-how; others will be experts at marketing, sales, logistics, service, and other vital activities. A well-run industrial platform will find ways to tap these sources of information and ideas. Platform managers may launch co-creation, collaboration, and crowdsourcing activities that will generate valuable insights for other business users of the platform.

Other valuable network effects will be generated by growing numbers of business users. Companies that purchase the same raw materials—the same kinds of metal powder for 3D printing, for example—can use the platform to pool their orders and so qualify for bulk discounts, special shipping and warehousing services, and other favorable business terms.

Companies that produce goods and services relevant to overlapping customer groups will use the platform to join forces, creating product packages that will be especially compelling to consumers. (For example, companies that make baby clothes, nursery furniture, diapers, toys, and children's books can collaborate to develop complete packages for layettes or baby showers that can be sold on the platform's consumer side.)

Companies in the same market sectors will also accrue significant value by sharing data about their consumers. Information gathered from the Internet of Things along with shopping activity, survey results, and other data will enable businesses to perform in-depth analysis of their customers and of potential customers. The insights so gained will help companies create products that serve customer needs better, and also help them market those products more effectively.

In short, there's almost no limit to the kinds of network effects that an industrial platform will be able to create for its business users. Over time, these beneficial effects will tend to "lock in" business users of the platform. They'll be reluctant to abandon the platform or to consider changing platforms because of all the benefits they've been able to tap. Affiliation with a great industrial platform will become one of the chief differentiating factors that separates successful manufacturing businesses from those that falter.

Most important, the companies that own the best industrial platforms—and enjoy the self-reinforcing benefits of those massive network effects—will be well positioned to grow into pan-industrial giants.

*Industrial platforms will* not *be dominated by winner-take-all effects.* Finally, the winner-take-all dynamics commonly found in consumer platforms will probably *not* be prevalent among industrial platforms. Instead, within any given industrial marketplace, it's likely that a number of industrial platforms will survive and compete with one another.

We've seen how network effects tend to be self-reinforcing. All things being equal, a big network attracts more users, which increases the power of network effects, thereby attracting still more users . . . with the logical end point being a single giant network to which virtually all users in a particular category belong. This explains how platforms like Facebook, Google, and Uber come to dominate their specific market sectors.

Competition among industrial platforms is not likely to work in this way. There are a number of reasons. One is the desire of business managers to protect the secrecy of their proprietary data—product designs and formulas, customer data, strategic plans, and the like. The importance of confidentiality as a competitive advantage will create natural, inherent limits in the amount of sharing companies will permit . . . especially with companies that are direct rivals for the same customers. Thus, it's unlikely that (for example) Ford, General Motors, Toyota, and Volkswagen will all end up as users of the same industrial platform.

A second reason is the relative complexity of the services and benefits that an industrial platform will offer. I've described some of the many ways that the work of industrial platforms will be more complicated and sophisticated than that of consumer platforms. This added complexity will create opportunities for smart rivals to emerge—specialists in technology, management, marketing, finance, logistics, or other fields with creative ideas about how to expand or improve the services offered by the platform.

Finally, there is the potential for government intervention. The possibility that a single platform could amass vast centralized accumulations of data, capital, and marketplace influence would likely attract the scrutiny of lawmakers and regulators. Antitrust laws could well be invoked to break up such an overwhelming force.

For these reasons among others, the world of industrial platforms will look and behave very differently from the world of consumer platforms. I expect to see a number of industrial platform marketplaces characterized by a long-term push and pull among a number of rival firms, each continually jockeying for advantage and competing for the loyalty of both business and consumer users.

## How the Power of a Platform Can Turbocharge Manufacturing: The Zara Story

In Chapters 2 and 3, we saw how firms armed with the new tools of additive manufacturing will be able to achieve (almost) boundless scope and scale. I explained why the ability to make almost anything in almost limitless quantities will bring with it economies of scope and economies of scale, which will reduce costs for the new AM-based manufacturers and make them more profitable than rival businesses. A self-reinforcing cycle of growth will be triggered that will put these businesses on a path toward global dominance.

But until recently, one big piece of the puzzle has been missing—namely, a system for organizing, managing, and operating these emerging giants that will enable them to take full advantage of the benefits inherent in their vastly expanded scope and scale. That's where the new digital industrial platforms come in.

An example of a contemporary company that is using a digitized global platform to create remarkable efficiencies is the Spanish-based apparel giant Zara. Although Zara currently relies on traditional manufacturing methods rather than additive manufacturing methods, it is a pioneer when it comes to using digital tools to organize complex design, production, and logistics operations around the world. A look at Zara offers a glimpse into the ways industrial platforms are likely to transform manufacturing of all kinds in the years to come.

Zara's "fast-fashion" clothes are sold at over 2,100 retail stores in 88 countries around the world. Few companies match Zara's ability to recognize and respond quickly to emerging fashion trends, whether they originate in New York's Soho, student hangouts in Singapore, or coffeehouses in Rio de Janeiro. The nerve center of the entire operation is located at Zara headquarters in La Coruna, Spain. Here a team of market analysts studies daily updates from stores around the world—which garments are selling fastest? Which items are being returned by dissatisfied shoppers? What new looks from other fashion companies are getting the most buzz? Based on this feedback, the team issues guidance to more than three hundred in-house designers, whose job is to translate the hottest fashion ideas into affordable garments for rapid shipment to Zara stores — usually in twenty-one days or less.

Tight linkage between all of Zara's upstream and downstream activities is controlled through IT. Headquarters sets product prices to cover distance costs, address local competitive conditions, and meet overall company goals. The headquarters team also sets regional and local performance goals and rewards, and shares best practices gleaned from exchanges with country managers.

Headquarters also oversees several key steps along the value chain, such as fabric preparation, sewing, and inspection in its wholly owned factories in Spain. Production for "fast imitation" products, for which time to market is the most crucial success factor, is carried out in Spanish factories close to company headquarters. When price-sensitive staple products are being produced, factories in Bangladesh, China, and other Asian countries are favored, while products for which a balance between speed and price is desired are made in Eastern Europe and North Africa. The headquarters team also handles material sourcing and inspection aspects of the value chain, thereby retaining tight control over quality.

Zara's highly centralized manufacturing system presents several risks. These include a potential overdependence on Spain, which could be dangerous in the event of an economic or natural disaster there; higher costs associated with maintaining many key operations in Europe; and the increased time to market resulting from the relative lack of manufacturing presence in other geographical areas. Still, the system has managed to implement Zara's fast-fashion, low-cost model quite successfully. It has enabled Zara to grow into a fashion titan that sells more than 450 million garments annually and reached sales of $15.9 billion in 2016.

Does the Zara system qualify as a full-fledged industrial platform? Not yet. Zara employs a centralized industrial IT system managed through use of various software packages, but this is not yet a fully integrated platform. If all the software were put together, it would constitute a nearly complete industrial platform.

When I toured Zara's facilities in La Coruna, I wondered how Zara's system might be transformed by the AM revolution. If Zara were to combine a complete industrial platform with the manufacturing advantages of AM, it could substantially enhance its already significant advantages in the areas of innovation, imitation, and time to market. AM could drastically simplify Zara's production system at many stages along the value chain, reducing or eliminating tasks such as cutting and sewing by printing entire garments all at once. AM could also allow the company to download 3D printable designs into a widely dispersed manufacturing system at the speed of light just by transmitting design files over a secure Internet connection. The industrial platform could enable coordination, communication, and control throughout the entire network, ensuring high quality and responsiveness despite the vast geographic distances involved. Transforming the Zara network into a more decentralized system would make the company even faster, nimbler, and more efficient, fueling further global growth in the decades to come.

Given what Zara has been able to achieve with today's technology, imagine what manufacturers of tomorrow will be able to do when true industrial platforms powered by additive manufacturing are in full operation.

Business leaders today are finally starting to recognize the potential of digital industrial platforms to turbocharge the productivity, profitability, and growth of manufacturers. But many are still hesitant about taking the steps necessary to pursue this vision.

In February 2017, the expert consultants at the Digital McKinsey Practice published a study that attempted to measure the value-adding benefits of various forms of digital investment. They compared the revenue- and profit-enhancing impacts of investments in digitization of five areas of business activity: products and services, marketing and distribution, ecosystems, processes, and supply chains.

They found that all five kinds of investments can pay dividends — but that digitization of supply chains was the area with the greatest future promise for handsome returns. Paradoxically, however, supply chain digitization was also *lowest* on the list of priorities for most business managers surveyed, with just 2 percent mentioning it as an area of focus.

As the stories of Jabil and Zara make clear, supply chain optimization is one of the key benefits that an industrial platform can provide. The McKinsey study suggests it may also be low-hanging fruit, offering big benefits to the companies that recognize the value it offers and move quickly to take advantage of it.

# 5

# CODING THE FUTURE

*Building the World's First Industrial Platforms*

**AS YOU'VE SEEN,** Jabil's InControl is much more than just an online store where businesses can merely order parts from suppliers. Instead, it helps companies dramatically improve their ability to plan, manage, and optimize their entire operations. After seeing Jabil's dashboard, I was mesmerized by the potential it offered. When a manufacturing executive gets a glimpse of the InControl dashboard and samples some of the benefits it provides, it's hard to imagine why he or she would choose to do business elsewhere.

## The Recipe for a Pan-Industrial Firm:
## AM-Based Scope + Scale + a Strong Industrial Platform

InControl is an early example of the kinds of digital industrial platforms that are likely to emerge in the years to come. These new industrial platforms will be capable of connecting and coordinating vast, diverse arrays of customers with far-flung, often localized manufacturing centers, together with specialists in design, marketing, sales, branding, finance, and other business activities. They will include all of the production-control capabilities currently boasted by InControl, along with many more functionalities. For example, they'll likely develop the ability to share data and processes with the popular Enterprise Resource Planning (ERP) software tools, which most big companies already use to monitor and control their sales, marketing, billing, and customer service activities. They'll also link up with software systems designed to handle common human resources functions, such as recruiting, hiring, onboarding, training, scheduling, and benefits management.

As the industrial platforms grow and expand, they'll offer a number of capabilities that will enhance both the economies of scope and the economies of scale that I've described — enabling still further growth on the part of the companies that control the platforms. Here is a list of some of the activities industrial platforms will make possible.

*Using new analytic tools to take full advantage of scope and scale.* The organizational challenges inherent in building a vast, multifaceted industrial company have traditionally played a big role in limiting the size and complexity of businesses. They were a major reason for the inability of companies to benefit from both economies of scope and economies of scale. Instead, companies were forced to choose one or the other. Now software will calculate the optimum mixture of scale and scope to achieve the company's growth and profitability goals.

The emerging powers of big data analytics, artificial intelligence, machine learning, and digital communications, as deployed by the new industrial platforms, will make it possible for companies to grow to giant proportions while also being highly diversified — and all without becoming too complicated to manage. Smart software tools capable of continually re-analyzing the schedules of workers and production facilities will constantly be fed a flood of up-to-the-minute data from smartphones, sensors, and terminals. This data will enable the apps to track the health, safety, movements, and accomplishments of those workers, as well as the ever-changing status of every machine in the organization's entire network.

Armed with this information, the industrial platform will be able to automate countless decisions that now require highly skilled human labor. The platform will be able to make and execute smart choices about everything from setting production levels for specific products based on minute-by-minute fluctuations in demand to identifying and taking advantage of arbitrage opportunities created by price differentials across international markets.

The result: One more major limitation on the scope and size of industrial firms is on the verge of falling. In the near future, manufacturing companies will have the management systems needed to make giant, complicated operations run more smoothly than ever. The industrial platform will make this possible.

*Jump-starting industrial productivity — a cure for Baumol's disease.* In many industries, much of the work on the factory floor has already been automated. But the managerial work required to organize manufacturing firms has not.

A simple example: A global company that makes and markets industrial machinery like factory equipment needs to employ thousands of workers who handle the installation, servicing, repair, and replacement of machines. These workers all need to be deployed, scheduled, tracked, and supervised by hundreds of administrative personnel. And as the size of the organization grows, the number of administrators grows disproportionately. Hence the huge administrative headquarters, often filling city skyscrapers or suburban office campuses, that big industrial firms have traditionally maintained.

The problem is that when it comes to information-based work that must be carried out personally by human workers, economies of scale don't exist; in fact, as the size and complexity of the conceptual challenges increases, the amount of intellectual firepower necessary to carry out the work may actually *grow* relative to the size of the organization. The difficulty of introducing automated methodologies to human-based intellectual activities has long been recognized as a root cause of stagnant productivity in many industries. The phenomenon is sometimes referred to as *Baumol's disease,* named after the economist who first diagnosed it. It helps to explain, for example, why the costs of healthcare delivery and education tend to keep rising despite the advent of supportive technologies like CAT scan machines and laptops. Most of the work in these fields is still done by individual doctors and nurses, teachers and principals, and it's virtually impossible to increase their productivity beyond a certain level.

In some fields of business, digital technology has already begun to make inroads in the battle against Baumol's disease. Consider, for example, that in the 1940s the word *computer* was not the name of a machine but rather a job title. Manufacturing companies employed thousands of men and women armed with calculating machines to perform the countless tedious mathematical tasks that complex engineering and financial systems demanded. The most skilled mathematicians served in management roles, combining the work of their subordinates and supplying the solutions the factory managers needed. During the 1970s and '80s, those human computers vanished, replaced by electronic devices with the same title, which could perform the same analytic tasks tirelessly, less expensively, more accurately, and far faster than people. It was an early triumph of automation over Baumol's disease.

In the years to come, many more areas of human activity are due to give way to digital replacements. AI, for example, is likely to weaken the grip of Baumol's disease on many fields where productivity now relies on human expertise. The rise of the industrial platform will ensure that manufacturing is one of the first fields that will be transformed in this way.

You've seen how a pioneering company like Zara is already experimenting with some of the possibilities that an industrial platform creates. Other companies, such as the multinational construction materials supplier Cemex, have been deploying platform-like systems for years. Cemex's IT system monitors every plant around the world for key performance metrics like capacity utilization and cost per ton. Gaps between plan and actual results are reported daily to headquarters in Monterrey, Mexico. Using sophisticated algorithms, GPS systems, sensors, and mobile computing devices, Cemex is able to automatically route and reroute thousands of delivery trucks, many of them carrying time-sensitive cargos such as wet concrete ready for use at job sites. As a result, it saves fuel costs, reduces supply wastage, and above all avoids costly construction delays — all while employing far fewer schedulers and dispatchers than were needed in the old, pre-digital days.

The coming of industrial platforms will bring similar savings to manufacturing. Just as Amazon can fill millions of product orders without employing hundreds of thousands of sales clerks, and Uber can book millions of car pickups without employing thousands of dispatchers, the industrial platforms will be able to organize the work of many thousands of workers with a much smaller management force than the Fords, Honeywells, DuPonts, and Boeings of the past once needed.

For individual companies, huge cost savings will result. In the over-all economy, productivity growth will enjoy a noticeable spike. And for the society as a whole, white-collar technological unemployment will become a significant problem. (I'll address its implications later in this book.)

*Bringing the benefits of competitive markets inside an organization.* Another way that industrial platforms will help to drive new efficien-cies is through the creation of self-organizing competitive markets — internal or external — that can drive decisions about pricing, resource allocation, and the like. Such markets can help to make entire layers of hierarchical decision-makers superfluous.

Consider, for example, how the giant automakers were once orga-nized as vertically integrated giants. A supplier of auto parts like Del-phi operated as a subsidiary of its parent company, General Motors. Orders about what parts to make, how, when, and at what cost were driven by executives at GM, and were only as accurate as the expec-tations and plans of those executives regarding the emerging shape of the car market. The result was a relatively inefficient system that de-manded thousands of paper-pushers at both companies to plan, man-age, monitor, and adjust production plans.

One of the main reasons that vertically integrated companies are now few and far between is the realization that market-based systems for managing supplier relationships are more efficient. Today Del-phi and other suppliers are freestanding companies that can sell their products to many automakers, while GM is free to buy parts not just from Delphi but from competing firms. Efficiencies, including lower prices, faster delivery times, and higher product quality, are driven by the pressure of competition and by the greater ease and flexibility of changes available when a network of firms interact with one another.

Industrial platforms will take the efficiency-driving powers of such networks and turbocharge them. The platforms will enable suppli-ers and customers around the world to remain in touch constantly, in-stantaneously, and in detail. Complex, unpredictable changes in mar-ket needs can be registered immediately, generating responses from a multiplicity of potential partners. If a sudden shortage of a crucial part emerges, excess capacity anywhere on the planet can be identi-fied and quickly tapped, often without even the need for human intervention. And if more than one supplier is available to address the shortage, competitive bidding will help ensure that the single most economical producer will get the job, increasing the efficiency of the entire interlocked system.

*Enhancing companies' innovative capabilities.* History shows that attempts to innovate in technology, products, and processes often fail because of weaknesses or missing links in the surrounding business ecosystem. One example: the failure of Nokia's groundbreaking 3G telephone handsets because the company's ecosystem partners failed to develop video streaming, location-based services, and automated payment systems in a timely fashion. Another: Philips Electronics' revolutionary 1980 high-definition TV set, which failed because of the lack of high-definition cameras and supportive transmission standards.

An industrial platform can support innovation by facilitating communication and partnership among its users. When a company that is a platform user is developing a new product idea, other users can support the innovation by helping to develop a reliable supply chain, adopting related technologies, producing ancillary goods and services, and coordinating efforts to distribute and market the new product.

*Creating economies of scope across multiple geographies.* A company that relies on traditional manufacturing methods finds it very difficult to serve any market with low product demand. If a particular country or region can't support production on a mass-market scale, most companies will choose either to ship in units from another location (which may make the product unaffordably expensive) or skip the market altogether.

The industrial platform will provide a number of solutions to this dilemma. The ability to electronically monitor or control small factories in far-flung markets, combined with the flexibility to change production plans quickly and inexpensively, will make it possible for companies to build multimodal plants even in low-density regions. By closely tracking demand, the manufacturer can make accurate decisions shifting production from one product or part to another as needed, making it possible to affordably serve even small markets with a variety of useful goods.

Alternatively, an industrial platform can make it easier for a multinational corporation to closely track shifts in demand for a product across many countries or regions. Up-to-the minute knowledge of consumer preferences and trends will help companies tailor their production plans to match demand more precisely, thereby reducing losses from the costs of producing, shipping, and warehousing unsold goods. The platform can also identify ideal local sources for parts and raw materials, helping to optimize the company's supply chain, reduce risk, and further boost profitability.

As yet another option, a group of companies that use the same shared platform can combine orders for various products from the same region or country, creating a high-quantity, high-value order they can fulfill efficiently and affordably. The industrial platform can help not only by tracking and combining orders but also by identifying the best shipping routes and methods, and by taking advantage of price discounts available at particular times.

These and other increased efficiencies generated by the industrial platform can help corporations serve multiple, smaller markets more profitably than is possible today.

*Making smart business decisions faster and better than humans can make them.* The integrating, organizing, and coordinating powers of a digital industrial platform will enable businesses to take full advantage of the benefits of scope and scale that AM promises. The end game will arrive when manufacturing businesses can be run almost entirely automatically, taking full advantage of the unsurpassed analytic capabilities of well-designed software to make strategic and managerial decisions without the need for human intervention.

Is it far-fetched that machines equipped with AI will soon be able to handle the kinds of complex decisions needed to run a giant manufacturing firm with virtually no human help? Not really. Over the last twenty years, many industries have already adopted *manufacturing execution system* (MES) technologies, which automate many of the data-gathering, analysis, and decision-making processes involved in manufacturing. An MES system can make sure that tools, equipment, and supplies are delivered at the right time to the right location on a factory floor; provide the detailed information needed to price products correctly and offer accurate delivery forecasts to customers; and adjust production schedules as needed when circumstances change.

The new industrial platforms will apply similar methods on a bigger scale, integrating and controlling not just the activity in a single plant but across hundreds of locations that may be thousands of miles apart.

Making this leap will be a big job, yes. But here is a story that may put it into perspective. In mid-2017, during one of my interviews with the executives at Jabil, I asked about whether their InControl system currently provides automated decision execution capabilities to client companies. In other words, can the same InControl system that notifies a manager about a production shutdown at a crucial supplier, and simultaneously offers the name of an alternative supplier capable of filling the slack temporarily, go ahead and switch an order for a vital part to the second supplier without waiting for human permission?

The answer was that InControl does not handle such decisions autonomously. It provides what's called *decision support* in the form of real-time data, but leaves the actual decision-making and execution to human managers.

"Will Jabil be incorporating automated decision execution into InControl anytime soon?" I asked.

"That's a long-term possibility," I was told. "We'll go that route if our customers want it."

"And what's the time frame for implementing it?" I asked.

"The next eighteen months" was the answer.

"Are you kidding me?" I asked.

"Well, that's only for the millions of tasks where off-the-shelf software and programmable logic controllers are already available. But if the manufacturing tasks are performed by 3D printers, we won't need eighteen months. We can program them in a day or two."

*Eighteen months — or a day or two!* That's the kind of "long-term" thinking today's best platform builders are practicing.

In other words, the ability of industrial platforms to take over most of the functions of human managers in running giant manufacturing operations is really just around the corner.

The transformational impact of industrial platforms on manufacturing will be astounding. They'll lend a huge impetus to the virtuous cycle already beginning to take shape. As this cycle accelerates, manufacturing companies that take advantage of the economic advantages of AM and the power of the industrial platform will be empowered

**TABLE 5-1: HOW THE RULES OF MANUFACTURING HAVE CHANGED**
Summarizing the combined impact of additive manufacturing and industrial platforms on the economics of manufacturing.

| TRADITIONAL MANUFACTURING: EFFICIENCY FIRST | PLATFORM-MANAGED AM: AGILITY FIRST |
|---|---|
| Standardized parts are used to reduce costs and simplify processes | Standardized, customized, or unique parts are used, depending on customer needs and preferences |
| Products are made from simple, interchangeable parts for easy assembly | Products are built all at once, eliminating assembly and permitting internal complexity |
| Specialized equipment and workers are used to reduce the cost of making a small range of products | Flexible equipment and workers are used to make a broad range of products at affordable cost |
| Economies of scale reduce costs of operations; economies of scope are generally sacrificed | Economies of scale are combined with economies of scope through smart software and flexible AM technologies |
| Heavy capital intensity is necessary to minimize labor costs | Lower capital intensity is combined with minimal labor costs |
| Steep manufacturing learning curves serve as a barrier to entry | Shallow learning curves facilitated by software, AI, and machine learning make innovation and entry to new markets relatively easy |
| Long supply chains are used to take advantage of cheap product inputs and convenient factory locations | Short supply chains move production close to customers and minimize costs of transportation, warehousing, and inventory control |
| Periodic product launches require costly retooling and marketing campaigns | Constant incremental product improvements eliminate need for periodic product launches |
| Business model assumes high fixed costs plus some variable costs | Business model assumes low fixed costs plus higher variable costs |

TABLE 5-1: HOW THE RULES OF MANUFACTURING HAVE CHANGED (cont.)
Summarizing the combined impact of additive manufacturing and
industrial platforms on the economics of manufacturing.

| TRADITIONAL MANUFACTURING: EFFICIENCY FIRST | PLATFORM-MANAGED AM: AGILITY FIRST |
|---|---|
| Supply chain management software based on traditional manufacturing methods | Platform-enabled supply chain management software incorporates real-time transparency, distributed manufacturing, continual analysis of data from the business ecosystem, and combination of AM and TM methods |
| Human-centric organizations with only routine tasks automated | Brilliant machine-centric organizations use big data and AI to automate many analytic, managerial, and strategic decisions |
| Manufacturing companies vie for competitive leadership based on transient product and marketplace advantages | Manufacturing companies linked to industrial platforms use economies of scope and scale to achieve self-reinforcing competitive advantages; they experience a virtuous cycle of continuing growth and increasing marketplace dominance |

to outgrow their rivals, ultimately achieving a level of dominance few businesses in history have enjoyed. See Table 5-1 for a succinct summary of the ways the combination of AM with industrial platforms is in the process of transforming the manufacturing sector — and, ultimately, much of the world's business landscape.

## Companies Now at Work on the First Industrial Platforms

So far in this book, I've detailed how and why the new industrial platforms are going to have a dramatic impact on business — especially when combined with the abilities of additive manufacturing to produce unheard-of economies of scope and scale. But is the concept of the full-fledged industrial platform as I've envisioned it actually going to become a reality anytime soon?

The answer is yes. The evidence lies in the number of big, powerful, well-respected companies that are already vying to become the world's leaders in developing and deploying the powerful industrial platforms of the future.

Jabil's InControl is just one of the pioneering industrial platforms now being developed to help drive, and take advantage of, the ongoing manufacturing revolution. Another is being pieced together by the industrial giant General Electric.

GE's Brilliant Manufacturing software is a cornerstone of the company's industrial platform-in-the-works — a portfolio of interlinked tools and capabilities that will position GE to compete with Jabil in the race to become the premier orchestrater of industrial activities. The company employs some 26,000 software developers, most of them based at GE Digital, a company division based outside San Francisco that is dedicated to software design. The results so far include GE's Predix operating system, which enables "industrial-scale analytics" and "real-time control and monitoring" for machines that are digitally linked through the rapidly expanding Internet of Things. Just a year after its initial release, Predix was ranked as one of the most advanced platforms for the industrial Internet by the research firm Forrester. Software tools in the "Predix portfolio" are now being sold to GE's industrial customers, with the possibility of broader markets in the future.

Another participant in the race to build the first true industrial platform is the manufacturing giant Siemens. It is working to combine the vast capital infrastructure that traditional manufacturers have amassed over the past century and a half with 3D printing, digital controls, and other modern tools in an effort to drive extreme improvements in flexibility and efficiency.

Included in this effort is Siemens's $24 million 3D metal printing plant in Sweden for making parts for industrial gas turbines using laser melting technology. Siemens is also using Ultimaker desktop 3D printers to print parts for its rail automation division, using a technique in which plastic parts are dipped in a ceramic slurry and left to harden. Firing them in an oven burns off the plastic, leaving a cavity mold into which molten metal is poured.

Siemens is also moving beyond the factory floor to reconsidering the entire value chain in order to bring the entire process closer to customers. Its Digital Enterprise Suite incorporates a cloud-based Internet of Things operating system known as MindSphere. Using big data drawn from every stage of a product's life cycle, MindSphere connects designers, suppliers, logistics experts, and operations managers into a single, seamless process.

Now Siemens is moving aggressively to improve these networking capabilities on several fronts. For example, the company is partnering with Georgia Tech University to improve Siemens's product-life-cycle management software by contributing new product designs and simulations that mimic manual workplace processes and identify areas for improvement. Siemens and 3D printing giant HP are also collaborating on software that will make it easier to design to print, offering new levels of design freedom, customization and speed. The goal is a unified CAD/CAM system that supports advanced design and analysis for 3D printing, including development of lighter, stronger products and products with combined parts to reduce assembly.

Progress has apparently been rapid. In September 2017, Siemens announced the launch of NX AM, a software module certified by HP that it says combines "design, optimization, simulation, preparation of print jobs, and inspection processes for HP Multi Jet Fusion 3D printed parts in a managed environment." It's a big step in Siemens's effort to create "a digital global part manufacturing collaboration platform."

An intriguing variety of other companies may also be preparing themselves to enter the industrial platform sweepstakes. Few are going public about the broad scope of their ambitious plans, but those who understand the power of the platform and can envision how it will transform the world of manufacturing are able to piece together the fragments of information revealed in press releases and news stories to see how corporations are jockeying for positions in the race. Here are some examples.

- The 3D printer maker HP — already mentioned above as a partner in Siemens's platform-building efforts — is creating an extensive business ecosystem of its own. In August 2017, HP announced an alliance with the consulting giant Deloitte, whose goal will be to help companies "accelerate their product design, speed production, create more flexible supply chains, and optimize the manufacturing lifecycle." Partner companies with whom HP is already collaborating include BMW, Johnson & Johnson, Nike, BASF, and others.

- IBM's Watson division, dedicated to applying artificial intelligence to a wide range of industries and activities, is offering an array of tools that use the Internet of Things to improve manufacturing capabilities. Core products of the Watson IoT project include a Plant Performance Analytics tool to enhance productivity, a Prescriptive Maintenance on Cloud tool to identify and manage reliability risks, a Visual Inspection for Quality tool that improves product consistency while reducing labor costs, and more.

- United Technologies, a multinational manufacturing conglomerate with annual revenues of more than $56 billion (2015), is investing $75 million to create an Additive Manufacturing Center of Excellence in East Hartford, Connecticut. Many of United Technologies' subsidiary companies in locations around the world are already deeply involved in 3D printing. These include the aerospace manufacturer Pratt & Whitney, which includes an aircraft engine business that competes with that of the 3D printing leader GE. It's easy to see the global network of United Technologies operations serving as the proving ground for UT's own industrial platform.

- Dassault Systèmes, a French software company, has launched a software platform called the 3DExperience. It offers managers throughout Dassault's client companies — in departments including marketing, sales, and engineering — a collaborative, interactive, virtual reality environment within which to work on 3D design, analysis, and simulation projects. Available remotely through the cloud, the 3DExperience platform can also be accessed at Dassault centers such as its 3DExperience labs, where clients can work for one to two years on specific projects under the guidance of Dassault consultants.

- Sumitomo Heavy Industries, a Tokyo-based manufacturer of many kinds of industrial equipment somewhat comparable to GE, is making rapid inroads into the world of AM. In April 2017, it purchased Persimmon Technologies, a Massachusetts company that has been making breakthroughs in both 3D printing and robotics. Most intriguing to Sumitomo is a new spray-forming 3D printing technique that Persimmon has developed to produce the winding metallic core of an electric motor — a part that is crucial to the motor's performance. Persimmon claims its new manufacturing method "enables smaller lighter motors with higher power output and better energy efficiency" — a huge advantage for companies in many industries if Sumitomo and Persimmon can quickly perfect and commercialize it. Sumitomo already has extensive software capabilities — for example, its Intelligent Transport Systems division, which manages complex "telematics" systems for cities in Asia. It would be a relatively small leap for Sumitomo to position itself as a platform player alongside companies like GE, Siemens, and United Technologies, whom it already views as competitors.

The companies listed above are all well-known corporate giants. Others that are less familiar — though already famous in additive manufacturing circles — also appear to be positioning themselves as players in the AM platform universe. Examples include the following.

- Carbon, the California maker of 3D printers mentioned earlier as the developers of the proprietary high-speed technology called CLIP, has created a partnership with the software giant Oracle to use its cloud-based enterprise applications to provide "a comprehensive 360-degree view of each customer." Carbon plans to run its own HR activities, financial services, supply chain processes, and customer experience management using the Oracle Cloud. If Carbon chooses to make this suite of services available to its customers, the result could well be an industrial platform-in-the-making.
- PTC, a Boston-based company that originated as a maker of systems for computer-aided design and manufacturing (CAD/CAM), has a software tool, dubbed Creo, that provides improved methods for designing, testing, and prototyping of products. For example, Creo offers an augmented reality system that provides engineers with a "real-life" experience of a product before it is made. Now PTC has developed a platform called ThingWorx that integrates Creo and a number of other advanced applications, allowing companies to de-

sign AM-ready products with built-in connections to the Internet of Things, digital sensors, and other enhancements. And tools like the so-called Advanced Assembly Extension make it easier to share design information across multiple design and manufacturing systems — for example, by capturing design requirements for customers and flagging whenever these requirements are not met during the design process.

- GKN, a British-based engineering firm with divisions that specialize in automotive, aerospace, and powder metallurgy technologies, is rapidly expanding its additive manufacturing capabilities. This expansion includes partnerships with other companies that can complement GKN's expertise — for example, a memo of understanding signed with GE in October 2017 under which the two corporations will share knowledge about innovative materials uses, final parts certification, and other elements of AM technology. Underscoring this commitment, GKN also announced in 2017 the formation of a new company brand — GKN Additive — that will bring together all of its AM initiatives and drive them forward aggressively.

It's possible — though less likely — that some existing companies that appear to be unlikely players in the world of AM platforms could jump into the race. Consider, for example, UPS, the shipping and storage giant. UPS already runs an enormous business specializing in supply chain and logistics services. It also has a growing AM business in the United States, which includes 3D printers installed in sixty UPS stores as well as a collaboration with AM service supplier Fast Radius. The company also offers an expanding array of 3D printing services in Europe and Asia, and it has plans to build AM factories in Cologne, Germany, and in either Singapore or Japan. UPS has also partnered with SAP, the enterprise software giant, whose rapidly growing portfolio of businesses built around the Internet of Things includes one called SAP Distributed Manufacturing. I spoke with Alan Amling, UPS's vice president of strategy, who runs the company's 3D printing business. He explained their overarching strategic goal: to provide networking and software tools that can help make 3D printing and other technologies for digital manufacturing more widely available around the world. He also mentioned that distributed AM was intended as UPS's counter to Amazon's expansion of its distribution and logistics capabilities.

Is a company best known for its brown delivery vans about to become a dominant player in digital AM platforms? Perhaps not... though stranger things have happened in business history. And it's certainly conceivable that an alliance that includes UPS, SAP, and other companies with complementary talents and resources could emerge as a potent rival in the race for platform leadership. Meanwhile, UPS's giant delivery rival FedEx has upped the ante by announcing a new venture called FedEx Forward Depots, which will use 3D printing to provide just-in-time parts production and inventory management services.

Each of the entrants in the platform race has unique strengths that grow naturally out of its original core business. What do all these companies have in common? Not much, except for the potential to be connected via a powerful web-based platform as building blocks for a giant future organization with strong manufacturing capabilities.

Jabil, for example, has vast experience in managing a complex supply chain network designed to provide varied products and services to a wide array of differing corporate clients. Jabil's InControl system reflects the benefits of that experience. GE's biggest advantage is its long history of successfully managing big machines — turbines, generators, locomotives, and the like — manufactured by GE and operated by the company's industrial clients. Siemens has focused on developing and deploying its expertise in managing the product life cycle, enhancing the efficiency and profitability of equipment from the design phase through retirement and beyond. IBM brings to the race its unique capabilities in the field of artificial intelligence and its experience in helping to build and manage the Internet of Things. And companies like Carbon have unmatched understanding of the latest AM technologies, which should enable their platforms to do an especially good job of helping client companies choose, deploy, and take full advantage of innovative tools as they become available.

Twenty years from today, we'll be able to look around us and see which of these companies were able to take advantage of their unique capabilities to build leading pan-industrials. If past history is any guide, it's likely that the lists of winners and losers will both include a number of surprises.

## Will the Software Titans Be Able to Compete?

A fascinating phenomenon is that companies most people consider to be pure information managers, such as Alphabet (parent company of Google), have begun making forays into the worlds of AM, digital manufacturing, or industrial platform-building. But it's an open question whether a company with its roots in Silicon Valley will be able to compete successfully in the effort to build one of the first great industrial platforms. Whereas GE, Jabil, Siemens, and others are beginning the evolutionary process with roots in the world of manufacturing, Alphabet is starting with a software platform that it is gradually supplementing with a portfolio of manufactured products. It's a very different path, to which Alphabet brings a unique set of strengths and weaknesses.

The core platform is Google's software, comprising cloud computing, the Android and Chrome operating systems, search, YouTube, Google maps, online advertising analytics, Google Docs, social networking, web browsing, instant messaging, Gmail, and numerous applications. Complementing or leveraging off of the Google platform are a series of other projects, including Google Fiber (superfast Internet service for crystal-clear digital HDTV and video game delivery), Google Capital (investment in long-term technology trends such as big data, financial technology, security, and e-learning), Google Ventures (investment in startups working on Internet software, and hardware for cybersecurity, AI, and life sciences equipment), Google X (a lab working on big breakthroughs, including self-driving cars, delivery drones, augmented reality, Google Glass, high-altitude balloons for Internet connectivity, robotics, AI, and neural nets), and Nest (smart-home automation products for security and HVAC).

No one knows which of these projects will work or fail. But it's clear that Alphabet is focused on putting together a vast array of products and services for which the only obvious connection is their ability to be tied together by its current Internet-based platform. To become a pan-industrial firm, Alphabet would have to add new software to its operating systems in the cloud, covering such functions as enterprise resource planning (ERP), business process management, and digital manufacturing systems. And it would have to include additive manufacturing capabilities for tasks such as printing electronics — for example, by acquiring a printer farm with mass production capabilities. Neither of these extensions seems to lie outside the capabilities of Alphabet.

Other leading companies in the high-tech universe are following Alphabet's lead with moves into a wide variety of markets and technologies with no apparent connection to their core businesses. Amazon is building big businesses in cloud computing, online services, and bricks-and-mortar retailing. Apple is experimenting with self-driving cars. Facebook is investing in 3D printing for electronic devices, drones, artificial intelligence, and virtual reality hardware. And Elon Musk is diversifying from cars into batteries, aerospace, AI, and even tunneling.

Today, technology experts and business pundits are struggling to get their arms around the enormous powers — economic, social, cultural, even political — wielded by the giants of Silicon Valley. A host of recent books and articles testifies to the challenge. It's now looking as if giants like Alphabet, Amazon, and Facebook are already working on what they hope will become their *next* new empires, which will be deeply connected with the old world of manufacturing. In their efforts to conquer this huge, lucrative new arena, the titans of software will face older, stronger, and smarter competitors of the likes they've never faced before.

The fact is that manufacturing is much more complicated than the information sector. It's true that an infotech giant like Amazon delivers physical, finished goods, as well as fresh and perishable food to customers, via FedX, UPS, and local couriers. But managing the logistics and inventory of information and finished physical goods is relatively easy compared to coordinating supply chains for making complex products. Today's software titans don't have the industry and production knowledge to conquer the world of manufacturing. They'll be in unfamiliar territory when they see how the digital AM platforms are connected to broad ecosystems of companies and government agencies than they are used to dealing with.

The apparent exceptions among today's Silicon Valley giants are more illusory than real. For example, while Apple manufactures cell phones and other complex electronic devices, remember that the vast majority of Apple products are actually made by Foxconn in Asia. It's simply too difficult for Apple to make its own products in a cost-effective way.

Similarly, while Amazon has used its excellent customer interface and popular sales platform to squeeze not only retailers but also manufacturers, it has been able to do so only because it is so dominant in the world of retail. When manufacturing firms start using their own platforms, they will have a choice that will undermine Amazon's control over access to a large community of buyers.

The software titans will have trouble creating great industrial platforms because to do so would require software from rivals and the formation of relationships with industrial companies, a battle that will be hard for them to win in competition with manufacturing firms that have been involved in similar supply, legal, and sharing relationships for decades. And if the software titans try to consolidate or create alliances to get access to all the necessary knowledge and software to build an industrial platform, governments (especially in the European Union) are likely to block such activities. They are already concerned about the software titans' "monopolization of information." Already, regulators in Europe and the United States are starting to go after the software titans. The EU just slapped Google with a $2.7 billion fine, and Facebook is now in the crosshairs.

Complicating matters further, the software titans have grown remarkably quickly based on their asset-light approach to business. Manufacturing is asset-heavy, so the software titans' balance sheets would struggle with major acquisitions. That makes it harder for them to build manufacturing expertise through gradual acquisition. They could still compete as pure software-based industrial platforms, with the advantage that this would allow them to license their software to a large number of firms, thereby enjoying a large market with extensive revenues. However, their lack of manufacturing expertise could make that a tough play. It's going to be easier to pull off what Jabil is doing, starting from a manufacturing base but gradually building software chops and pushing a platform into the world.

If anything, rather than the software titans taking over the world of manufacturing, the software titans may find themselves being challenged on their own turf by manufacturing companies with new levels of expertise in software.

Here's a story that illustrates how that could happen. In recent years, farmers have shown growing interest in boosting their yields through better information. Monsanto, a seed provider, responded by investing in software algorithms to tell them exactly when to lay the seeds, depending on temperature, soil moisture, and other factors. And John Deere partnered with Monsanto by building harvesters and other farm equipment that collected all of the required information. The benefits proved so large that Monsanto and Deere were able to charge farmers a big premium for the privilege of loading the monitoring hardware and software on tractors.

A Silicon Valley company could have done the same, and perhaps extracted a similar premium from farmers. But Monsanto and Deere got there first. In the future, industrial firms are more likely to identify similar opportunities from the world of manufacturing than the software titans are, simply because they have a deep, immersive knowledge of customers and their needs.

All of these factors make it unlikely that the software titans will simply swoop in and take the market for industrial platforms by storm. To be sure, Alphabet and other giants of Silicon Valley will play some part in the coming revolution, but it's likely to be a limited one. The starring roles will probably be reserved for companies that already have deep roots in manufacturing.

It will be fascinating to watch how the varied capabilities of companies like Jabil, Siemens, GE, Carbon, and Google may play out in the arena of competing industrial platforms. The platforms that become dominant will leave their individual imprints on vast portions of the world economy.

Will all of these potential industrial platforms be successful? Surely not. Will new contenders not currently on our radar screen enter the fray? Almost certainly yes. As this nascent industry takes shape, winners and losers we can't presently imagine will emerge — and the precise outlines of the marketplace will evolve in ways no one can foretell. But while the fate of specific entrants in the industrial platform arms race can't be predicted, a general outline of what's to come can be discerned.

# 6

# THE TRIUMPH OF BIGNESS

*The Coming of the Pan-Industrials*

**YOU'VE SEEN HOW THE** advent of additive manufacturing is providing an unprecedented range of strategic advantages to the companies that are embracing and adopting it. In particular, AM is abolishing the old opposition between scope and scale, making it possible for companies to take advantage of both economies of scope and economies of scale. The result is businesses that are capable of making almost anything, anywhere — and doing so with levels of quality and efficiency once thought impossible.

So far, so good. But the opportunity for companies to both dramatically diversify their product offerings and grow to enormous scale would not be easy to seize using traditional management systems. This is where the newly developing industrial platforms will play a crucial role. By using the latest digital technologies for communication, information gathering, data analysis, and decision making, industrial platforms will enable giant, diverse businesses to operate with greater speed, flexibility, and efficiency than ever before. The result will be a remarkable transformation of the entire landscape of world business.

The idea that new methods of manufacturing could change the global economy may feel a little strange. For the last century and more, most of the dramatic changes in the economy have been driven by technological advances in other sectors, such as transportation (railroads, autos, airplanes), medicine (antibiotics, miracle drugs, genetic therapies), communications (radio, movies, television), and information (telecom, digital computing, the Internet). By contrast, changes in manufacturing methods have mostly been modest and incremental.

But the coming transformation of the economy by technological changes to manufacturing is not unprecedented. History shows that in any given era, the dominant form of manufacturing can have a profound effect on the overall economic landscape.

Beginning in the eighteenth century, the first industrial revolution transformed the economies of Europe and North America, then went on to produce equally sweeping changes elsewhere on the planet. This happened largely because of innovations in manufacturing methods — the invention of the steam engine, which made possible the mechanization of mills and factories, and developments like the cotton gin, the spinning wheel, the loom, and the use of interchangeable standardized parts in various products (beginning with firearms).

Of course, these breakthroughs in production methods were augmented by other technological advances. The invention of the telegraph encouraged the rise of business hierarchies as near-instantaneous communication became possible between local operations and headquarters. The creation of networks of canals and roads, along with the spread of railroads, made it possible for the new mass-produced goods to be widely distributed.

The result: Prior to the 1800s, markets were atomized, with small firms trading locally and selected goods being passed along traditional trade routes. Large organizational hierarchies didn't exist. By the end of the 1800s, nationwide markets embracing millions of customers had emerged, and multistate business organizations were being created to manage these vast new markets. All of these changes were driven, in large measure, by the revolutionary changes in manufacturing methods that the industrial revolution produced.

In the 1900s, a new stage in the march to bigness took shape. Henry Ford and others developed the modern assembly line, which made possible even larger mass manufacturing markets fed by giant factories that could churn out products at unprecedented speed. Giant centralized plants fed by widely dispersed supply and distribution chains led to a series of economic and managerial shifts, including the emergence of big economies of scale, the need for huge new financial institutions to provide capital for the huge new factories, and arms-length bargaining between buyers and suppliers.

These changes produced enormous frictions. Running giant, complicated operations like these proved to be extremely difficult. So managerial hierarchies that were capable of running the vast new corporations of the twentieth century were gradually developed and perfected. Practitioners experimented with systems for making these new forms of organization work efficiently, as Alfred P. Sloan explained in his classic memoir *My Years with General Motors* (1963). Scholars like Peter F. Drucker developed theoretical models for optimizing the management of giant corporations that guided later generations of corporate leaders. And new institutions like graduate schools of business and management consulting firms sprang up to provide executives with the insight and skills they needed to help run the new giant corporations.

Once again, the very nature of business had been transformed by a series of changes that started with new technologies on the factory floor.

***The rise and fall of conglomerates.*** But by the 1960s, most of the technological advances focused directly on manufacturing methods had played themselves out. As firms reached the limits of economies of scale and vertical integration, business leaders sought other advantages that could be derived from bigness and managerial hierarchies. Large diversified companies with adjectives like *consolidated, amalgamated, united, associated, combined,* and *general* in their names became commonplace. Conglomerates that included a wide array of disparate companies and therefore enjoyed the benefits of diversification were considered the epitome of advanced managerial thinking.

Harold Geneen at ITT was hailed as the "emperor of acquisitions," regarded as a business genius for his methods of running companies strictly "by the numbers." He used to say, "Telephones, hotels, insurance — it's all the same. If you know the numbers inside out, you know the company inside out." That's no surprise coming from a trained accountant, but Geneen's boldness was something else. He bought 350 companies, building ITT from a telegraph equipment maker into a multinational, diversified powerhouse.

In conglomerates like ITT, savvy executives took over underperforming companies, gave them sophisticated management techniques and control systems, and ran them in a nicely balanced portfolio. Some divisions that were profitable but slow-growing were milked of their cash in order to invest in other divisions where growth was rapid and profitability high. Headquarters provided low-cost capital to capture opportunities in the booming economy of the 1950s and '60s, while the diversity of industries kept earnings stable. The strongest conglomerates, such as General Electric, included management training centers and other support services that promoted managerial excellence and up-to-date accounting control systems throughout sprawling business combinations.

Some conglomerate theorists believed that operational synergies across divisions could provide additional economic benefits, but most practitioners eventually gave up on this idea. Larry Bossidy, who was vice chairman at GE and later CEO at Honeywell, once told me that the elusive operational synergies between unrelated companies aren't worth the money it takes to capture them. In Bossidy's view, superior financial performance driven by strong financial discipline and professional management was valuable enough to justify the existence of conglomerates.

The conglomerates also achieved strategic advantages through other, less reputable means. Geneen, for example, was widely viewed as a corporate autocrat who treated foreign governments like subsidiaries. Under his leadership, ITT was allegedly involved in everything from military coups to U.S. presidential campaigns. People compared Geneen to General Patton, Napoleon, and Alexander the Great. Some said he would have bought up the world if he had the chance.

Other conglomerates came to dominate such a large part of the U.S. economy that antitrust regulators, Wall Street, and citizens interested in the protection of democracy became concerned. Evidence was mounting that the overlaps among different conglomerates was resulting in quasi-collusive behavior, often leading to less-aggressive pricing and noninnovative behavior due to *mutual forbearance* — a kind of "cold peace" that arises when conglomerates tacitly or quietly agree to avoid competition that would erode their profits or stock prices.

Thus, an antitrust case in the 1960s demonstrated that GE had tacitly divided up the high- and low-end segments of the turbine power generator market with Westinghouse. GE was found to be disciplining Westinghouse into the small and midsize generator segments, which were less technology-heavy segments of the market. And GE was supposedly teaching Westinghouse to be a "good competitor," that is, to stay in "its niches," to be less aggressive with price and technological attacks on GE's more profitable niches, and to avoid teaming up with European and Japanese electric power conglomerates to get better technology or to outsource turbine production. The cartel is estimated to have cost consumers some $175 million per year. In this way, conglomerates as operated in the 1960s threatened the very nature of capitalism and its reliance on free, fair markets.

A few of these giants are still going strong in the United States, including Honeywell, 3M, United Technologies, Graco, ITW, and Textron. GE continues to operate its traditional conglomerate structure, though under strong pressure from investors to sell off some holdings and convert itself into a smaller, more tightly focused company. In any case, all of these corporations are stragglers from a conglomerate era that came crashing down in the 1980s and 1990s. Wall Street argued that firms should avoid wide diversification due to the "diseconomies of scope" created by the high costs of having a large headquarters, extra layers of management, lack of managerial focus, culture clashes among divisions, brand confusion, and the complexity and non-transparency of internal transactions, work flow, and accounting methods. Wall Street argued that the market can allocate resources better than any empire-building executive at a top-heavy headquarters.

Wall Street won the argument. Most diversified firms, including ITT, were eventually broken up and sold for more than the parent was worth. Today, *conglomerate* is a dirty word on Wall Street. The few remaining American combines appear to trade at a "conglomerate discount," while antitrust regulators keep a watchful eye for any misbehavior that would warrant the government to step in and break up firms.

So much for the theory of economic dominance through diversification. The end of the conglomerate age was also the end of economic control by a group of "old money" elite families that started family businesses in the 1800s, and expanded by issuing stock to build the conglomerates of the 1900s.

The era of the conglomerate could be viewed as representing the ultimate corporate structure for organizing the systems that underlay twentieth-century mass production. The end of that era revealed the limitations of those systems. Once a giant Fordist factory centered on a traditional assembly line has been made as efficient as possible, any economic gains to be achieved by combining it with other businesses around the world are elusive at best.

Now, however, that conventional wisdom is about to reach its expiration date. The advent and spread of additive manufacturing, together with the rise of industrial platforms that will digitally connect and control production operations around the world, is about to transform the global economy yet again. Companies are beginning to use additive manufacturing and digital platforms to take advantage of the economies of scope, real-time change, customization, a range of process efficiencies, complex product designs, local production, and other new capabilities. Over time, these firms will use their digital platforms to replace markets and managerial hierarchies in ways that were impossible in the past, and will do so with far-reaching effects.

## The Advent of the Pan-Industrials — The Next Wave in Bigness

Ultimately, economic logic suggests that proliferation and growth of business platforms and the expanding, highly flexible, and very efficient AM systems they will drive are likely to evolve into voracious, ever-expanding industrial titans that I call *pan-industrials.*

A pan-industrial company may possibly look like a conglomerate on the outside, but it will run quite differently. It will be driven by a software platform that monitors, facilitates, and optimizes operations, from product development to customer delivery, across a disparate product line. Although pan-industrials will need a certain level of focus — unlike some of the sprawling conglomerates of the 1960s — they will be able to operate in much broader areas, with much greater scope, than today's more targeted manufacturers. So the pan-industrial "Universal Metals" might use its underlying expertise in metal 3D printing to manufacture products ranging from medical equipment and home appliances to cars and airplanes.

Over time, technologies from these differing fields of activity will increasingly connect and merge — for example, imaging technology now used in MRI machines will find applications in factory equipment, aerospace controls, home security systems, and traffic monitoring devices. Gradually, the boundaries between what were once separate businesses will increasingly blur. Eventually, the pan-industrials will find themselves competing not in a range of distinct industries but rather in a single, giant pan-industrial market.

This vision is not a mere speculative fancy. A company like Siemens, United Technologies, or GE may, in fact, be the forerunner of tomorrow's Universal Metals. The recent moves these companies have made into additive manufacturing are positioning them to become some of the first pan-industrial companies, making thousands of different products with unprecedented flexibility and efficiency, serving numerous industries in every region of the globe. The investments these businesses have been making into software development foreshadow the central role that a great software platform will play in the creation of a pan-industrial.

In the early years of the pan-industrials, there's likely to be a fair amount of confusion between them and the conglomerates of old. In fact, today, as companies like Amazon, Alphabet, and others are beginning to assemble the disparate pieces that could go to make up tomorrow's pan-industrials, critics are already emerging and wondering whether they aren't simply old-fashioned conglomerates dressed up in high-tech garb. Thus, the financial journalist Andrew Ross Sorkin asks:

> When it comes to Amazon (or Alphabet, or any of the new conglomerates), the question is whether there is something fundamentally different about these businesses given their grounding in digital information — especially as they expand into complex brick-and-mortar operations like upscale supermarkets.
>
> In an age of big data and artificial intelligence, are businesses that look disparate really similar? And can one company's leadership really oversee so many different businesses? When does it become too big to manage?

Sorkin's question is a natural one — but his skepticism is rapidly becoming outdated. It's increasingly clear that the age of big data and artificial intelligence — as well as additive manufacturing, industrial platforms, and the other technological breakthroughs I've been discussing — has indeed created a new managerial environment in which (some of) the old rules no longer apply, or at least apply far less powerfully than in the past. Thanks to these trends, the pan-industrials will have a number of huge areas of unique strength that will enable them to accomplish feats of profitability and efficiency that the old conglomerates could only dream about.

**The information edge.** The owners of effective industrial platforms will ultimately become information overseers, making their money less from manufacturing and more from using the information available on the platform and among the users of what I call a pan-industrial platform. The platform owners will have access to semi-secret information not available to the public or, perhaps, even to other users of their platforms, which will allow the platform owners to expand into arbitrage, brokerage, private equity, venture capital, lending, and other financial and business/market information services. In the long run, this dynamic will help drive the restructuring of the economy by promoting the convergence of several business sectors, including manufacturing, IT services, communication, and financial services.

The pan-industrials won't be the first companies to parlay their exclusive access to a wide array of competitive information into a rich stream of profits. Some of the companies that have pioneered this business model are among the world's most successful — though they are often relatively unknown to the general populace. For example, take a look at Cargill, one of the biggest and (reputedly) most profitable privately owned companies in the world. (The bulk of the firm is owned by members of the Cargill and MacMillan families.) Cargill came into existence as a middleman, equipped with warehouses and transportation services, to help farmers get their grain to market. Over time, it built up a uniquely powerful platform connecting sellers and buyers of agricultural commodities.

Cargill's position as a middleman eventually gave it the ability to see trends in the agricultural economy better than most sellers or buyers. It observes the purchasing behavior of its customers, the large food manufacturers, and uses what it learns to develop ingredient solutions for those customers — for example, creating new products that offer unique tastes and textures, health benefits for consumers, or reduced production costs.

The company has also used its information access to establish lucrative businesses in trading, purchasing, and distributing grains and other agricultural commodities, such as palm oil; trading companies that manage contracts for energy, steel, and transportation services; firms that produce food ingredients like oils, fats, syrups, and starches; companies that raise livestock and produce cattle feeds, and other, remarkably disparate businesses. In fact, Cargill has diversified so extensively that it now owns some seventy-five business units that operate in sixty-five countries. It bundles together the services it offers to provide complete, multifaceted "customer solutions" for food and agriculture companies. Cargill also has a large financial services company that manages risks in the commodities markets. In 2003, it split off just a portion of its financial operations into a hedge fund called Black River Asset Management, with about $10 billion of assets and liabilities.

Cargill's leaders have been very deliberate in their pursuit of a strategy that maximizes the value of their insights into many businesses with complex links to one another. For example, in a 2013 interview, the CEO Greg Page explained that the company's participation in the iron ore market might seem anomalous for an agricultural business, "unless you understood that there are huge ore shipments in Asia with a big impact on Cargill's ocean shipping of other commodities." It's precisely the complicated interactions among the businesses, and their effect on one another, that makes Cargill's network of companies so powerful — and so profitable.

Cargill is not currently involved in additive manufacturing. However, it's a vivid example of how a company can turn information access into a collection of profitable businesses. The industrial platform owners will eventually know so much about the manufacturing economy that they can create value purely through the information they control.

One way they may do this is by creating information-driven markets for goods and services among the users of the industrial platform.

The platforms may eventually resemble trading pits where members bid for designs, production capacity, or distribution contracts. Unlike commodity exchanges, however, industrial platforms will be private, and the platform owners will have unique access to the bidding activity. This will give them asymmetric information — knowing something that others don't. They'll profit not just from a percentage on all the transactions, but also from selling that information, buying and reselling for their own account, and perhaps even trading on their unique information in stock and bond markets.

Does that sound far-fetched? Consider that it's not so different from what Facebook or Google does with all the personal information it collects from users and then repackages for advertisers. Platform users may seek a share of the profits from these information-based transactions, or bargain for a degree of privacy, but in most cases their leverage will be limited.

Pan-industrials will be the first to learn about innovative designs or emerging consumer trends. They'll see the choke points, discover unused production capacity, and detect raw material price differences around the world. As the Internet of Things grows in importance, they'll automatically gather the data from billions of connected sensors embedded in industrial organizations and other end-users across the globe, crunch the numbers, and set the best prices — perhaps enjoying handsome profits realized through arbitrage. They'll use the data for many other purposes as well, including designing products tailored to the needs of specific markets, taking advantage of emerging AM trends before competitors, and so on. The more information a pan-industrial has, the better it can position itself to create many forms of value for its users — and the better it can fend off rivals.

Will the information edge be sustainable? Logic suggests that it will. Other trading entities, from the New York Stock Exchange to the great merchant banking houses of Europe, have endured for centuries. Trading goes on forever because it meets a fundamental human need: *People always want what others have.*

What's more, the pan-industrials will have unique advantages traditional trading organizations could not match. Because of the informational power of industrial platforms, most companies, even small makers, will need to join an established and large pan-industrial network. The makers could try to organize a rival platform of their own, in order to keep more of the profits for themselves. But even if they can recruit enough makers into a collaborative network, they're unlikely to capture enough information to stay reasonably competitive.

Meanwhile, the users of established platforms probably won't defect from them due to the advantage of being part of a bigger and better network, as well as the switching costs from having to convert digital files and production software. And history suggests that such cooperative arrangements fail to innovate over time. Assuming the established pan-industrial platforms stay reasonably diligent, they'll have a strong and sustainable advantage in the marketplace by cherry-picking the users of the less established platforms. Again, the sustainability of today's major media platforms points the way.

The platform controlled by the core company and those of user companies may all be interoperable and interconnected, much as the Wintel and Apple desktop operating systems for computers became over time. But the pan-industrials will resist becoming interoperable and interconnected with rival pan-industrials, because in that case they would lose their access to asymmetric information — a benefit far greater than anything Microsoft or Apple ever derived from their operating system platforms.

*The speed-and-flexibility edge.* Most traditional conglomerates exert little control over their operations. Each division has its own research and development (R&D), factories, and distribution network, and tends to share few suppliers with the rest of the conglomerate. Headquarters gets involved primarily in finance, management development, and expansion decisions, because it simply can't know enough to make more specific decisions responsibly in such diverse industries.

Pan-industrials will be very different, because they'll rely on sophisticated software platforms that coordinate most steps in the value chain. Conventional supply chain software can't handle such diverse operations; it would be overwhelmed by the myriad potential options. But platforms with advanced cloud-based analytics can. They'll integrate the value chains of the various business units and generate savings in purchasing, production, distribution, and overall risk management. Digital manufacturing platforms can reduce costs by coordinating supply chains, optimizing production plans, minimizing inventory carrying costs, and accelerating the prototyping and introduction of new products. Additive manufacturing makes these processes so easy that they can be achieved in real time and on the fly.

Any individual action will be more valuable because the platform will have more options in carrying it out efficiently. As for production, additive manufacturing will increasingly replace inflexible, scale-intensive subtractive manufacturing, and the platform will direct factories when to switch from slow-moving products to the hot sellers. Factories will enjoy higher rates of utilization than is possible now, which is key to manufacturing efficiency.

Headquarters will use the platform to centralize most of the supply chain decisions, and eventually the production decisions as well. As a result, managers of the individual divisions will have less and less to do. Over time, the pan-industrial will organize less around industries and more around geography, with smaller plants and supply chains located close to customers in order to boost responsiveness.

With advanced digital manufacturing platforms, pan-industrials will be able to locate and control factories close to the market. Because each factory can supply a broad product line, smaller factories are possible. Companies can situate them near to customers and learn more about what customers really want. We'll get regional factories with locally adapted goods, rather than global plants putting out standardized products that don't quite satisfy everybody. They'll help to make the economy much more responsive to customer demand.

At its core, a pan-industrial firm will integrate and improve its additive and digital manufacturing capabilities. That means that a pan-industrial business model will constantly be evolving. Two pan-industrial firms will not necessarily look alike, even if they happen to overlap in several industrials and buy the same 3D printers. They will differ with respect to the markets they have diversified into, their overall size, and the machine learning that their additive and digital equipment have absorbed. Again, the result will be greater flexibility and responsiveness to the needs of specific market segments, no matter how those needs may change over time.

There will be one more ancillary benefit from the speed-and-flexibility advantage of the pan-industrials—namely, a reduction in the need for contracts, onerous contract-enforcement mechanisms, and labor-intensive checking of product or service quality. Pan-industrials armed with digitized information systems will be able to monitor compliance with standards automatically and instantaneously. In the long run, even the notorious litigiousness of American industrial society may be minimized as a result.

*The innovation edge.* The pan-industrials will develop an advantage when it comes to innovation through their deep knowledge of markets and customers. They'll also benefit from the creative capabilities afforded by leading-edge additive manufacturing — advantages we've already mentioned, such as the increased speed of prototyping, the new design options AM makes possible, the ability to easily customize products, and more.

The giant pan-industrials that will emerge in the next few years will also have some surprising innovation competencies that small "makers" and traditional manufacturers won't have, even when these are armed with 3D printers and other new technological tools. The advantages they'll enjoy will strike some as counterintuitive. After all, it is conventional wisdom that small companies are generally more innovative than large ones due to the slowness of large bureaucracies. It's also widely assumed that big firms are inherently risk-averse. Furthermore, they're generally believed to be susceptible to the so-called *innovator's dilemma* — the reluctance of successful companies to commit to innovation because of the size of their investment in old technologies, the high cost of change, their past track record of accomplishments using the old technology, and the possibility of continuing to improve the old technology up to a point.

These beliefs have some validity. But the pan-industrials will be able to overcome the barriers to innovation by taking advantage of the speed and flexibility that AM, digital manufacturing, and industrial platforms provide. Because it's so easy to design and try out new products in the marketplace, pan-industrial companies can flood the market with experiments at modest cost — and because pan-industrials are large and well known, with extensive distribution chains, they will have little difficulty convincing customers to give their new products a test drive.

The same flexibility will make it easier for pan-industrials to minimize the risk in innovation. When a new product idea surfaces, it will be quickly modeled and prototyped using AM. Then it can be tested in one or a few low-quantity, high-value-added niches using small quantities of goods produced at relatively low cost. For example, imagine a new design for a mountain bike that is particularly light and durable and both flexible and strong. A few dozen 3D-printed models of this new design could be made available to competitive bicycle racers who are eager to test any promising innovation, with little concern about cost. When and if it is justified, the quantity can be increased to supply larger niches using advancements in printing methods that increase speed and reduce waste. Along the way, steps in the supply chain will be shortened or eliminated by moving the production nearer to the place of consumption. To that end, small production plants for the new bikes could be quickly established at a dozen locations where world-class cyclists tend to cluster, from Laramie, Wyoming, to Dunedin, New Zealand. This will reduce costs further and make the marketplace innovation even less risky.

Pan-industrial firms will be able to switch over to new kinds of products more easily and affordably than traditional manufacturers. Once a company makes the fundamental commitment to additive and digital manufacturing, no individual product choice is terribly risky. The same web-based digital platform and 3D printer farm that produces product A can be switched to producing product B, C, D, or E very quickly and at minimal cost — and if the new product fails, the pan-industrial firm can switch the capacity over to making something else that is in demand. The same applies on a larger scale to experiments with new markets; additive manufacturing skills and materials will likely transcend industry boundaries as we know them today, making it relatively risk-free to test the waters.

Finally, remember that shorter supply chains, local production, and quicker turnaround times all help companies get closer to customers — and this provides another big assist to would-be innovators. Pan-industrials that take advantage of all the benefits of new manufacturing technologies will be able to read and respond to customer needs with remarkable speed. Digital manufacturing platforms will enable up-to-the-minute product changes in response to customer feedback or safety issues. They can also launch co-creation programs to collaborate with customers or suppliers, making new product designs better, developing them faster, and reducing the number of failures.

All of these factors will lower the risk inherent in innovation, encouraging pan-industrials to produce a continual flood of new goods. Some will fail, some will succeed — but the net effect is likely to be a Golden Age of creativity that promises incredible benefits for consumers, as well as huge profits for the pan-industrials.

*The deep-pockets edge.* The industrial platforms I'm describing — those capable of managing the complexity of real-time optimization — are expensive. Besides the up-front software and hardware costs, there's also the implementation and training time required, as well as the work of converting supply chain and production data into a consistent format readable by the platform. Pan-industrials will be able to spread those costs across multiple industries. They'll be able to move faster down the learning curve in each industry because of what they've learned and developed elsewhere. They will automate the routine transactions and build out a richer menu of options to handle new kinds of activities. They'll have the heft to invest in machine learning to speed things up as well. So they'll realize the efficiencies, quality improvements, and innovation from digitization a good deal faster than smaller, less diverse companies.

After all, digital integration is not a one-time decision. It's a gradual process of installing the software platform ever deeper into operations. Pan-industrials will gradually remove legacy structures that get in the way of realizing the new capabilities. They'll develop entirely new ways of organizing production, much as manufacturers did when they electrified their plants in the early twentieth century. At first, the factories simply replaced their central steam engines with electrical equivalents, but eventually they gave each machine its own electric motor and created a much more efficient layout.

An even better analogy is from the 1950s and '60s, when new accounting and management methods gradually spread through the U.S. economy. Conglomerates that had already perfected these methods bought up smaller operations and whipped them into shape. The marketplace eventually caught up, and now consultants and private equity companies provide this service better. But for decades, conglomerates had a decided competitive advantage. A similar process will play out with the digitization of manufacturing.

This will just be the start of the financial advantages enjoyed by the pan-industrials. Because pan-industrials will be created through the combination of many companies from a wide range of industries, they will have access to a deeper pool of capital than most businesses enjoy. Furthermore, the financial stability of the pan-industrials will be enhanced by the same diversification effect that the old conglomerates enjoyed: Their access to differing markets and geographies will make it easier for the pan-industrials to weather temporary or market-specific economic upheavals, and to take on giant projects too big for any conventional business. Thus, one characteristic virtually all of the giant pan-industrials will share will be very deep pockets — a giant reservoir of wealth they can call on as needs or opportunities require.

This deep-pockets advantage will benefit the pan-industrials in several ways. It will enable them to survive and thrive even if they end up in face-to-face competition against today's richest companies — the digital giants Alphabet, Apple, Amazon, and Facebook. The pan-industrials will be able to respond quickly and decisively to opportunities that arise due to market shifts — for example, when a particular city or region enters a period of rapid economic growth, a big pan-industrial will be able to fund a series of factories in the area within months, turning out a stream of cars, appliances, furniture, electronic devices, and other goods to supply the burgeoning population. When a product becomes an unexpected hit — for example, when demand for a particular model of phone, toy, or gadget suddenly rockets — a deep-pocketed firm will have the resources to quickly shift dozens or hundreds of local production facilities to manufacturing the hot product, so none of the urgent demand ends up going unfilled.

Big pan-industrials will also have the money needed to fund research into new generations of manufacturing and digital information technologies, and to implement those new technologies as soon as they become available. They'll have the sophistication and resources to develop the powerful security systems needed to fend off hackers, terrorists, and others malicious actors who might seek to corrupt AM software for their own purposes. Most important, with the ability to sell so many products in so many markets, pan-industrial firms will be able to climb the learning curves of new technologies, processes, or systems more quickly than smaller business. This will help them to gain first-mover advantages, proprietary intellectual property, and tacit knowledge that other types of businesses find it hard to accumulate.

*The reputation edge.* The pan-industrials will develop a reputational advantage through their sheer size and power. As AM goes mainstream and the secret gets more widely spread, customers will naturally prefer buying from big companies with deep pockets and reputations on the line. Bigness will help legitimize the technologies and products. And buyers and suppliers will be more inclined to work with large, stable pan-industrial firms, rather than sell to or buy from makers that could disappear at any moment.

Pan-industrial firms will offer an important degree of reassurance to customers trying out this new technology. They'll be able to afford to engineer and manufacture goods to the very highest quality and safety standards, and to implement testing, guarantees, liability coverage, and other measures that consumers find reassuring and attractive when considering the purchase of a new or untested product. People will naturally prefer buying from big companies with well-known reputations on the line.

In brief, pan-industrial firms will become too smart to fail, too agile to fail, too innovative to fail, too rich to fail, and too respected to fail. Pan-industrial firms will be gigantic juggernauts unlike any the business world has ever seen.

As the pan-industrials grow and diversify, will traditional Wall Street financial firms regard them with the same skepticism they've learned to apply to old-fashioned conglomerates? Is it possible that activist investors, hedge funds, and institutions like banks, endowment funds, and mutual funds will use their clout to try to break up the pan-industrials through proxy fights or a continual barrage of criticism in the media?

They may—for a while. But if I'm right about the overpowering advantages that the pan-industrials will wield, it will eventually become clear to all sensible observers that they've managed to overcome the weaknesses of the old conglomerates . . . and that smart investors should join them rather than fight them.

At first glance, the pan-industrials of the future may sound a bit fantastic. But their predecessors are already among us, assembling the building blocks for the evolutionary changes to come — much as the late dinosaurs of the Cretaceous period developed hollow bones, feathers, nesting behavior, and other features of the birds to whom they would one day give rise.

You recall from a few pages back the partial list of companies that are currently at work on developing entrants in the race for the industrial platform of the future. The list included a varied array of companies, from manufacturing giants to software companies to business service providers.

As the variety of that list suggests, the pan-industrials of the future may grow from a variety of different core businesses. Some could emerge from contract manufacturers, like Jabil, Flex Ltd., or Foxconn; others from diversified manufacturers, like GE, Siemens, or Honeywell; others from software providers, like IBM, Dassault Systèmes, or Oracle; still others from consumer platforms, like Google or Amazon; and still others from B2B exchanges (not yet in existence) that connect hundreds or thousands of businesses into a production network.

Whatever their origins and their specific corporate form, over time, the pan-industrials will gradually come to occupy powerful roles in the new industrial order of the twenty-first century. They'll compete by developing the flexibility and agility to serve as many markets as possible, building spheres of influence that will span industries, markets, and geographies. Companies that are the first to master breakthrough production methodologies and develop the computerized capabilities to manage the complexity of a pan-industrial will attract the lion's share of customers for particular categories of products — for example, metal goods created using metal additive manufacturing techniques. As individual pan-industrial companies emerge victorious from these races, they'll gather additional advantages from the information flows to which they'll gain access.

Organizations that become the centers of big, vibrant production networks will know more about the ever-evolving marketplace than their rivals. As a result, they will be positioned to develop new, better products more quickly than anyone else, thereby tightening their grip on the market even further. Thus, definitive, relatively long-term marketplace victories will once again be possible. Just as the first industrial revolution helped create many of the corporate giants that dominated the business world for decades — companies like DuPont, GE, Ford, Kodak, and U.S. Steel — the pan-industrial revolution will create titans that will likely bestride the economic scene for many years to come.

## Beyond the Maker Myth

As I've noted earlier, the coming rise to power of pan-industrial companies means that, contrary to one popular myth, the future of additive manufacturing does *not* lie in a world of "makers" — hobbylike small-scale craftspeople producing a few items at a time in little workshops scattered all over the world.

The maker myth is a vision that has been popularized by a number of 3D printing enthusiasts who see the technology as a vehicle for "democratizing production." They believe that 3D printers will enable artisans to produce bespoke objects designed according to individual creative visions, ushering in a new age of unique goods and liberating the world from the marketing and financial power of big corporations. This vision is supported by organizations like Fabfoundation, which is encouraging the building of many small fab labs all over the world, under the rubric of the "democratization of making." Their dream is that additive manufacturing and related technologies will take production out of the hands of giant companies and put it in the hands of millions of ordinary people.

A different but related trend is the spread of manufacturing service companies — Xometry, Fictiv, Proto Labs, RapidMade, Forecast 3D, and Fast Radius — which are "Uberizing" manufacturing by making parts or devices on demand for other companies. In an era when 3D printing was a brand-new technology that big companies were hesitant to invest in, these service firms played a valuable role by providing expertise, advice, and access to machines that companies could use to experiment with the new methods and to tackle small one-off projects, such as prototype designs. The work of service firms is also valuable to small businesses that don't need or can't afford their own 3D printing operations. However, some prognosticators have extrapolated from the success of these service companies to envision a world in which most additive manufacturing happens in thousands of small, independently owned shops that act as contractors to the big firms that design and ultimately market the products.

The small service shop vision of 3D printing isn't quite the same as the maker myth. But they share the idea that independent people and small, independent organizations will come to dominate the new world of manufacturing, taking much of the power and innovative capacity away from big corporations.

It's an appealing vision in some ways. David beating Goliath is a fun story — after all, everybody loves the underdog. But this is not a story that is likely to reflect much in the real world of the major industrial future.

The maker myth ignores many realities about what makes products and companies successful in a world of hundreds of millions of customers — the powers of branding, marketing, advertising, and the global reach of sales messages spread via mass media, and social networking. It ignores the learning curve benefits that favor big firms, as well as the asymmetric information advantages and network effects that only large firms will be able to capitalize upon. It ignores the reality of the cost savings that digital manufacturing platforms can bring to large firms by coordinating, optimizing, and predicting demand when running an additive manufacturing–based supply chain. And it ignores the fact that deep-pocketed large firms are already betting big on 3D printing to speed their new product development costs, closing the innovation gap that individual artisans originally opened up in the earliest days of the maker movement.

The notion that service firms and small-scale, independent fab factories can be the main locus of additive manufacturing by operating as contract suppliers to big companies in the long term is equally short-sighted. The reasons are simple. They include the fact that large corporations with national or global markets need to be able to create hundreds of thousands or millions of products quickly in response to changes in demand — a level of manufacturing that small producers, even numbering in the thousands, would find very hard to provide.

Equally difficult is the challenge of establishing and maintaining exacting standards of consistency and quality across hundreds or thousands of separate suppliers. Even when the software programs and the printing machines themselves are precisely the same, hard-to-control variables like air quality, temperature, humidity, elevation, cleanliness, and handling methods can have a noticeable impact on fine details of production — details that can make a big difference when parts from multiple sources need to be combined or used in some standardized process.

Technological advances, including improved software programs designed to monitor and address environmental variables, can't solve these problems all by themselves. Human factors will always play a crucial role. As long as people are tempted to cut corners — for example, by ignoring the warning signals being sent by quality-control software — there will be a risk in outsourcing production to hundreds of small makers. A larger plant, organized and run by a big company with a reputation to protect, will always be a safer bet.

Small 3D printing firms have still other competitive disadvantages. Modest, low-priced printing systems like those that most makers can afford have limited capabilities. As new, more powerful AM machines are developed that are able to use a wide range of materials and create products of many sizes, costs are steadily climbing, into regions that are far more affordable for giant corporations than for individual entrepreneurs or small startups.

The same problem is even more acute when it comes to complex hybrid fabrication systems that include not just 3D printers but robotic arms, conveyor belts and gantries to move items around according to precise timetables, advanced drying and finishing systems, and multiple sensors feeding data to artificial intelligence programs. These new-style factories are smaller and much less expensive than the gigantic plants characteristic of traditional automakers or aerospace manufacturers. But they are well beyond the capacity of most makers operating out of small workshops.

These disadvantages of small AM shops are one reason many of the service companies that flourished in the early days of 3D printing have already begun to consolidate, some under the ownership of big businesses like Stratasys. Bigness simply offers too many competitive advantages for the small players to overcome.

The maker myth is not completely baseless. It is true that small, inexpensive AM systems can and will be used by hobbyists and craftspeople in a variety of creative ways. Some of the goods they produce will appeal to niche markets and some may even influence broader tastes, just as low-budget films and indie pop music productions can sometimes attract a cult following and help to shape tastes beyond what one might expect. In that way, the maker movement is likely to continue to flourish, providing artistically minded individuals with a community to support and encourage their efforts. Similarly, the service shops that provide small-scale 3D printing on demand to companies will continue to play a useful function, just as the photocopy shop in the local strip mall serves as a handy supplier of printing services for nearby small businesses and individuals.

Nevertheless, it's simply not realistic to imagine that individual workshops turning out a few items at a time are ever going to become major sources of goods for markets numbering in the millions of people.

The advent of the industrial revolution in the eighteenth century, together with the rising world population and advances in transportation and communication, all conspired to create the era of the mass market in the nineteenth century. Artists like William Morris and other avatars of the so-called arts and crafts movement protested against mass production toward the end of that era, but they could do little to slow the trend. Nostalgia for one-at-a-time production can't change the mathematical realities of today's global economics — and the development of AM, in the long run, will do nothing to reverse the tide of history either. The logic of the pan-industrial revolution — and the power of the virtuous cycle of growth that it will set in motion — will make the drive toward bigness practically irresistible.

# PART TWO

# WHEN TITANS RULE THE WORLD

Part 1 described the new technologies that are transforming manufacturing, including various forms of additive manufacturing and the rise of industrial platforms. It explained how these new technologies are leading to far-reaching changes in manufacturing processes and capabilities, including the ability of industries to achieve unprecedented scope and scale. It also discussed how and why these new capabilities will lead to the rise of a new kind of company, the *pan-industrial*.

Now, Part 2 will explore the competitive consequences of the changes described in Part 1. It will show how the transformation of additive manufacturing and capabilities will eventually transform the economic landscape and the nature of competition itself. It will describe the various kinds of pan-industrial entities we can anticipate, the characteristics of each, and explain how they are likely to emerge and evolve. It will explain the characteristics that will make the most powerful firms of the new manufacturing era markedly different from those that have dominated the last several decades.

It'll show why, after a period of hypercompetition in which the traditional concept of "sustainable competitive advantage" appeared to be all but extinct, new forms of sustainable advantage are now likely to re-emerge. I'll analyze the new forms of competition that will be practiced by the giant pan-industrials that will dominate over the next few decades — and by other companies that will strive to survive in their shadows. And I'll show how the new phenomenon of superconvergence will rapidly erode boundaries between business functions, individual companies, markets, and entire industries. In effect, super-convergence will turn the world economy into a single giant ocean in which the pan-industrials will freely swim.

Finally, Part 2 will explain how the pan-industrials will present new challenges to democratic governments — a throwback to the Gilded Age, with its battles over wealth and political power between trust-builders and trust-busters. The pan-industrials will drive such changes as unprecedented levels of unemployment and seismic shifts in global trading patterns. There will be many losers, and a few very big winners. I'll discuss these challenges while also showing the enormous potential benefits that the age of the pan-industrial titans may provide.

# 7

# NEW PLAYERS

*Inside the World of Pan-Industrials*

**AT SIX O'CLOCK ON** Thursday morning, April 2, 2027, Mary Ramirez's smart pillow began to vibrate gently, just as it did practically every weekday. It didn't make much noise; even Mary's cat ignored the quiet hum. But it was enough to wake Mary, who'd always been a light sleeper. And just as she did practically every weekday, Mary popped out of bed within sixty seconds and headed for her kitchen, ready to launch herself into another day as Chief Platform Officer of Universal Metals, the third-fastest-growing pan-industrial firm in the world.

As she poured herself a second cup of coffee, Mary tapped the dome-shaped silver-and-gold digital assistant squatting on her kitchen counter. The gadget was itself a Universal Metals product. "Good morning, Theresa!" she called. "What's on the agenda for today?"

"Good morning, Mary!" the friendly, faintly Italian-accented voice replied. "It's April second — the fifth anniversary of your first day at Universal Metals. Happy anniversary! Your agenda includes the following: Your daily operations review. A ten o'clock meeting with the design management staff to review progress on implementing third-generation generative design. Lunch with Peter Kim to discuss having his company join the Universal Metals platform. Strategy meeting about the potential for entering the water treatment equipment industry. Coaching session for next month's legislative hearing in Geneva." A short pause. Then, as usual, a concluding comment from Theresa: "A very full day ahead, even by *your* standards, Mary. Better finish that second cup of coffee!"

Mary laughed. "Thanks, Theresa. Catch you later!" She headed out the door of her apartment.

Her fifth anniversary — she'd almost forgotten! As she rode down in the elevator, Mary thought back to her first weeks at Universal Metals. She remembered seeing the Universal Metals name and logo everywhere she went. It had long been there, she realized; she'd just never been primed to notice it before. Around her apartment, it appeared on everything from the coffeemaker and instacooker in her kitchen to the light fixtures on the walls and the video screens in every room. Outside, she spotted it on the elevator control panel, the frames of the advertising kiosks on the street outside, and even on the nameplate of the self-driving taxi she hailed for the ride to the office ("Zephyr-Wheelz, a Universal Metals brand"). She remembered feeling quietly proud to be part of such a vast organization — over a million employees worldwide — that made so many products essential to daily life.

Mary arrived at her workplace, a curvilinear building of metal, glass, and concrete bearing the Universal Metals logo, just two stories high and occupying less than half a city block in downtown Denver, Colorado. Not a very imposing footprint for such a powerful and ubiquitous corporation — until you realized that this was just one of seventy-eight Universal Metals facilities staffed by some 8,000 employees in the Denver area. As one of the company's twenty most important executives, Mary had the freedom to work in almost any location she found compatible with her lifestyle. As an avid skier and hiker, she'd chosen Denver. Of course, she spent almost half her time on the road, visiting Universal Metals operations around the world. She also attended periodic meetings with other members of the executive team at the corporate headquarters in the suburbs of Milwaukee, Wisconsin. Like other cities in what had once been America's rust belt, Milwaukee was enjoying a resurgence thanks to the pan-industrial revolution, which had transformed manufacturing from a moribund industry into a newly booming economic sector.

By 7:20, Mary had settled into her office, with its grand view of the mountains, and reconnected with Theresa via the transmitter on her desk. As she'd left the office the evening before, Mary had switched on the Manufacturing Execution System, or MES, to fully automate the global production system overnight, leaving smart machines running smart 3D printers based on AI and IoT sensors. It was just as easy as turning off her office light.

Now she started the day the same as always, by logging in to Universal Metal's Global Activities Platform, or GAP. The platform's summary page filled a video screen that stretched from one end to the other of a wall in Mary's office. It displayed a world map in vibrant colors. Some 1,100 glowing nodes represented Universal Metals facilities in 140 countries, while shifting, pulsing patterns of lines connecting those nodes represented flows of raw materials, work in progress, and finished products from one location to another. Numerous dashboard dials showed the ecosystem's current status as well as how it had performed over the past twenty-four hours.

When Mary joined Universal Metals from a smaller manufacturing firm, it had taken her a couple of weeks just to master the various colors, symbols, and patterns on this screen. But she'd now become so proficient at reading and interpreting its visual messages that she could spot potential trouble spots and opportunities within a few seconds of logging in. As usual, she spent the first fifteen minutes this morning reviewing utilization and efficiency ratings from a few dozen of the corporation's biggest supply centers. Nodes glowing in shades of green, yellow, orange, and red gave her an instantaneous visual sense of which plants were operating at full capacity and which were not. On this particular day, just three factories, all blinking scarlet, required a bit of attention. Mary zeroed in on them quickly, briefly diagnosed the apparent problems — a worker shortage here, a power blackout there — and dictated short messages to the local managers with her recommendations for corrective action. Nothing very challenging on that front, she observed with satisfaction.

"Theresa," she said, "please show me the overnight production adjustments."

The screen suddenly changed. Most of the nodes and lines vanished, replaced by a simplified image in which about ninety glowing spots represented locations where production plans had been altered during the last ten hours. Mary could read the details by pointing to one of those spots or by speaking the location name or number to Theresa. Most of the changes had been minor ones, implemented automatically by GAP in response to market fluctuations, production problems, or economic developments. For example, six out of thirty-eight factories in West Africa had been instructed to shift from producing tractors and other farm equipment to making sporty self-driving cars, thanks to an unexpectedly strong demand for the new roadster designs Universal Metals had introduced this week. In Jakarta, street protests by anti-government demonstrators had slowed truck deliveries to and from seven Universal Metals plants; production quotas had been shifted to nearby facilities instead.

Most distressing to Mary, she learned that mudslides in Northern California had heavily damaged a factory that had been making airplane parts, car engines, washing machines, and other goods, as well as destroying the homes of at least a dozen Universal Metals employees. Of course, production had quickly been shifted to nearby local facilities, but Mary had other concerns. "Theresa, please make sure we're delivering food, water, medicine, and other supplies to the area, and that we've provided shelter to anyone who needs it," Mary said. "Our employees and their families get top priority. Convert another warehouse if needed, but be sure to reroute the inventory to the most economical locations."

"That's been done," Theresa replied after a moment's pause. "Delivery drones have brought three point six tons of supplies to the local high school, which is managed by our California Community Engagement nonprofit subsidiary. A Universal Metals warehouse four miles away has been turned into a shelter with beds, showers, and food. Overnight guests included twenty-seven adults, thirteen children, six dogs, four cats, one parrot." The screen displayed photos of workers in yellow jumpsuits bearing the Universal Metals logo, setting up cots, unloading cartons of meals, and offering blankets and stuffed toys to kids with tearstained cheeks.

Mary was satisfied. "Thanks, Theresa. Please update later today."

This morning, the GAP screen highlighted just one proposed production change that required Mary's attention. An image flashed onscreen of a powerful-looking teenage girl in a bright green nylon jersey and shorts, riding an electric-powered 3D-printed skateboard up an impossibly steep incline. The adjacent text explained that Angelina Georgescu currently held a twenty-nine-point lead in the first Universal Metals Competitive Skateboarding Challenge, due for completion within the next two hours. If Angelina held on to win the tournament, as expected, her victory was likely to boost demand for the brand-new motorized skateboard she was riding — a double-axle hyperflexing model that Universal Metals' generative design team had released within the past eleven days. GAP was recommending that six plants in Mexico and Canada be instructed to deliver 50,000 units of the new board to retail outlets within the next three days. "If those boards sell out," Theresa observed, "we can shift worldwide production to deliver another one hundred thousand 3D-printed units by this time next week. Is it a go?"

Mary pondered. Thinking that Georgescu's name sounded familiar, she clicked on the cyclist's photo. The screen lit up with a dozen pictures of young Georgescu attending film premieres and art galas in Bucharest, Vienna, and Prague. She sported a wild hairstyle of corkscrew curls in an amazing shade of violet. A caption noted that the Romanian native had already attracted a cult following among teenagers in her native country. Mary spoke to Theresa: "Add three plants in Eastern Europe to the plan, and expand production quantity by twenty-five thousand. With those changes, the plan is approved."

As the GAP screen faded for Mary's five-minute midmorning break, giving way to a panoramic view of a trail in the Rockies, she sat back, gave a deep sigh, and thought about how far she'd come joining Universal Metals. At her previous job, as production manager for the Taiwan-based Qijan Components, she'd spent most of her time figuring out ways to boost efficiencies within a single factory — for example, by developing enhanced layouts for machines, assembly lines, and supply routes. At Universal Metals, those kinds of challenges had almost all been solved with the help of systems-optimizing AI tools built into GAP. Now Mary could focus her attention on improving performance across a much bigger universe — more than a thousand factories on every continent on Earth. The roster of plants included the three factories she'd managed for Qijan Components, which had joined the Universal Metals platform two years ago.

At ten o'clock, three members of Mary's local design management team arrived at her office for the first big meeting of her day — the review of progress on implementing third-generation generative design ("3G Gen," as Mary dubbed it) across the company's worldwide platform. Six other managers logged in using Microsoft's hololens — a virtual reality room — from locations in Boston, Barcelona, Cairo, Ankara, Sydney, and Shanghai. Mary knew the conversation would be delicate. Designers throughout the corporation understood and appreciated the benefits that generative design had already produced — brilliant, counterintuitive innovations that no human would be likely to imagine, taking advantage of the unique, molecule-by-molecule production capabilities that only additive manufacturing offered. The new skateboard that Angelina Georgescu was now riding to victory and to worldwide acclaim was just the latest example. The people of Universal Metals were justly proud of their ability to innovate the skateboard's colorful designs and lightweight, durable honeycomb structures as quickly and cleverly as any company on the planet, and they knew that generative design was a big contributing factor.

But the planned implementation of 3G Gen, in which entire new products and manufacturing plans — not just parts or components — would be conceived, designed, and built by computer/printer combinations equipped with AI and machine learning... this idea made even the sophisticated designers at Universal Metals nervous. Was this the step that would finally make creative *human* designers redundant?

Mary listened closely as each member of the team offered a progress report. As she expected, the results were mixed. Although none of the managers spoke candidly about negative attitudes among local designers, Mary sensed that some of the delays in full implementation of 3G Gen had stemmed from such resistance. For half an hour, a mood of uncertainty and anxiety quietly mounted in the room.

The breakthrough happened when Mary called on Hany Ozman, the leader of Universal Metals' research team in Egypt. Mary knew that Hany was one of the most enthusiastic supporters of 3G Gen. She'd been hoping his team would be pioneers in demonstrating the benefits it could offer to everyone in the company. Now Hany came through for her, with flying colors.

For ten minutes, Hany described how he and his design team had fully implemented 3G Gen in all their operations over the past two months. "The results have been amazing," Hany recounted. "The new applications have boosted our innovative capacity by forty percent.

Last year, during February and March, we introduced four hundred and seventy-eight new products. This year, during the same months, we introduced six hundred and sixty-nine. And the quality is better! One hundred twenty-seven of the new products are already the best-selling items in their markets — a new bathroom cabinet design, an improved home trash compactor, a storage system for airplane cargo, and many more." As he spoke, a series of amazingly novel 3D printable designs appeared on the screen beside him.

"Most important, my people love it! Three months ago, my best designer — you know Magdi, that smart young kid who earned every award at MIT — was threatening to quit if we insisted on 3G Gen. Now he's having a ball. He's spending his days listing ideas on a yellow pad, dreaming up crazy, imaginative product challenges for the computers to play with. He is so grateful that I forced him to upgrade to 3G Gen!"

Hany's report instantly transformed the mood in the room. Mary could see the skepticism and anxiety in her team members' faces beginning to melt away. She smiled gratefully at Hany's image on the screen. "Thank you for that report," she said.

"You're welcome, Mary," Hany replied — and gave her just the very briefest wink. *You owe me one,* it seemed to say. Mary nodded and made a mental note to take Hany out for an especially nice lunch the next time she visited Cairo.

As the meeting continued — now in a far more upbeat atmosphere — Mary found her thoughts drifting to the rest of her day's schedule. She'd be having lunch with Peter Kim, who was being wooed to bring his company into the Universal Metals family of businesses. She'd already planned to introduce Peter to a couple of her former colleagues at Qijan Components, who could tell him all about how their company's productivity, speed, and flexibility had soared since joining the Universal Metals platform. Now she was thinking that she ought to connect Peter with Hany Ozman in Cairo as well, so that Hany could get Peter jazzed about the potential for 3G Gen — and about how far ahead of the other pan-industrials Universal Metals was in implementing it.

Lunch would be followed by an executive team discussion about entering a new market — specifically, the market for water treatment equipment, generally sold to municipalities and giant utility firms.

Like the other big pan-industrials—corporations such as Additive BioTech, Omnium Engineering, Local Globalistics, MacroNanoBuild, and Synthesis, Inc.—Universal Metals was engaged in more or less endless debates concerning how widely to diversify. Mary would be asked to weigh in on whether the new industry fit the scope dynamics of the company's existing assets. Mary had already gathered some great customer insights and predictive analytics from the data collected by Universal Metals' platform. But the right answer might be revealed only through trial and error.

Mary had seen enough cases of overexpansion to make her adopt a fairly cautious approach to expansion, especially in cases where the new customer groups differed significantly from those already served by the corporation. But Universal Metals' counted local governments and big utility companies among its existing customers for products like fleets of vehicles, tools for road building and maintenance, energy-generation machinery, and so on. The platform data made her feel that marketing water treatment equipment would be a natural extension. And her experience with GAP gave her confidence that the platform and AM equipment could easily handle any design, production, and logistics challenges associated with the new product line. The discussion that afternoon would be an interesting one.

Mary's day would end with one of her least-favorite activities—a coaching session for her upcoming testimony in March before the World Legislative Assembly's Economic Activity Committee. Back in graduate school, when Mary had chosen operations management as her field of study, she hadn't bargained on getting involved in politics. But Universal Metals, like other pan-industrials, had become so big and powerful that the governments of the world inevitably felt pressure to monitor, regulate, and sometimes control its activities. And the pan-industrials, in turn, had felt obliged to mount extensive lobbying efforts to defend their prerogatives and to try to shape legislation that would be friendly to business interests—especially those of the pan-industrials.

So when Mary was asked to join Universal Metals' executive team, the CEO, Felix Granchelli, had mentioned, almost as an aside, "Of course, we're also hoping you'll serve as one of the public faces of the corporation, especially when it comes to explaining the impact of our daily operations on local economies. I do the same for our biggest international markets."

Over the next five years, Mary had learned what being a face of the corporation meant: periodic calls to testify about upcoming legislation before national, regional, and global government agencies. It involved a lot of time-consuming homework as well as travel; legislators liked to question powerful business executives in person rather than electronically. Sure, most of this was play-acting — kabuki drama designed to show the constituents back home how "tough" their elected officials could be in defending the public interest against the powerful pan-industrial titans. But it was all part of the price a pan-industrial had to pay for enjoying a level of economic, social, and political power comparable to that of many nation-states.

Mary's drifting thoughts were brought back to the present as the meeting about 3G Gen neared its close. "Thanks to all of you for your fine reports," Mary said. "Let's check in again the same time next month. I'm hoping to hear about even greater progress."

But before her team members could sign off, Theresa's disembodied voice was interrupted. "Excuse me, Mary," he said. "But I've been asked to introduce a surprise guest — our CEO." And there, suddenly dominating the screen, was the looming, smiling face of Felix Granchelli, to whom everybody in the room ultimately reported. Felix was a remarkable man — holder of PhDs in chemistry and material science, and fluent in four languages: English, German, Italian, and Spanish. In the office window behind his left shoulder, waving branches thick with pale pink buds were visible; spring was well under way in Wisconsin.

"*Buongiorno*, Mary!" Felix said. "Sorry to interrupt your meeting, but I thought you and your team members might have a minute for me this morning."

Mary collected her thoughts. "Sure, Felix. I suppose you'd like an update about our progress with 3G Gen."

"Absolutely!" Felix replied. "But let's do that another time. Right now, I have a more important matter to address. Theresa, have you made the necessary arrangements?"

"Yes, sir," Theresa replied, and the office door swung open. A smiling, white-jacketed attendant wearing a chef's hat rolled in a cart bearing a big 3D-printed pink cake in the shape of the figure 5. Mary's three team members broke into grins. "Happy anniversary, Mary! And many more," Felix declared. The attendant began slicing portions of cake and handing them out.

Pleased and a little embarrassed, Mary cried out in mock dismay, "Felix, you're the worst! This is going to completely ruin my lunch." And she dug in for a giant forkful.

## Breaking Boundaries: The Expansive Logic of the Pan-Industrials

In Chapter 6, I introduced pan-industrial companies and explained why they matter. The story of a day in the life of Mary Ramirez, central platform manager for Universal Metals, has given you a little glimpse of what the operations of a pan-industrial might look and feel like from the inside. Now let's take a step back and consider the essential characteristics of a pan-industrial, and how it differs from other kinds of big companies.

A pan-industrial has three key defining features:

- It operates in multiple industries and makes products that span multiple industries.
- It relies on additive manufacturing for much of its production, taking advantage of the economies of scope and scale that AM makes possible.
- It uses an industrial platform to connect and optimize the multi-industry factories it operates.

These three elements enable pan-industrials to expand into a wide range of activities while achieving extraordinary operational synergies across its products and operations, especially by sharing the industrial platform, AM production centers, and crucial suppliers.

By contrast, traditional focused companies have none of these three elements. Conglomerates operate in multiple industries, but they need not use additive manufacturing, and they have no platform to optimize production across divisions. Conglomerates have tried to coordinate their production across industries, and have either failed utterly or discovered that the cost of the efforts was greater than any gains.

Companies that invest in Industry 4.0, employing new technologies such as artificial intelligence, all-purpose robots, and the Internet of Things, may or may not use AM, and they most likely have not developed digital platforms to optimize their production capabilities. Nowadays, almost every manufacturer of size uses complex information systems to monitor and adjust its operations. But these systems lack the power to truly optimize operations across industries, or to achieve scope and scale benefits at the same time.

Platforms are, of course, a central feature of the big tech giants such as Apple, Amazon, Alphabet, and Facebook. But these companies use platforms to optimize their sales and marketing efforts, not their manufacturing capabilities. You could say they use platforms to create valuable services, such as Facebook's user-generated newsfeeds. But these are information-based, not physical product-based.

As you can see, none of these tech giants is a pan-industrial, because none includes all three of the essential features that makes a pan-industrial unique.

Pan-industrials will operate in a sweet spot of diversification. They'll go beyond merely adjacent industries, in order to capture wide economies of scope. They'll focus on manufacturing (as opposed to information goods and services), with varied specializations based on related categories of physical goods. One pan-industrial might concentrate on consumer appliances, another on high-tech electronics, another on heavy equipment developed for business-to-business markets. Some pan-industrials may be built around particular types of materials. Our fictitious Universal Metals is an example.

As of today (2018), a few companies have started to put in place the three key elements that will define the pan-industrials of tomorrow; none have so far fully leveraged them to create the economies of scope and scale that will drive pan-industrials to economic dominance. But the economic and strategic logic underlying the pan-industrials is already becoming clear. And a crucial element of that logic is the breaking down of barriers once felt to define and limit the nature of what a company could do.

In the straightforward view of the business world that many people still have, most companies are identified with a brand and a product. In this simple business world, Ford = cars, Starbucks = coffee, Converse = sneakers, and Lego = toy building blocks. A bit more broadly, other companies are identified with a group of closely related products, all sold to the same basic market: Procter and Gamble = soaps and other household necessities sold to supermarket shoppers; Kohler = sinks, toilets, faucets, and other plumbing fixtures sold to people building or renovating their homes; and Sony = TVs, Playstations, cameras, and other electronic devices sold to individuals seeking entertainment and fun. Many great businesses have been built following these linear, easy-to-understand models.

Today, however, the business world is increasingly being dominated by companies whose products, markets, and activities can't be so neatly defined. Boundaries between markets, product categories, and company types are rapidly blurring. And corporations are freely roaming into competitive spaces they might once have hesitated to explore.

Some obvious examples come from the dot-com world: Amazon, which has become not merely the "everything store" but also a major player in businesses such as electronic devices and corporate cloud computing services, and Alphabet, built around Google's search engine but now including forays into everything from drone delivery services to self-driving cars.

But the story of blurring boundaries isn't restricted to just dot-com players. There are a growing number of other, less obvious examples of boundary-busting businesses. Many are industrial companies that are building complex ecosystems of alliances, investments, and partnerships to attain access to resources, information, and markets they'd otherwise be unable to reach. As highlighted earlier, Jabil is a leading example. It's working with a growing array of companies to expand its connections into new geographies, technologies, processes, activities, and markets.

There are other examples you may find more surprising. For instance, you may be accustomed to thinking of the venerable manufacturing company Corning as a relatively simple business: Corning = glass. It was founded in 1851 as the Bay State Glass Company, and over the next century-plus, Corning Glass Works (as it was known until 1989) became famous for developing many specialized uses of glass, from the glass used in Edison's first light bulbs to glass-ceramic Pyrex and Corelle cookware.

Today, though, Corning, Inc. is involved in joint ventures, partnerships, and investment relationships that give it a hand in businesses that include catalytic converters, optical cables, glass for stem-cell research, wireless network antennas, and nose cones for tactical missiles. At the same time, Corning is still involved in glass-related industries — for example, as a leading supplier of touchscreens for Apple's iPhone. So Corning still equals glass, but it also equals a whole lot more.

Similarly, you probably think of Ryder System, Inc. as being a relatively simple company: Ryder = delivery. But today, Ryder has built partnerships with companies that include Delphi Automotive Systems, Toyota Tsusho America, Frigidaire, and Mansfield Clean Energy. They are working together on technological and managerial solutions for challenges in logistics, warehousing, energy efficiency, and vehicle self-driving. Ryder still equals delivery, but it is rapidly expanding beyond those boundaries to provide services of many other kinds.

Other companies are also using boundary-breaking alliances to overcome literal, geographic boundaries as well as industry boundaries. Consider NTT DoCoMo, the leading mobile phone operator in Japan. In the traditional view, DoCoMo = Japanese phone service. Now DoCoMo has created partnerships with companies like Google (to facilitate YouTube viewing by DoCoMo customers), Nintendo (to create and distribute video games), and GE (to develop a new Internet of Things tool combining technologies from the two companies). In addition, DoCoMo has also created a network of international telecom companies, including KG Telecommunications (Taiwan), Tele-Sudeste (Brazil), U Mobile (Malaysia), and Tata Teleservices (India). In this new world of blurred boundaries, DoCoMo is not bound by national limitations.

These boundary-breaking businesses represent the future — and the technologies described herein are going to help make that future happen. The powers of the new additive manufacturing systems and the emerging industrial platforms will make it possible for fast-moving, information-rich companies like Jabil, Corning, Ryder, and DoCoMo — among others — to grow into pan-industrials.

The pan-industrials will manage ecosystems of customers, suppliers, distributors, and others in conjunction with their internally owned companies, providing access to manufacturing systems and services for consumers, and services and information to the firms it owns. These pan-industrials will focus on developing tightly knit organizations with centrally driven command-and-control platforms. They'll have the disadvantages that centralized organizations usually exhibit, including a vulnerability to being blindsided due to short-sightedness or flawed judgment on the part of the team that controls the firm from headquarters. But they will also have many huge advantages. Most important, they will be highly coordinated and extraordinarily nimble, able to turn on a dime when market changes demand it.

In the decades to come, the emerging pan-industrials are likely to take three distinct forms:

- *pan-industrial firms* — single companies that use industrial platforms to build flexible supply chains and powerful business ecosystems, enabling greater product diversification than practiced by any corporation of today;
- *pan-industrial federations* — loose networks of independent firms that share one industrial platform as well as selected additional assets, such as market data and financial resources; and
- *pan-industrial collectives* — closely interconnected corporate entities in which member businesses that share an industrial platform are coordinated by a central authority that orchestrates overall strategic, market, and financial goals for the entire group.

Let's consider each of these business structures in turn.

### Pan-Industrial Firms

The pan-industrials of the near future will emerge in stages as companies move to tightly integrate their existing business ecosystems. The first stage will occur when individual companies adapt AM, digital IT and control tools, and other technological innovations to expand their manufacturing capabilities in ways that have long been considered impractical. The result will be what I have termed *pan-industrial firms* — single companies that use additive manufacturing and industrial platform capabilities to enable wider product diversification than practiced by any corporation of today.

In pan-industrial firms, the siloed structures found in most traditional corporations will largely disappear. Instead, their functional departments will tend to merge. For example, R&D, marketing, and product launch departments may converge into a single operating unit as incremental product changes are made continually, in real time, rather than being scheduled in discrete "seasons" or development cycles. Instead of having several separate teams that will work on a new product design and hand it off from one to another sequentially, a pan-industrial firm is more like to employ a single team of people with a wide range of talents and functions. Artists, engineers, programmers, customer interface experts, marketers, sales reps, service specialists, and more will work together using networked software tools, crafting the new product design collaboratively and rapidly building multiple prototypes and samples for testing.

In pan-industrial companies, a product development process that today takes months and includes numerous administrative steps to ensure effective handoffs from one department to another will be reduced to days or even hours. As a result, new products can be rushed to market more quickly than ever before. In a similar fashion, other neighboring functions now organized and run separately will be so tightly integrated that they will effectively constitute a single department.

We already see glimpses of the emerging pan-industrial model in the vast array of thousands of products and sophisticated services offered by the global supplier Jabil. Other industrial giants from around the world, including U.S. companies like GE and United Technologies, Japan's Sumitomo Heavy Industries, and Germany's Siemens, are also making moves that suggest they plan to pursue the same path. They are investing in 3D printing and in other technologies crucial to the future of manufacturing, such as robotics, sensors, and the Internet of Things. They are also developing the tools and systems needed to build industrial platforms that can link, organize, and coordinate the operations of many far-flung production facilities. And as we've seen, a number of today's Silicon Valley giants — already operating like souped-up twenty-first-century versions of the conglomerates — may be positioning themselves to jump into the pan-industrial fray.

As the adage goes, the best way to predict the future is to create it. Those who don't create the future must accept the world created by their competitors. Today's most far-reaching business giants are determined to create the future. They foresee a future of what I call superconvergence, in which market and industry barriers are enormously permeable, and in which companies with powerful analytic and data-crunching capabilities can run operations across a wide range of businesses. That explains why they are positioning themselves to compete with one another in the race to become some of the first successful pan-industrial firms.

### Pan-Industrial Federations

The development of pan-industrial firms will likely represent just the first stage of our pan-industrial future. In the second stage, pan-industrial companies will gather around themselves loose groups of independent firms that share the same industrial platform as well as selected additional assets, such as market data and financial resources. The platform owner's purpose will be to sell the platform to companies outside their immediate ecosystem. This will generate revenues that reduce the cost of developing and upgrading the platform for its owner's use. The groups that emerge will constitute what I call *pan-industrial federations.*

A pan-industrial federation will include a company that owns and governs the platform as well as a small group of select, invited, or preferred manufacturing firms that will use the platform. The platform-owning company will invite or disinvite users to the federation. The users will act independently of each other and delegate only selected powers to the platform owner. They'll have considerable autonomy in action from the platform-owning company and from one another, because they will be independently owned and operated, each with its own corporate management and separate board of directors.

But these user firms will benefit greatly from having access to the platform. Creating, running, and continuing updating a really powerful industrial platform is no small task. Outsourcing this job will be an attractive, cost-effective choice for many manufacturing businesses.

A pan-industrial federation may serve, in part, as a kind of testing ground for the platform-owning company. It will generally have to invest in building a "system of systems" to which all the user companies can seamlessly connect. Over time, it will work to enhance the power and flexibility of the system of systems, thereby building a platform that users will find increasingly useful. The more the platform can do, the greater its value, both for the company that owns it and for the users who have access to it.

The platform-owning company may sell or lease access to its platform software, charge by the transaction, or charge subscription fees for use of its basic and premium services and software. It may offer a patent or design library in exchange for additional fees. The platform owner will have a core software platform. It may also have additive manufacturing facilities, standards of quality, and technology knowledge that user companies can use. These user companies may be offered a menu of software and services to choose from as they see fit. For example, users may choose whether or not to take advantage of the AI and machine learning capabilities of the platform — for which an additional service fee may be charged by the platform-owning company.

In addition to strategic "preferred customer" or "preferred supplier" relationships with user companies, the federation will involve additional value-creating connections. For example, the platform-owning company will have access to vast streams of information about user companies. This data will have enormous potential value, much like the consumer data that Google currently gathers and resells. This information-sharing may be required by the rules of the federation, or it may be limited according to individual user contracts. The degree of confidentiality and data access individual users enjoy will be one of a number of issues that the users of the federation will need to hash out through negotiation.

Other companies may connect with the platform in a more limited way. For example, companies that act as suppliers and distributors to the user companies might simply hook their information systems into the platform to facilitate management of the extended supply chain.

As you can see, a pan-industrial federation is not a tightly knit alliance. The federation has no common goal other than to share the platform's resources for the betterment of the users as well as for the platform owner.

Some platform owners will choose to maintain the pan-industrial federation structure permanently. For others, the federation stage will turn into a transitional step as they develop over time into the more close-knit form of pan-industrial organization described below.

### Pan-Industrial Collectives

In the end, some federations will evolve into tightly interconnected corporate entities that I call *pan-industrial collectives.*

A pan-industrial collective will be built around a *core company* that owns and manages an industrial platform connecting a host of other companies. This core company will have greater authority than the platform owner in a federation. It will develop overall strategic, market, and financial goals for the entire collective and play the role of a central authority. It will own the platform, invite companies to become members of the collective, and offer members the right to plug in to its AM supply chain and other value-adding services — pooled purchasing arrangements, online selling sites, co-marketing efforts, a shared brand, joint R&D programs, shared financing opportunities, and more.

There are already corporate groups that show some of these characteristics — for example, GE, with its finance arm and its ability to share managerial and technological strategies with outside companies through training programs at its Crotonville center and elsewhere. Corning, Inc., which invests in startup businesses, helps fund their R&D programs, and shares other resources with companies with overlapping strategic goals, is another business of today that could be considered a proto-collective.

However, if and when these corporate alliances evolve into true pan-industrial collectives, they will feature a much greater level of centralized control than they now exhibit. As a result, they will enjoy operational efficiencies and other advantages that are impossible to imagine today.

A pan-industrial collective will operate very differently from a federation. A collective will seek member companies with closely convergent interests that are ready to cooperate directly with each other on common causes and joint ventures. The core company may use its AM capabilities and its industrial platform to become the outsourced contract manufacturer for its members if they so desire. In this role, it will consolidate supply chains and distribution across primary members to gain economies of scope and scale, improved levels of service, enhanced quality control, pricing advantages, and many other benefits.

The core company will control membership in the collective, set the fees charged to member companies, and certify the quality of members' products and processes to be sure they warrant continued access to the platform. However, the power of the core company over a particular member won't be absolute. Instead, it may vary, depending on a number of factors: the member's size and prestige; any special value the member brings to the collective; the member's interconnections with other members; the strength of a member's need for the central authority's services, and so on.

While members may interact with one another separate from the central platform, the core company will add value to those interactions by reducing operational frictions and transaction costs. For example, the core company will monitor members for compliance with delivery, quality, and other standards. It will also offer a forum for quick conflict resolution, making it cheaper for members to deal with each other — more trust, simpler contracts, fewer lawsuits. The process might be comparable to the way disputes between cardholders and vendors of American Express are resolved today. If an Amex member has a problem regarding a transaction with a vendor firm, the complaint can be resolved through pre-agreed rules under the guidance of an arbitrator employed by the "core company" — in this case, American Express itself. Vendors guilty of repeat transgressions may be punished by expulsion from the American Express network — a threat that suffices to keep most businesses in line. In a similar fashion, members of a pan-industrial collective will be incentivized to treat one another fairly and responsibly in order to maintain their good reputations and to retain access to the valuable services and information of the collective.

The core company in a pan-industrial collective will offer member companies a variety of financial services — loans, public stock offerings, equity infusions, and so on. Because the core company will capture vast amounts of real-time information about the collective's members — capacity utilization rates, raw material holdings, and parts and products inventories, and more — it will be able to arbitrage products, parts, materials, and capacity in real time. It may offer derivatives, futures, puts, and other transaction types based on this information, enabling members to hedge their bets or cover high and low peak times of production. The core company may also sell the real-time information to brokers for a fee so that a limited financial market develops within the collective.

The core company can add value to the collective in many other ways. For example, it could act as an *orchestrator,* seeking out business opportunities and pulling together *ad hoc* supply chains from within the collective. Such orchestrators already exist in *industrial clusters* in Italy — regions in which many closely related companies combine efforts to produce large quantities and varieties of goods in a particular product category, often dominating entire business sectors throughout the country. The core company could set up a venture capital board using its own money, funds from members, or even money from outside investors. The board would invest in projects that would benefit the collective — for example, developing a new standard for products made by members of the collective, building a new technology that member companies could use, or inventing products that combine the technologies of several members.

Perhaps most important — though most difficult to define — the core company will be the center of gravity of the pan-industrial collective. It will perform any task essential to the survival and success of the collective. When a unique resource on which several members of the collective rely is in short supply, the core company will be responsible for finding a source or inventing a substitute. When a crucial distribution channel is threatened by political unrest or violence, the core company will take steps to ensure its safety. When a crisis arises that could harm the value of the collective brand, the core company will mount a public relations offensive to protect it.

## Which Model Is Best?

As the taxonomy above may suggest, each of the three types of pan-industrials will have its strengths and weaknesses; each will provide a unique set of advantages and disadvantages to the companies it serves.

The pan-industrial firm will find it easiest to control and coordinate its activities, since all its key parts will share a single corporate ownership. This unified business structure will also have inherent weaknesses. For example, the firm's scope and scale may both be constrained by the fact that it has only as much investment capital to use as a single company (though a very large one) can generate.

The structure of the pan-industrial federation will be attractive to many companies because of its relative freedom. Users of a particular industrial platform that is managed along federation lines will be able to pick and choose which services they buy and which activities they participate in. Such flexibility will attract user companies that value their independence. However, that same flexibility will also limit the ability of the federation to orchestrate multicompany activities among users and so achieve economic dominance over major pan-industrial marketplaces. That flexibility will also limit the political and social influence of the federation. A loose grouping of companies that share an industrial platform but speak with a multiplicity of voices will inevitably lack the power enjoyed by a single entity with a strongly unified identity and vision.

The pan-industrial collectives will have greater unity than the federations. The collectives will have the scope and scale — including the financial clout — to wield enormous power over vast pan-industrial marketplaces. Because the core company will set broad business and financial strategies for the entire group, the collective will be able to develop a strong brand identity and a forceful political presence.

For these reasons, it's likely that, over the next few decades, the emerging pan-industrial collectives will become some of the most powerful entities on the global stage, with a profound influence on economic and social trends the world over.

There will be a high degree of difficulty for platform owners when managing a pan-industrial collective. Getting companies to act in concert is a bit like herding cats. So strong incentives to cooperate will be necessary. When the interests of a member of the collective conflict with the interests of the platform owner or those of other members of the collective, reconciling those differences while maintaining the balance of power among all parties will be time-consuming.

In the pan-industrial world I am sketching, not every company will evolve into a pan-industrial. Some will retain the familiar outlines that characterize most of today's businesses: They may continue to serve niche markets with specially designed goods that they manufacture and market through traditional channels. Over time, however, many if not most of these firms will probably end up dying out, being acquired by a pan-industrial firm, or joining a pan-industrial federation or collective. Being forced to choose one of these alternatives will increasingly be the cost of survival in the new era. As the pan-industrials grow in size and power, many traditional businesses will be required to focus on making themselves attractive to a leading pan-industrial — and then on gaining as much power as possible within the pan-industrial system.

Given the pressure that companies like GE are now facing — from Wall Street, big investors, and business analysts — to become smaller, more narrowly focused, and therefore easier and more profitable to manage, it might seem strange that I'm predicting the rise of a host of companies that will do just the opposite. How will the pan-industrials become enormously larger, more broadly diversified, and more complex, while still remaining manageable and highly profitable? The answer has several parts.

First, the pan-industrials will be able to manage bigger and more complicated combinations of businesses thanks to powerful, flexible new tools like additive manufacturing, big data, AI, machine learning, the Internet of Things, and especially industrial platforms. These innovations will make it possible for company leaders to monitor, analyze, coordinate, and control their operations with far greater speed and efficiency than ever before.

Second, the ability to participate in a broader array of markets will open the door to economies of scope. These will allow pan-industrials to experience real operating synergies — which the old conglomerates could never achieve — on top of the financial synergies (lower cost of capital) and management synergies (broad-based strategic and budget planning tools and procedures) that conglomerates did enjoy. The flexibility, speed, and broad market penetration of the pan-industrials will boost their profitability and help them to grow even bigger.

Third, the vast information flows to which the pan-industrials will have access because of their participation in so many varied markets will generate huge value in themselves — especially when the data is dissected, studied, interconnected, and monetized with all the power of today's ever-improving IT tools. For example, the data they'll collect regarding markets, prices, supply, demand, and resources will enable the pan-industrials to become adroit commodity traders, giving them another source of profits that traditional conglomerates did not enjoy. In a similar way, pan-industrials will be well positioned for success in venture capital, arbitrage, money market investing, and other financial arenas.

As these various advantages of being a pan-industrial kick into high gear, other stakeholders in the national and international economy will take notice. Big investors and Wall Street firms will gradually shed their skepticism and jump on the pan-industrial bandwagon. Analysts will recognize that the pan-industrials are reaping benefits such as their information advantage directly from the range of cross-market activities they engage in — which will discourage the analysts from pressuring the pan-industrials to narrow the scope of their activities through breakups or divestitures.

Furthermore, government regulators who might want to break up the pan-industrials because of concerns over their market dominance will find it difficult to do, given the huge economic, social, and political clout the pan-industrials will inevitably wield. Once the influence of the pan-industrials grows to rival that of some countries, the political power brokers will likely be forced to seek an accommodation with them.

Any one of these factors might not suffice to enable the pan-industrials to overcome the challenges currently faced by today's biggest diversified firms. But the combination of all of these factors will.

## Pan-Industrials: The Zaibatsu of the
## Twenty-First Century?

You can see that the pan-industrials that will evolve during the next two decades will be complex, diverse, and, above all, very large. The pan-industrial firms will use the powers of AM and industrial platforms to produce an extremely wide variety of products and serve an extraordinarily broad array of customers, all with unprecedented efficiency and flexibility. The pan-industrial federations will connect additional manufacturers to a single industrial platform, making the potential range of products and customers wider still. And the pan-industrial collectives will unify the activities of many companies behind a single overarching strategy and turbocharge their capabilities by providing valuable financial, administrative, marketing, orchestrating, and other services.

Armed with these powerful weapons, all three kinds of pan-industrials — but especially the pan-industrial collectives — will enjoy incredible expansion. The virtuous cycle of growth launched by the combination of AM with industrial platforms will kick into high gear as the pan-industrials take shape.

As they evolve and grow, the pan-industrials — especially in the form of pan-industrial firms — will increasingly resemble the *zaibatsu* that traditionally dominated the economy of Japan (as well as the similar but less-well-known *chaebols* of Korea). The pre–World War II *zaibatsu,* including the Mitsui, Mitsubishi, Yasuda, and Sumitomo groups, operated much like the pan-industrial firms of the near future. Each *zaibatsu* was a conglomerate made up of companies held together through interlocking stock ownership, with the companies sharing resources, employees, and a common strategy. Membership was exclusive, controlled by ultra-wealthy families who had dominant positions in the overlapping corporate boards.

Instead of competing with each other, the *zaibatsu* pursued oligopolistic strategies aimed at maximizing market control, stability, and a steady stream of profits. Each *zaibatsu* operated its own bank, providing access to capital and financial services, as well as businesses involved in a wide range of industries. For example, the Mitsui *zai-*

*batsu* was engaged in mining, textile manufacturing, food processing and production, machinery manufacturing, importing and exporting, shipping, and many other businesses. Pan-industrial firms will resemble the *zaibatsu* in their enormous size and diversity, as well as their tight control over operations.

Does this mean that the pan-industrial firms are likely to grow into pan-industrial collectives without limits? Probably not. Their ability to continue to expand in size and scope will be limited by four main factors.

*Capital constraints.* The evolution of pan-industrial firms into federations and then collectives will be driven in part by the hunger for more and more capital. Once the collective stage is reached, pan-industrials will include their own financial companies with the ability to raise investment funds without outside help. They'll have very deep pockets, to be sure. Some will respond by using mergers and acquisitions to grow ever bigger. But even the biggest of the pan-industrial collectives will eventually run up against size limitations based on the sheer cost of further expansion.

Over time, as the biggest pan-industrial collectives gobble up the smaller ones, we may well reach a point when the global economy is largely dominated by five to ten giant pan-industrial collectives. But is the number likely to shrink even further, say, to two or three? Probably not — because each of the ten giants will be so huge and so valuable that it will be too expensive for even one of its titanic rivals to absorb.

*Resistance from member firms.* The second limiting factor will be the need of the pan-industrial collectives to retain their members. The power of members to leave a collective will also impose some implicit limits on the ability of the collective to behave in whatever ways it likes. For example, some member firms might object to rivals or potential rivals that want to join the collective, and the collective or the platform owner might not have the power to force approval of a new member.

*Political constraints.* The third limiting factor will be political forces beyond the control of the pan-industrials. Governments may seek to restrict the power of pan-industrial firms, federations, and collectives through licensing, antitrust, and other regulations. As I've noted, imposing such restrictions won't be easy. But resistance from government regulators will surely have some impact on the growth prospects of the pan-industrials.

*Technological constraints.* The fourth limiting factor will be the technical limitations of the collective's additive manufacturing assets. Some collectives may have capabilities to work only with metals, but not with electronic circuits. Others may have design and customer knowledge related to medical implants, but not to bioprinting of tissues. So pan-industrial leaders will have to decide the age-old question: Should I leverage my core competencies and assets into markets that my existing capabilities allow me to go after, or should I find the best market opportunities and then gather the assets and capabilities needed to pursue those opportunities?

The existence of these and other constraints will mean that the pan-industrials will not enjoy unlimited growth. Rather than a single pan-industrial collective swallowing up an entire industry, competing collectives will create sprawling empires of associated companies that will compete with each other for spheres of influence. This ongoing competition will provide one more growth-restraining factor. It's unlikely we'll ever see the ultimate stage of pan-industrial consolidation — the emergence of a single giant collective that organizes and runs the business activities of an entire national economy (as envisioned, for example, in the influential 1888 novel *Looking Backward* by Edward Bellamy).

Nonetheless, the many economic and managerial advantages that the pan-industrials will enjoy will enable them to grow much larger than even the biggest companies of today. And this means they will attain power and influence even beyond the economic sphere.

Once again, the *zaibatsu* offer some useful parallels. During the 1920s and '30s, these giant business groups gained enormous political and social power as well as economic clout in Japan. The Mitsui group, for example, was closely connected with both the Imperial Army and the *Rikken Seiyukai* political party, while the Mitsubishi group had ties to the Imperial Navy and the *Rikken Minseito* party. Though the policy stances of the parties varied over time, the *zaibatsu* generally used their influence to promote big-government programs, conservative social policies, and a militaristic foreign policy aimed at gaining access to resources and markets sought by the *zaibatsu*. Many historians say they contributed to the rise of aggressive militarism in Japan that helped to bring on World War II.

When the U.S. general Douglas MacArthur took over Japan during the period of occupation that followed the war, he targeted sixteen of the *zaibatsu* for dissolution as part of a general program of modernizing the Japanese economy as well as the national culture. But he found that the *zaibatsu* were so deeply entrenched in the Japanese economy that he couldn't break them up entirely. What's more, with the rapid emergence of the cold war between East and West during the postwar period, the United States decided on a policy of quickly reindustrializing Japan to serve as an Asian bulwark against the spread of communism. With this goal in mind, the U.S. administrators rescinded the orders that would have dissolved the *zaibatsu*. Instead, they worked toward a peaceful transformation of the *zaibatsu* into more loosely connected business groups. Some of the most powerful controlling families had their assets confiscated, a few of the major holding companies were broken up, and the interlocking directorships and stock ownership that were the main source of unified corporate control were outlawed.

As a result, the *zaibatsu* gave way to looser networks of related businesses that are now generally referred to by the term *keiretsu*. In this new postwar form, the *keiretsu* became collections of companies with separate ownership that nonetheless coordinate much of their strategy and share many services, including financial services provided by a semi-official bank.

Whether in the form of the older *zaibatsu* or the modern *keiretsu*, this system of networked corporations is a new kind of economic structure that few in the West understand and that few are fully prepared to deal with. As one scholar put it, "Western business executives are familiar with cartels as informal — and usually illegal — agreement among companies to control prices and curb competition among themselves. In Japan, cartels are a way of life and keiretsu a structural vehicle that ensures their continued success."

This perspective characterizes the *keiretsu* as a product of Japanese culture, fundamentally alien to Western minds. Yet now we are at the threshold of an era in which new forms of technology will create the opportunity for largely automatic, instantaneous coordination among businesses far more powerful than any employed by would-be business cartels. It seems unlikely that cultural forces alone will thwart this trend. It's possible that the pan-industrials of the twenty-first century will amass powers comparable to those enjoyed within Japan by the *zaibatsu* of the 1930s — and because the pan-industrials will operate across national borders, their influence will extend far beyond any one country. In fact, armed with today's technological tools, the pan-industrials will be like *zaibatsu* on steroids.

As a result, one of the biggest challenges the citizens of the world will face will be dealing with the enormous influence of the pan-industrial titans. Rather than allowing them to exacerbate such problems as economic inequality, environmental degradation, and concentrated political power, our goal should be to encourage the pan-industrials to use their powers to bring about a fairer, greener, freer, and more prosperous world.

# 8

# NEW MARKETS

*Pan-Industrial Markets, the End of
Hypercompetition, and the Rise of Superconvergence*

**IT'S NOT OFTEN THAT** a student of business has the opportunity to witness a major sea change in the nature of corporate competition and to describe that change as it is happening. I've been lucky enough to have the chance to study not one but two such transformations in my career.

In my book *Hypercompetition: Managing the Dynamics of Strategic Maneuvering* (1994), I showed how national oligopolies were being destroyed by disruptive business models and technologies. I also showed how the once-accepted model of competition most often associated with the work of Michael Porter was becoming outmoded. That model was based on the idea that companies could create sustainable forms of advantage that would enable them to remain on top for decades, even generations. However, I posited that, in the emerging era of hypercompetition, four types of sustainable competitive advantage — based on product position, know-how and resources, barriers to entry, and deep pockets — would be eroded faster than ever before. I predicted that, for the foreseeable future, no incumbent business would feel safe because of the frequent emergence of disruptive, competence-destroying business models, organizational forms, and technologies.

In the years that followed, much of what I forecast came to pass. Many old, wealthy, and powerful companies found themselves toppled from their market-dominating thrones by upstarts that used new business models and radically transformative technologies to destroy the protective walls the incumbents once relied upon. Many of the successful upstarts found themselves beleaguered in turn by even newer entrants. The firms that achieved lasting success in this age of disruptive turbulence did so by stringing together a series of temporary advantages, adopting the philosophy of constant reinvention implied in the famous motto of Intel's Andrew Grove: "Only the paranoid survive."

Many companies adjusted successfully to the era of hypercompetition. Others failed to navigate the transition successfully. Some of those no longer exist, while some are still struggling to find their way.

Now it seems that another major transformation is on the way. The era of hypercompetition is coming to an end. The concept of sustainable competitive advantage is making a comeback, though in a new form. The four Porteresque advantages once considered impregnable sources of long-term competitive success are not returning. But new kinds of sustainable advantages based on additive manufacturing and digital AM platforms are beginning to emerge.

In this new environment, the nature and frequency of market disruptions is about to change dramatically, as Figure 8-1 illustrates. The old Porteresque world was one in which powerful companies that mastered the art of developing sustainable advantages could impose a state of equilibrium. In this world, markets were basically stable, shaken only by small-scale disruptions that did little to weaken the core competencies on which the leading companies relied. The two images in the top half of the figure capture the nature of disruption in this world. They explain how great businesses like General Motors, Sears, IBM, AT&T, U.S. Steel, and others managed to stay on top of their industries for decades and even generations.

In the 1980s, businesses largely shifted into the world of hypercompetition, illustrated in the lower right quadrant of the figure. Disruptions capable of destroying the core competencies of great businesses became frequent. In this unpredictable world, no company was safe for long.

The new stage we're now entering is depicted in the lower left quadrant. I describe it using the term *punctuated equilibrium,* borrowed originally from the work of the evolutionary biologists Stephen Jay Gould and Niles Eldredge. It refers to an era in which periods of stability are interrupted occasionally by major competence-destroying disruptions, which then give way to renewed stability. Unlike in the age of hypercompetition, well-run, powerful organizations will be able to seize and maintain control of pan-industrial markets, sometimes for extended periods ... although the possibility of their being unseated by a cataclysmic upheaval can never be completely ignored.

The older patterns of competition are not going to vanish completely. In a few markets, frequent disruptive changes may still occur — just as Porteresque oligopolies can still be found in a handful of other markets. But the unmistakable trend is toward punctuated equilibrium in more and more markets.

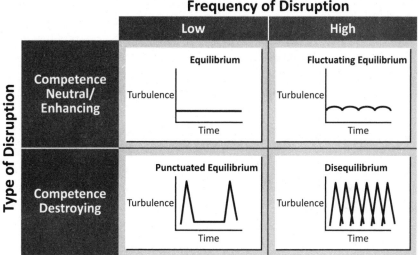

FIGURE 8-1: Much of the business world is now moving from the type of markets shown in the lower right, characterized by the disequilibrium caused by hypercompetition, to the type shown on the lower left, characterized by punctuated equilibrium, featuring periodic bursts of disruption in otherwise stable markets. CREATED BY RICHARD D'AVENI. USED BY PERMISSION OF SLOAN MANAGEMENT REVIEW.

## New Forms of Sustainable Advantage

In this new age of punctuated equilibrium, the pan-industrials will gradually obtain positions of greater and greater power thanks to an array of operational and competitive strengths their new technological capabilities will provide. In particular, a handful of pan-industrial organizations will become especially large, wealthy, and powerful. And unlike in the age of hypercompetition, the edge these champions will enjoy will not be short-lived but rather sustainable, likely leading to decades-long positions of leadership.

Here are the four kinds of sustainable advantage that I believe will be key to long-term business success in the years to come.

*The first-mover advantage.* Pan-industrial firms that are quickest to develop, deploy, master, and learn from the powerful new manufacturing technologies will gain an edge on rivals that cling to traditional production methods. They will have the opportunity to transform the short-term benefit of being first to market with the new technologies into a long-term advantage by forging exclusive partnerships with suppliers (such as 3D printing firms and platform software developers). They can maintain and even expand their lead by climbing the technological learning curve earlier and faster than other companies, using machine learning and AI to figure out ways to apply the new digital tools to specific production processes, materials, product types, and markets more effectively and efficiently.

*The economies-of-scope-and-scale advantage.* Companies that use the new technologies to develop the greatest range of manufacturing competencies will be able to outcompete their industry rivals through their increased flexibility, speed, and nimbleness. A pan-industrial that uses its industrial platform, its array of 3D printer farms, and its other advanced manufacturing facilities to serve an array of varied industries will enjoy big economic benefits as a result. When economic conditions shift to create opportunities in one market while others falter, the pan-industrial with a broader base of operations will be positioned to reap the rewards. The ability of those pan-industrials equipped with AM and industrial platforms to combine economies of scope with economies of scale will make them almost impossible to outcompete.

*The network-effects advantage.* Pan-industrials that build the best industrial platforms and use them to attract the largest array of affiliated companies will enjoy benefits driven by the sheer size and breadth of the network. These are the network effects that reward the most attractive platforms. The industrial platforms that are judged best in the early competition will attract participation by the most numerous, the largest, the richest, and the most respected manufacturing firms. And this will trigger the cumulative power of network effects: Other companies will reason that Platform A, with its wealth of great corporate users, is likely to have a richer store of information, skills, expertise, and information to share than Platform B, which has fewer and less prestigious corporate users. Other things being equal, this will enable Platform A to grow and expand even more, thus creating a sustainable competitive advantage for the company that owns and manages that platform.

*The integration-and-coordination advantage.* Pan-industrials that are more skilled at using their industrial platforms to make smart, fast decisions about how to employ their resources efficiently will be more profitable than their rivals. They'll be quicker to recognize opportunities implicit in shifting market conditions. They'll be better positioned to take advantage of arbitrage opportunities that arise when raw materials, products, or services are priced differently in different markets. And they'll be more proficient at working with other firms in their ecosystem to direct resources (such as factory availability) where the prospects for profit are greatest and most urgent. Over time, even a small, consistent edge in these skill areas will grow cumulatively, helping the pan-industrial that enjoys this advantage to steadily outgrow its rivals.

Building on these four sustainable advantages, the biggest and strongest of the pan-industrials will seize and maintain a dominant role in the global economy.

Make no mistake: The new era of punctuated equilibrium is *not* about a return to the Porter era. The Porter view of competition, as you may recall, was based on the persistence of national or regional oligopolies — automakers in Detroit, steel companies in Pittsburgh, optical firms in Rochester — that drastically reduced competition in a particular industry by barring the entry of potential rivals. Such oligopolies will not be a feature of the decades to come. In fact, as industry barriers fall, companies will no longer even identify themselves as automakers, steel companies, or optical firms. Instead, they will become pan-industrials, making products and serving customer groups that span the old industry sectors.

Furthermore, the four sustainable advantages bear no real resemblance to the old barriers Porter described. Instead, they are expensive, hard-to-replicate advantages that are based on AM and industrial platform technologies that can be continually upgraded and improved without destroying the underlying competitive advantage of the pan-industrial.

Over time, individual businesses will feel increasingly pressured to join one of the pan-industrial firms, federations, or collectives simply in order to survive. In the words of the technology writer Christopher Mims, "Existing businesses that can't respond by becoming tech companies themselves are going to get bought or bulldozed, and power and wealth will be concentrated in the hands of a few companies in a way not seen since the Gilded Age."

Eventually, much of the industrial economy will fall within the sway of the gargantuan pan-industrials. Industrial platform owners will exert the same kind of sway, and draw the same kind of criticism, that Facebook is experiencing with its billion-plus users — only more so, because the pan-industrials will reach more deeply into our lives. They'll tend to exacerbate existing trends toward inequality and corporate power — and governments will have the same difficulty stopping them that they're having with Google. Eventually, the platforms will become so powerful that science-fiction buffs will start to invoke parallels with the Skynet system that wreaks havoc in the *Terminator* movies.

## Losers in the Pan-Industrial Market

If giant pan-industrials enjoying new forms of sustainable advantage will be the big winners in the pan-industrial markets, who will be the losers?

The biggest losers, of course, will be those companies that fail to recognize or understand the transformations now beginning to sweep the economic world — and therefore fail to respond in time.

But in addition, there will be several specific kinds of market participants whose importance and influence can be expected to suffer substantial declines in the years to come. Here are four of the most significant.

*Owners and operators of giant, capital-intensive manufacturing facilities.* In the pan-industrial age, the flexibility of AM will favor production that is widely dispersed and localized. Not all manufacturing will experience the same level of decentralization. Various factors will shape the decisions made by particular companies about how widely to disperse their production facilities, including the relationship between capital costs (machinery, real estate) and warehousing and shipping costs, and the degree to which customers themselves are clustered or dispersed. But the trend will be away from capital-intensive plants toward smaller, more localized facilities.

Thus, over time, large, centralized factories that produce specific goods for large national, regional, or global markets will often give way to smaller facilities that produce a varying, ever-changing array of goods that are mainly intended for local consumption. Why build hundreds of thousands of cars in a giant plant in Detroit and then spend thousands of dollars shipping them around the world when you can instead build hundreds of cars at a time in small, inexpensive plants scattered throughout your customer base? Under the new regime of decentralized production, companies will save millions in shipping and warehousing costs, and customers will enjoy faster deliveries of goods that may be more specifically designed and made to meet their local needs and preferences.

The losers from this trend: companies that cling to the old model of big specialized factories with inflexible equipment that source globally and ship goods across a broad geographic area. Most will find themselves quickly outmanuevered by nimbler pan-industrials. Also likely to suffer: cities and regions that rely heavily on traditional, giant manufacturing plants to drive the local economy and provide employment to thousands of workers. As these big factories become obsolete, the communities they once supported will experience declining fortunes — unless they recognize how the world is changing and move quickly to adjust their economic development strategies.

*Companies and regions dependent on import and export markets.*

One side effect of the trend toward localized production will be the relative decline of import and export markets. More local production means more in-country sourcing and production, and less shipping of work in process and finished goods across national borders. The fact that digitized manufacturing processes require less human labor will only strengthen the trend: The attractiveness of low-wage countries as manufacturing hubs producing goods for consumers in high-wage countries will decline as labor costs become a less significant fraction of total manufacturing expenses. As a result, businesses that have positioned themselves as centralized exporters of low-cost production for foreign markets may find themselves facing hard times. The same could apply to countries, such as China, that depend on large, vibrant export markets for their economic growth. The impact on the international balance of trade may be profound.

*Small to midsize companies that rely on free, atomistic open markets.* One by-product of the disappearance of most vertically integrated businesses and conglomerates has been the increasing dominance of free, open markets for almost all goods and services. Nowadays the vast majority of companies buy their raw materials, component parts, capital goods, and business services in uncontrolled, unrestricted markets where a large number of independent suppliers compete for deals on the basis of price, quality, and other benefits.

Classical economic theory says that this is the most efficient way to run an economy, because market forces will drive competition, reduce prices, improve quality, and encourage innovation. And the flourishing of these sorts of open markets has helped to support thousands of small to midsize companies that have enjoyed long-term success as suppliers of goods and services to bigger businesses.

As pan-industrial firms, federations, and collectives multiply and grow, these free, open markets will give way to relatively limited, controlled, and closed marketplaces managed by core companies and their platforms. Depending on the rules that govern a particular pan-industrial, member companies may be required to buy goods and services from other member companies — or they may be strongly incentivized or simply encouraged to do so. When a company keeps its purchases within its own digital business ecosystem, it will benefit in various ways, which might include preferential pricing, enhanced service, priority access in times of shortages, quicker and easier process coordination, and reliable and painless resolution of disputes. In addition, computerized allocation of goods among members of a collective may result in a more efficient marketplace by funneling raw materials and finished goods to those who can create the most value. Computerized markets can work better than supposedly open markets, especially where market liquidity is low, asymmetric information abounds, or ambiguous conditions make it hard for a human mind to develop the right strategy.

Thus, in the pan-industrial economy, trade will gradually move from free, open markets into the relatively closed ecosystems that are governed by particular pan-industrials — for better and for worse. Better, insofar as closed, protected markets will likely reduce the levels of uncertainty and risk that companies face when competition is open and unconstrained. Closed markets will also remove many of the frictions characteristic of the free market. When you work with reliable partners from the same pan-industrial collective, the costs associated with search, matching, contracting, monitoring, and enforcement are all reduced.

On the other hand, closed markets may also lack some of the dynamism and creativity that open markets enjoy. Flexibility and innovation may not decline in the pan-industrial world due to AM's design and time-to-market advantages — but this innovation may have to be driven mostly by leadership at the top of the pan-industrial ecosystems rather than by creative impulses percolating throughout all the levels of those ecosystems. And crowdsourcing of designs or creative design software may mitigate the problems associated with a more closed market.

In any case, the decline of free, open markets will force the thousands of small to midsize companies now thriving as supplier firms to find new ways to survive. Most will discover that their best option is to join forces with one of the growing pan-industrials, either by selling out to a pan-industrial firm, becoming a user company within a pan-industrial federation, or becoming a member of a pan-industrial collective.

*Activist investors in the market for corporate control.* Another dynamic feature of today's economy is the existence of a vibrant market for control of individual businesses. This market is driven by a number of independent players, from activist investors who ignite proxy battles to hedge fund managers, private equity firms, and investment banks that launch takeover bids when they spot companies they believe are suffering from poor management. In some cases, this market for corporate control leads to abuses, as when firms are saddled with huge debts to pay for their own takeovers or when new owners milk a firm for profits rather than investing in long-term growth. Most often, the market for corporate control forces boards and executives to pay greenmail or buy back stock to keep its price up. And the fear of losing control of a company often causes management to remain sharply focused on shareholder value so as to avoid the risk of takeover — sometimes at the expense of workers, retirees, local communities, and the company's long-term position.

As big pan-industrial collectives grow in size, wealth, and power, the market for corporate control will lose much of its influence. Many companies, if not most, will be members of collectives that include their own financial institutions — banks, investment banks, mutual funds, venture capital firms, and so on. The wealth controlled by these financial firms will provide a strong deterrent force that will protect member companies from fears of a hostile takeover. When businesses need an infusion of cash, they'll turn to the "family banker" rather than to any outside source, which will greatly lessen any pressure to modify company strategies or policies in exchange for funding.

## Superconvergence: From Industries
## to Pan-Industrial Markets

The word *convergence* is getting used a lot these days, in a variety of ways. We're hearing about *digital-physical convergence,* in relation to topics from additive manufacturing to driverless cars. There's *industry convergence,* with companies getting hit by rivals out of nowhere as borders between products or geographies fade. And there's *functional convergence,* with teams and departments of companies merging thanks to instant communication and digital tools for collaboration.

The pan-industrial superconvergence now about to hit us may superficially resemble some of these familiar forms of convergence. For example, it may call to mind the industry convergence of the 1990s, when consumer electronics, computers, and telephony converged to enable what many then called the New Economy.

However, the coming superconvergence will be much more far-reaching in its effects, transforming our traditional view of the economy. AM and industrial platforms will allow firms to make parts for automobiles, toys, airplanes, military equipment, power generation equipment, building materials, micro-electronics, and a whole host of other products in the same factories and even on the same machines. The era of dominance by diversification that ended with the passing of the conglomerate era will reappear in a very different form. And markets may lose their boundaries as part of this process, becoming pan-industrial markets without fixed barriers.

Not only will individual industries and markets tend to merge in the new pan-industrial economy, but the boundary between the manufacturing sector and the services sector will also blur and fade. Manufacturing itself will become a service in some industries. Products will be made to order, just like suits crafted by a tailor. In other industries, manufacturers will gather so much information from their platforms that they can become financial services firms, generating business credit ratings, making loans, and infusing private equity and pension money into members of their ecosystem.

The convergence of functional departments will be an outgrowth of the breakdown of silos within organizations. For example, the creation and sale of new products will no longer be neatly broken down into clearly demarcated stages — R&D, engineering, design, marketing, sales, distribution, and so on. Instead, all these functions will occur in parallel, involving teams of employees with multifarious talents working together to produce goods that respond to consumer demand and rush them quickly to market using flexible, ever-changing tools for design, production, and distribution. Product R&D may take over production scheduling as it generates a flood of new products for testing in the marketplace. Conversely, production may take over aspects of product design using generative design software embedded in 3D printers. In such a world, functional activities like these, which many companies now outsource, may migrate back in-house.

In some cases, manufacturing, warehousing, distribution, sales, and marketing may happen under one roof. For example, it's easy to envision an electronics store with a showroom in the front where customers can design their own smartphones, selecting individual components, apps, accessories, materials, and colors. The production facility might be just a few feet away, on the other side of a wall, where a few special parts are warehoused and the majority are produced on demand by banks of 3D printers, some turning out customized plastic cases, others electronic components, still others LED screens. The customer can wait a while in order to take her phone home, or have it shipped for overnight delivery instead. Again, the distinction between product and service will be far less clear and distinguishable than in the past.

However, the most dramatic form that superconvergence will take will involve the merging of entire industries into vast new combinations that I refer to as *pan-industrial markets*. A few examples of pan-industrial markets we can expect to see in the next couple of decades:

- *The home controller market.* Combine a centralized computer that controls systems for security, heating/cooling, lighting, major appliances, cable and Internet, entertainment, and you have a new pan-industrial market that spans all the products involved. Internet connections, sensors, and AI-enhanced controls will be embedded in appliances, lights, cameras, cleaning devices, sprinklers, water heaters, health monitoring devices, and more.
- *The agricultural equipment market.* Combine the familiar tractor, tiller, and harvester with an array of high-tech tools — self-driving skills, GPS, satellite communications. Then add the ability to analyze and respond to natural conditions of many kinds — weather, soil chemistry, insect infestations, blight — as well as agricultural market trends. The result is a new pan-industrial market for integrated devices capable of running a profitable, productive farm with minimal human help. Some will be more akin to a Mars rover than to a piece of traditional agricultural equipment.
- *The point-of-sale kiosk market.* Combine the corner ATM machine with an array of useful new services, from updating your driver's license and passport to buying theater and sports tickets, having your

house cleaned, or investing in a mutual fund. These and other services, and the equipment to deliver them, will be sold in a new pan-industrial market that combines a number of separate industries from today.

- *The cyborg-enhanced worker market.* Combine robotics, AM, digital sensors, medical prosthetics, cognitive computing, AI, and new human-computer interfaces, exoskeletons, and you get a new market for tools and systems that repair or replace injured or missing body parts — or enhance body parts by offering increased strength flexibility, or speed that allows workers to compete with machines in the factory. Prosthetic limbs and joints are already widely used. As improved systems for connecting such parts directly to the nervous system are developed, the psychological barrier that prevents people from wanting to become "cyborgs" will gradually fade. A pan-industrial market for human enhancement tools will spring up.

In the world of superconvergence, few companies will have the luxury of competing in the familiar, narrowly defined industries they currently occupy. The vast majority will find themselves thrust into a much bigger, more complex world in which products, services, processes, and activities that today form parts of many separate industries are all connected and jostling for attention.

## Responding to Superconvergence: Navigating an Ocean of Threats and Possibilities

The coming superconvergence obviously demands a thoughtful response from business leaders. But convergence tends to be like the weather: everybody talks about it but nobody knows what to do about it. Our conventional business strategies assume stable industries and economics. We're stuck in old mind-sets while business is being transformed. We've imagined our companies as portfolios of specific businesses working within defined boundaries, much like a family of wolves with defined territories. With the boundaries falling, it's time for a new metaphor, and my favorite is a school of fish swimming in the ocean that has no borders.

In this metaphor, each fish is a semi-autonomous being. Fish congregate in schools to improve their chances of finding food and in fending off predators. Each fish constantly watches its schoolmates to know what to do, based on a few simple rules, such as "Follow the majority" or "Move toward the successful (fatter) fish." In contrast, the scouting fish stay on the edges of the school looking for threats and opportunities, and they'll often veer off in response. At times, the school needs to scatter apart, but the school soon reforms when the danger passes. When a predator threatens a school, stragglers — slower and weaker fish — are sacrificed, so the strongest fish are protected. A migrating school gradually shifts direction as the scouts discover new leads and attract others to follow in their boundary-less world.

Think of any pan-industrial company as a school, with each fish representing a line of business. Because of convergence, each fish is free to swim in many directions. But if they cooperate and loosely influence each other, they generate collective motion that enables most of them to survive and prosper. Their flexibility and autonomy generate a kind of swarm intelligence that better responds to collapsing boundaries between industries and sectors.

This metaphor of the school of fish offers a vivid image of how pan-industrial organizations will operate. Here are some of the implications in business terms:

- *Borderless competitive space:* Rather than operating in a set of distinct and separate markets, a school of fish explores the open space for better customer groups or rival-free areas. This contrasts with traditional business methods of exploring new markets, where an individual fish is charged with the task. The entire school collectively self-organizes to explore, but nevertheless balances the risks and opportunities of changing path. A few fish wander away from the school, moving only a short distance. Nearby fish follow if they discover something good. The information then ripples throughout the school, causing the overall school of fish to change direction toward richer ecosystems.
- *Free-flowing organizations and collectives:* Each fish is free to move around the school to be closer to the other fish that can help the most, as well as to the outside opportunities. But just as fish on the

periphery of the school are easy for sharks to pick off, fish will want to stay in synch with the school as a whole. Fish stay together and avoid collisions not because of strict directions from headquarters, but because of a strict set of cultural norms or rules. The stronger the rules, the better your organization or collective will be able to diverge from what all the other schools are doing and pursue more profitable opportunities.

- *Migration strategies:* The school's biggest challenge is deciding where to move. It can't stay in one position for long, because it will exhaust the feeding ground or attract predators, but it's hard to sense where to go. Some fish detect warmer waters and lead the school in that direction. Other fish detect currents and tides, and lead the school to go with the flow. Organizations likewise need to hire more visionaries with good instincts on where opportunities or threats are likely to emerge. They need more Leonardo da Vincis and fewer analysts (especially since the latter can be replaced with computers). Leonardo could paint the *Mona Lisa* one day and sketch a helicopter the next; you need that kind of sharp agility to survive in open, continually shifting markets. Combine that with daring scouts who can tackle promising areas quickly. "Blue Oceans" can't be determined in advance; they have to be discovered.
- *New forms of leadership:* The time you were spending on controlling everything you can now use to better explore possibilities. Send out more scouts to check out potential opportunities or threats. Cast a wide field of investigation, in three dimensions, instead of the usual strategic analysis. And set simple rules for the roles and interactions of different types of fish in the school. Visionaries will be at a premium in a superconvergent, pan-industrial world.

Superconvergence will turn every business into a school of fish, wandering in a vast sea of boundary-less possibilities fraught with predators — and intriguing opportunities — at every turn.

# 9

# NEW RULES

*Collective Competition and the Battle
for Spheres of Influence*

**IN THE NEW SUPERCONVERGENT** pan-industrial markets, competition will shift its focus from battles between companies to battles among the pan-industrial ecosystems of large companies. The pan-industrials will compete to dominate converging industries that serve many markets and are linked primarily by shared manufacturing materials, processes, and methods.

Thus, pan-industrial markets will be characterized by what I refer to as *collective competition.* Competition among companies that specialize in particular products and markets will be replaced by competition among pan-industrials that amass market-based information about supply and demand, manufacturing technology, economic trends, consumer preferences, and the analytical intelligence to use its unique information to compete for dominance.

For example, in the pan-industrial world, the traditional rivalry among Volkswagen, GM, and Toyota will take a back seat to the bigger rivalries among the competing huge pan-industrial collectives to which the three automakers will belong. The pan-industrials that develop the most insightful analyses about market evolution and economic trends are likely to prevail in these new macro battles. Today, automakers focus much of their energy on creating the most broadly appealing new car designs to steal market share from their rivals. Tomorrow, this form of competition will still exist — but in the context of the broader competition among pan-industrial titans that are not only designing and selling cars but also rethinking local and regional mobility systems, and even developing infrastructure plans for entire nations.

The biggest pan-industrials will be so large, wealthy, and diversified that it will be almost impossible for any one of them to be seriously crippled or crushed by the actions of a rival. As a result, competition among the pan-industrials will probably resemble the kind of decades-long ebb-and-flow competition that has historically existed among global political empires — for example, the cold war rivalry of East and West, or the protracted "Great Game" that pitted Britain against Russia for control of Central Asia during the nineteenth century.

Like the great imperial powers of the past, each of the pan-industrial titans will be built around a powerful core surrounded by important tributaries. In the age of empires, the core and its tributaries consisted of nation-states; in the age of pan-industrials, they will be less about nations and more about pan-industrial firms with strong ecosystems and the industrial platforms to control those ecosystems. Further outside the core will be forward positions used as launching areas for attacks on pan-industrial markets currently controlled by rival powers. In the days of empire, these forward positions and neutral zones were geographic locations — the Indus River basin or the Hindu Kush. In the days of pan-industrials, they will be contested pan-industrial markets that might be characterized by various technologies, customer types, geography, demographics, product types, distribution channels, supply chains, or a combination of these features. Simple geographic-product markets, such as bicycles in the Netherlands, will no longer be enough.

Even today, we can see battles for spheres of influence already beginning to take shape. The convergence of industries and the collapse of global market boundaries are creating giant corporate entities that include cores, buffer zones, and forward positions in which struggles to control vast territories are based. For example, GE and Siemens are two industrial empires that are involved in many of the same rapidly converging industries. They are grappling with each other in the quest for long-term dominance, each building on a different set of core strengths, based partly on their geographic origins (GE in the United States, Siemens in Germany) and partly on their historical origins and industrial specializations. Other business rivalries that may be harbingers of protracted battles for spheres of influence include the competition among the online retail giants Amazon, Alibaba, and eBay, and the competition among leading AM platform architects like Jabil, IBM, and SAP.

## Real-Time Competition and the Reinterpretation of SWOT

In pan-industrial markets, massive disruptions in the competitive landscape will be relatively rare, since the giant combinations that will dominate markets will be too rich, powerful, and multifaceted to suffer lethal blows leading to wholesale collapse. Instead, the pan-industrial titans will continually jockey for marginal advantages, much as the United States and the USSR did in Cuba, Vietnam, and Angola during the cold war.

What's more, the coupling of AM with digital AM platforms changes the rules of the competitive game from periodic to continuous play, speeding up the action and making it more aggressive. This is roughly the equivalent of shifting from (American) football to English rugby, played without breaks or huddles between plays.

Real-time play in many simultaneous industries will necessitate a very different strategic mind-set. Consider SWOT (strengths, weaknesses, opportunities, threats) analysis, the most fundamental tool for strategic thinking during the traditional manufacturing era. As conventionally formulated, with its four-part examination of strengths, weaknesses, opportunities, and threats, SWOT analysis is based on two strategic maxims and one corollary. But in pan-industrial markets, the applicability of all three will be limited (see Table 9-1). Thus, the age of superconvergence and pan-industrial markets demands that SWOT analysis be reinterpreted.

Recall that, as shown in Figure 8-1, the death of hypercompetition is leading to a world dominated by punctuated equilibrium. Spikes of dramatic competitive change will occasionally interrupt periods of relative stability, when pan-industrials will take advantage of the new forms of sustainable advantage that are now possible. During those periods of stability, the old principles of SWOT will still be useful, as seen in the left-hand column of Table 9-1. But during the occasional upheavals, new strategic rules will apply, as described in the right-hand column of the table.

| TABLE 9-1: SWOT ANALYSIS FOR PAN-INDUSTRIAL MARKETS | | |
|---|---|---|
| | **TRADITIONAL SWOT ANALYSIS** | **SWOT STRATEGY DURING PAN-INDUSTRIAL UPHEAVALS** |
| **Maxim 1** | *Leverage Your Core Competencies.* Playing from existing strengths is less costly than building new ones and maximizes the firm's chance of winning. Profits from low-hanging fruit finance further market incursions, producing additional profits. | *Turn New Areas of Activity into Competencies.* Pan-industrials transfer learning across industries, creating next-generation competencies, transforming weaknesses into strengths, and changing the rules of the game. |
| **Maxim 2** | *Deploy Strength Against Weakness.* Firms use their strengths to attack the weaknesses of rivals. This strategy produces easy wins while avoiding costly wars of attrition. | *Attack Rivals at Their Strong Points as Well as Their Weaknesses.* Diversified pan-industrials can attack rivals at points of strength as well as weakness, paving the way for a decisive confrontation. |
| **Corollary** | *Seek Stability, Rather Than a Decisive Victory.* Avoid aggressive warfare; instead, seek stable industry structures. Use buffer zones to play defense, and stay in your niche if you are a marginal player. | *Press Rivals Continuously; Seek Chaos, Disruption, and an Expanded Sphere of Influence.* Use forward positions to attack rivals' cores or seize pivotal zones. Safe niches no longer exist. |

As Table 9-1 suggests, a key strategic challenge in pan-industrial markets will be to accurately determine your current position in the cycle of punctuated equilibrium. Companies that try to apply the less aggressive version of SWOT principles when they are in the times of upheaval will underutilize the powers of real-time learning, vastly increased speed and flexibility, and the potential to dynamically outmaneuver or surround rivals' core pan-industrial markets — and therefore are likely to fall behind in the competitive battle for advantage. They'll miss their chances to gain greater influence over their business ecosystems and to expand their spheres of influence.

### When Titans Clash: The Wars for Spheres of Influence

The pan-industrials will fight with many rivals, but they can't fight everyone, everywhere, all of the time. Each pan-industrial will have to focus on a few competitors who occupy spheres of influence that overlap with the pan-industrial's plans for its own sphere. To have the most influence in a pan-industrial market, a pan-industrial will have to capture the largest and most lucrative parts of the pan-industrial market, while weakening selected rival spheres of influence. Meanwhile, the pan-industrial will have to establish détente or mutual forebearance with other rivals by creating a favorable balance of power with the less salient rivals swimming in less vital profit pools.

A particular pan-industrial will seek to co-opt the rivals that are less important, as well as let allies or rivals fight the others it chooses to avoid in the short run. Alternatively, a pan-industrial might seek to ally with others in an effort to gang up on a particular rival. The goal: for the allies to encircle the rival's sphere of influence and thereby prevent it from expanding, or perhaps even to seize control of its sphere of influence and divide it up amongst themselves. This is the well-known cold war strategy of *containment*.

The pan-industrial titans will struggle with each other using a variety of other strategies. Some will employ variants of what has been called *judo strategy*, in which a fast, flexible competitor uses its opponent's size, strength, and weight against it. For example, judo strategists avoid direct conflict by moving swiftly into unoccupied markets or by redefining market spaces through innovative product and service offerings.

Others will employ an alternative *sumo strategy*, in which size, strength, and weight can play a decisive and positive role. Sumo competitors relish direct conflict and seek it out, knowing they can over-whelm the opposition through sheer force. Thus, they deploy mas-sive resources to take control of large, lucrative market spaces, hoping to weaken a competitor's sphere of influence and seize the initiative from the competitor. In some cases, the competitor may be weakened enough to make them ripe for conquest — most likely through acqui-sition.

Both judo strategy and sumo strategy could be attractive to pan-in-dustrial organizations. Remember that pan-industrials can enjoy both benefits of scope and benefits of scale. As a result, they'll be able to grow enormously while retaining the speed and flexibility that tradi-tionally characterized only smaller firms. Thus, a given pan-industrial could choose to compete using flexibility and rapid change against a key rival (judo strategy) or using size and resources (sumo strategy) against a different rival. In fact, it's likely that the pan-industrial mar-kets of the near future will exhibit both styles of competition in ev-ery possible combination: judo versus judo, sumo versus sumo, and judo versus sumo. What's more, given the nimbleness that will make the pan-industrials, we'll likely see prolonged competitive battles in which rivals switch strategies from time to time — as if a slender judo wrestler could morph, midbattle, into a massive sumo warrior, or vice versa.

Still other companies jockeying for position in a pan-industrial market may opt for a third possibility — *conflict avoidance strategy,* in which a competitor seeks a safe haven in a niche that others are unlikely to try to seize. Those who favor conflict avoidance may try to collude tacitly with rivals to divide a pan-industrial market into non-overlapping spheres of influence or to restrain the intensity with which they fight in overlapping pan-industrial markets.

## The Machine Wars and the Platform Wars

In the quest to achieve the new sustainable competitive advantages and to begin building expansive spheres of influence, a number of companies have embarked on the journey toward pan-industrial status. Most of these companies are already beginning to be embroiled in two simultaneous sets of arms races — struggles for mastery that so far have gone largely unnoticed in the business media.

One of these sets of races is focused on improving additive manufacturing, hybrid fabrication systems, and related technologies. I call these battles *the machine wars*. The second is focused on developing the best industrial platforms — *the platform wars*.

The machine wars and the platform wars will reflect the battles of pan-industrials to achieve network effects, information advantages, and economies of scale and scope across industries. The wars will also be costly, so spreading out their cost over many product and pan-industrial markets — another aspect of economies of scope — will be critical to victory.

To give you a better feel for these wars, let me provide some real-world examples.

## The Machine Wars

The competitive battle for technological leadership in the world of additive manufacturing is already well under way on a wide variety of fronts. As 3D printing and related technologies develop rapidly, dozens of companies are racing to develop or seize control of the tools they consider most promising. The outcome of the machine wars is likely to help determine which companies have the greatest initial success in launching the first powerful pan-industrial firms.

With the understanding that we are still in the early days of the machine wars, and that winners and losers are not likely to emerge until a few more years have passed, here are a couple of dispatches from the battlefield that will help you glimpse the nature of the competition.

In 2015, two major firms threw their support behind a new technology, called CLIP (mentioned earlier), that is now revolutionizing 3D printing. It's quite likely that CLIP could play a big role in transitioning these firms into true pan-industrial firms with powerful new manufacturing technology at their core. Alphabet is one of these businesses; Ford Motor Company is the other.

As you know, Alphabet (parent of Google) is a diversified $75 billion enterprise with interests in software platforms built around its search engine, email, and other applications, as well as its cyberdefense and cloud computing capabilities. But it is also deeply involved in developing hardware that might connect to its software platforms. The hardware projects that Alphabet supports include experiments with self-driving cars, robotics, optical fiber networks, telecommunication equipment pharmaceuticals for aging and age-related disease, flying vehicles (including drones for delivery of goods), Internet network balloons, and equipment for urban infrastructure and energy. Alphabet is also working on hardware for the life sciences, healthcare, transportation, and agricultural industries, as well as electronic devices like augmented reality headsets, cell phones, and wearable computing tools.

The $150 billion Ford Motor Company also has an opportunity to put additive manufacturing at the center of its operations, although it obviously joins the race from a completely different starting point than Alphabet. Ford is famous for its cars, trucks, vans, automotive components, and many other products that could benefit from AM, including electric drive vehicles, industrial engines, and components for military vehicles, such as the joint light tactical vehicle, tanks, half-track armored personnel carriers, and armored cars.

Alphabet and Ford have also partnered with a 3D printing startup called Carbon3D, now renamed simply Carbon. Historically, 3D printing has been based on repeated 2D printing of layers to build up parts and products. But Carbon founder Joe DeSimone and his co-inventors Alex Ermoshkin, chief technology officer at Carbon, and Edward T. Samulski, also professor of chemistry at UNC, came up with a 3D printing technology that doesn't use layering. Instead, it projects an almost continuous series of rapid-fire bursts of light and oxygen into the bottom of a vat of liquid photosensitive resin. The bursts of light, a bit like a high-speed animated movie, are a series of cross-sectional images that set the shape of the object and harden the resin. Meanwhile, the oxygen keeps the resin from hardening and sticking to the bottom of the vat. By controlling light and oxygen exposure in tandem, intricate shapes can be made in one piece instead of the many layers of material that usually make up a 3D-printed object. Bringing oxygen into the process makes 3D printing a tunable photochemical process that rapidly decreases production times, removes the layering effect, and takes 3D printing to a new level of speed, strength, and overall quality. DeSimone and his partners named the new technology continuous liquid interface production, or CLIP.

Carbon has taken many steps to perfect its technology in the field before release of its first printer for sale. In early 2016, Carbon partnered with Johnson & Johnson's Medical Devices & Diagnostics Global Services Division to make custom 3D-printed surgical devices. BMW is also working with the technology. Also in early 2016, Carbon announced four partnerships with 3D printing service bureaus to commercialize its technology: Sculpteo, CIDEAS, the Technology House, and WestStar Precision.

Then, in mid-2016, Carbon's first commercial printer, the M1, was introduced. It produces both functional prototypes and production-quality parts featuring resolution, surface finish, and mechanical properties required for most applications. It can produce small objects with a maximum size of 144 × 81 × 330 millimeters (approximately 5.7 inches × 3.2 inches × 13 inches, or 240 cubic inches). The M1 uses machine learning, collecting a million data points per day for each printer in use to determine what works and what does not — that is, which combination of materials, printer settings, design geometry, speed, stacking and orientation within the build area, and postprocessing methods will yield the fewest defective parts, the greatest consistency, and the lowest costs.

While CLIP now works only with resins and elastomers (rubbery substances), Carbon has already made the process compatible with silicones, epoxies, and nylonlike materials called esters, and is working to make it compatible with ceramics and biodegradable materials.

More recently (2017), Carbon introduced the M2 printer, with double the build volume as the M1. Carbon also introduced the SpeedCell System, a system for combining M2 printers and automated postprocessing stations for repeatable end-use production at any scale.

So Alphabet and Ford, as well as others testing out CLIP, are now fully engaged on one front of the machine wars. The first challenge they face is to get CLIP ready for mass manufacturing before other firms do. The second is to fully deploy and monetize CLIP before alternative technologies emerge that are even better.

The battle to enhance, diversify, and perfect the powers of CLIP before rivals grab a foothold with this new technology is just one place where the machine wars are being fought. A number of other big companies that are aspiring pan-industrials are investing in leading-edge manufacturing technologies, seeking a technological edge they can use to leapfrog the competition — for example, Sumitomo Heavy Industries, whose purchase of AM experts Persimmon I discussed earlier.

CLIP illustrates some of the ways that AM equipment is becoming faster, cheaper, more efficient, higher quality, and more agile. But CLIP hasn't taken the prize yet. Similar technologies, such as continuous stereolithography from 3D Systems, are nipping at CLIP's heels in the race for supremacy.

At the same time, there are many other ways to improve the speed and quality of other AM methods. When I interviewed S. Scott Crump, cofounder and chief information officer of printer manufacturer Stratasys, he quickly rattled off a series of them: reduce the postprocessing time; reduce the setup time for new product runs and different materials; slice the object into thicker layers; reduce the need for supports during the printing process; improve computer-aided design to overcome the limitations of traditional manufacturing; and improve the number-crunching capabilities of systems that control quality and yield rates. Some of these improvements sound modest in themselves, yet in combination they can generate significant gains.

In addition to printer manufacturers, users of AM equipment are also seeking opportunities to improve their overall manufacturing systems. In fact, 3D printer users are now receiving more patents for AM-related innovations than printer manufacturing companies. Thus, it is increasingly the users' job to modify or improve the printers they buy. Machine learning and AI are beginning to allow AM systems to run themselves, to learn from experience, and to compete effectively against one another with minimal human intervention.

Many of the competencies now being explored to give added efficiency and power to AM can be divided into five broad scientific areas:

- *applied chemical sciences,* in which chemical reactions are used to create, customize, or improve materials during the AM process —

for example, adding chemicals that speed the hardening of material, prevent cracks, or regulate air retention;

- *electromagnetic sciences,* which use electrical or magnetic fields to enable the 3D printing of innovative geometries or alter the shape of a part or product;
- *advanced material sciences,* such as the use of "memory materials" that change shape after printing nanomaterials, alloys, carbon fiber and nanotube composites, or unusual materials like chocolate, ceramics, or cellulose;
- *cutting-edge computer sciences,* including the use of AI, predictive algorithms, generative design, and virtual or augmented reality as tools to improve product design, material capabilities, or printer performance; and
- *other mechanical sciences,* such as the use of microbots, miniaturized printers, hybrid fabrication systems, conveyor belts, robotic arms, quadcopters, and remote devices for control or measurement.

Manufacturing firms will decide which of these areas of competency to focus on based on the nature of their businesses, the products they build, and the opportunities they perceive to outcompete rivals. As you can see, the machine wars will be continuing on many fronts in the years to come.

## The Platform Wars

At the same time that manufacturing companies are vigorously fighting the machine wars, other companies are beginning to engage in the platform wars — battles to determine which digital AM platforms will become dominant.

One precursor to the platform wars has been the competition to create what might be called a successful *digital utility* — a cloud-based business offering hardware management services and software to as many firms as possible to create economies of scale. At the moment, the biggest providers of digital utilities include Amazon, Microsoft, Google, IBM, and a number of other smaller players, such as Oracle, Adobe, Salesforce, and SAP. Of these, Amazon is by far the biggest — it entered the cloud management market earlier than the other competitors and now runs a digital utility business the size of those owned by Microsoft, Google, and IBM combined.

But digital utilities are no longer at the leading edge of the platform wars. As the digital utility market commoditizes, with prices and profits both shrinking over time, these firms are starting to move to AM platforms in small increments, adding more and more business functionalities to their platforms. IBM and Microsoft are probably the most advanced in moving to industrial platform–like functionalities. IBM Watson has developed its industrial Internet of Things platform with the ability to do advanced analytics and use AI to tackle tough management questions, while Microsoft has added Microsoft Hololens for 3D-augmented reality-based activities such as product design and business meetings.

But when it comes to creating the industrial platform that will enable the creation of the first true pan-industrials, the manufacturing and manufacturing software firms are much further along. Jabil, GE, and Siemens are the leaders in this area. Other diversified manufacturers, such as United Technologies and Sumitomo, and starting down this path. The platform wars will focus on integrating business functionalities, making different business software packages interoperable and compatible. The race is on to create and integrate real-time applications for supply chain management, asset management, product life cycle management, production and logistics scheduling, facilities management, enterprise-wide resource planning, product design, corporate accounting, compliance reporting, and many other functions into one soup-to-nuts platform.

The engineering giant Siemens illustrates one strategy aimed at victory in the platform wars. Its Digital Factory division is working to merge the real world of hardware with the virtual world of software. Siemens says the tools and systems are already in place to create a "digital twin" of a factory — in effect, to "build manufacturing automation lines and design processes before a manufacturing plant has been built." As the CEO, Josef Kaeser, explains, "We copy a real-time manufacturing process into the virtual world to optimize engineering, processing quality, uptime, and load time — and then we copy it back into the real world of manufacturing. That's pretty cool."

It is — and it shows how Siemens is determined to seize a large, lucrative share of dominance as the platform wars continue to unfold. In these wars, hardware matters, but leading-edge software and the information it controls and analyzes matters still more. As Kaesar says, "Our customers care about manufacturing and engineering data and intellectual property rights because [this type of data] is the holy grail of innovation." Siemens is already operating factories managed by their new "digital twin" control platform in Germany and in Chengdu, China.

Of course, in the rapidly developing world of AM software, good ideas tend to spread rapidly. Other corporations are already working on their own versions of the "digital twin" concept. Dassault Systèmes uses simulations in much the same way, to identify mechanical and structural issues related to a part or machine under construction. Meanwhile, experts at GE Additive are using their own digital twins as part of a real-time machine learning approach they hope will let engineers make on-the-fly adjustments to manufacturing processes with the goal of achieving "100 percent yield" — that is, ultra-efficient, zero-waste production.

As companies like Jabil, GE, and Siemens morph into burgeoning pan-industrials, they will gradually add member firms to create economies of scale and scope for their platforms. In time, they will form pan-industrial federations and pan-industrial collectives that are differentiated by their members, rules for member behavior, independence or interactivity among members, common purposes and projects, governance structures, resource sharing arrangements, information ownership rules, brokerage services, and other unique features.

But none of this will happen until the digital AM platforms that add huge value to prospective manufacturing customers are fully perfected and made available by the core companies. That's why these firms and others are investing billions in the race to be the first one with the most powerful platform.

## Pan-Industrials Versus the World

I've made the case that the pan-industrials will wield such powerful strategic and economic tools that they will gradually come to dominate the world of business. But history shows us that no particular outcome is ever foreordained. Big, powerful rivals will fight back against the pan-industrials, potentially threatening their control. It's possible to imagine scenarios in which the pan-industrials as I've described them will have to share power with other kinds of businesses.

Here are some of the battles for dominance we can expect to see in the decades to come, together with my best estimates of the likely outcomes.

*The pan-industrials versus the dinosaurs.* This scenario pits two kinds of manufacturing companies against one another. In one corner: the pan-industrial firms, federations, and collectives I've been describing, which will use AM, other digital manufacturing tools, and industrial platforms to build giant organizations capable of competing in the huge multifaceted, cross-border pan-industrial markets. In the other: the so-called dinosaurs — old, established deep-pocketed firms that are still using and improving traditional manufacturing systems.

At least a few of the dinosaurs are likely to survive for a while, even as the pan-industrials make increasing inroads into their markets. The dinosaurs will have a number of obvious advantages: long-standing relationships with suppliers, distributors, retailers, and other companies up and down the value chain; familiar, respected brands that provide a sales and marketing edge; access to capital from banks and investors; and big facilities (factories, warehouses, distribution centers, office complexes) they've built over decades at enormous cost. The smartest and best-run dinosaurs will invest in some technological upgrades in an effort to keep pace with the pan-industrials; they'll install robots in their factories and even make limited use of 3D printers to feed parts to their traditional assembly lines.

But within the next few decades, the traditional advantages of the dinosaurs will gradually be transformed into expensive weights that slow down the dinosaurs rather than empowering them. The pan-industrials will increasingly outcompete the dinosaurs using the many benefits of AM and industrial platforms that I've already explained, including speed, agility, efficiency, and economies of scope and scale. Eventually, the dinosaurs will become extinct, either by having their product portfolios and brand names absorbed by the pan-industrials or by quietly going out of business.

*The pan-industrials versus the West Coast technology giants.* This scenario pits the pan-industrials against high-tech companies that have been some of the fastest-growing businesses in recent decades. This category of competitors includes not just the "Big Four" firms — Alphabet, Apple, Amazon, and Facebook — but other information-based technology companies such as Oracle, IBM, and Salesforce. As I've shown, some of these businesses are already experimenting with acquisitions and experiments involving manufacturing and industrial platforms. Thus, it seems likely that some form of this scenario will come to pass — and it may evolve into a full-fledged war for control between the manufacturing-based pan-industrials and the giants of Silicon Valley and environs.

In this scenario, the West Coast tech giants will win if they retain and use the customer data they already control; acquire or develop industrial platforms; and use their innovative talents to create specialized software to improve business operations — for example, tools for voice recognition, natural language processing, image recognition, and deep learning.

The pan-industrials will win if they can induce large numbers of consumers to begin using their pan-industrial platforms, which will give them access to consumer data. They can also win if they are able to purchase consumer data from the tech titans. In this scenario, the balance tips in favor of the pan-industrials because they can create a unified value chain that will connect manufacturing companies both to other businesses and to consumers directly. In essence, this would disintermediate firms like Amazon by eliminating the need to use Amazon's website to sell the pan-industrials' products.

*The pan-industrials versus the telecom kings.* Telecom companies like AT&T and Verizon can be potential "dark knights" — surprise combatants with a chance to shake up the pan-industrial battlefield. They support all communications among IT companies, social media companies, manufacturing companies, and consumers — which means they have access to lots of consumer data if government regulations don't hamper them.

The telecom kings would have some real advantages in a war against the pan-industrials. One of the big advantages is the major investments they've already made in the physical communications networks, which any other company would find it very difficult to replicate. When 5g networking is introduced in the next few years, all smart devices will be connected to an efficient, reliable, scalable network, making truly AI-level services available to consumers.

The telecoms could win the war if they use the consumer data to which they have access to create personalized and customized product and service offerings. On the other hand, the pan-industrials will win if they maintain their big advantage — namely, their control over systems and infrastructure for physical manufacturing, which the telecoms currently do not have.

The critical determinant will be net neutrality and how the telecoms make use of it. If the telecom titans are able to act as bottlenecks for the delivery of information on industrial and B2C platforms, all bets are off. The telecoms would then be able to determine the winners and losers among the tech titans and the pan-industrials, or force them to find ways to communicate with customers and suppliers without using the Internet or telecom networks.

*The pan-industrials versus the Chinese warlords.* State-owned or state-linked enterprises based in China would have many advantages in a future contest for power against the pan-industrials: access to capital provided by the government, influence wielded by state-run or state-censored media (including online social media), and, of course, the vast size of their home market. China is currently "the world's factory" and could impose its choice of an industrial platform by governmental fiat, forcing the cooperation of non-Chinese businesses that want to include China's production skills and facilities in their ecosystems. If the Chinese warlords leverage these advantages internationally, they could achieve a powerful role in the pan-industrial markets.

However, the pan-industrials could defeat the warlords if other governments take steps to thwart Chinese expansionism. The Chinese powers that be would find it difficult to truly dominate international manufacturing without the help of local companies. Their goal will be to acquire foreign companies strategically or enter into joint ventures with them. Both of these could be stymied by determined governments making aggressive use of antitrust laws and regulations designed to protect intellectual property (which Chinese firms are widely known to flout). Trade wars may ensue, aimed at forcing China or the U.S. to back down and allow access to their markets.

The pan-industrials will certainly face some tough, determined competitors as they strive for dominance of the new, superconvergent markets. But in the end, it's likely that they will win out over other companies that fail to match their use of the unparalleled powers offered by AM coupled with industrial platforms.

## Pan-Industrial Brand Rivalries

In addition, the pan-industrials will also compete with one another by pursuing a variety of branding strategies. Some will probably choose to develop a tightly defined core of technologies and markets built around a single strong brand, as automotive giant Ford markets cars, trucks, and other products under the same brand name. Others may choose to develop a strong brand that unites a loosely defined set of technologies serving a variety of markets, as Richard Branson's Virgin Group has done with businesses in various sectors that range from travel and hospitality to media, finance, and healthcare. Still others may pursue a strategy that emphasizes the unifying technological thread that connects and adds value to an array of otherwise distinctive brand identities (the "Intel Inside" branding approach). And others may try to seize a particular market position, the way brands like Gucci and Bulgari strive to claim the high-end luxury mantle for each of the products they sell.

In any case, one of the central questions that all the pan-industrials must wrestle with will be this: What does *brand* mean in an era when products are continually being redesigned, and when the same company or group of companies provides a complex array of markets with a multiplicity of products that may lack any obvious unifying thematic or stylistic quality?

Every pan-industrial will develop its own answers to this question. The persuasiveness of the answers will help to determine the relative winners and losers on the giant, increasingly unified chessboard of business.

# 10

# NEW WORLD ORDER

*Utopia, Dystopia, or Both?*

**DONGGUAN IS A CITY** in the Guangdong province of southeastern China. An industrial hub, it has grown in tandem with the rest of the Chinese economy in recent decades thanks in part to the country's vast reservoir of workers. If there is any country on earth where corporate executives might be tempted to cut costs and to speed up processes simply by applying the power of abundant labor, it should be China.

Which makes it paradoxical that Dongguan is home to one of the world's first "unmanned factories" — a facility where hundreds of thousands of cell phone parts are turned out every month by an assembly team that consists of sixty robots. The robots are guided by computerized sensors and controls, and automated trucks and warehouse equipment move the products from the assembly line to the storage and shipping facilities — *and no human being is ever required to touch a single component* (Figure 10-1).

In reality, "unmanned" is a slight exaggeration. The factory, managed by Changying Precision Technology Company, actually employs about sixty human beings, who monitor the ten production lines by gazing at computer screens and occasionally checking on what is happening on the factory floor. But those sixty workers represent just a fraction of the 650 who were employed in the same facility as recently as early 2015 . . . and the company's general manager, Luo Weiqiang, says that, in the near future, their numbers will be reduced to twenty. What's more, as robots have replaced human workers, the overall production quantity has soared by 250 percent, while the rate

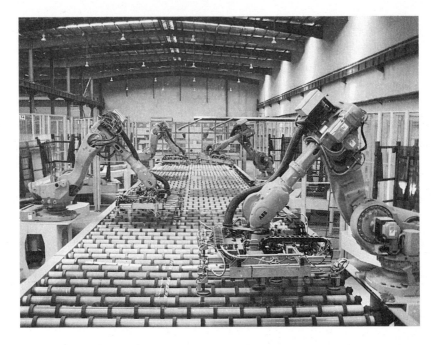

FIGURE 10-1: Robots operating assembly lines at a virtually "unmanned factory" in Dong-guan, China.

of product defects has fallen from more than 25 percent to less than 5 percent.

Given these realities, it's hard to imagine why Changying Precision Technology would ever consider rehiring any of the hundreds of employees who no longer have jobs in the factory. It's a vivid illustration of how technological change can produce dramatic economic, social, and human impacts. In the years to come, we'll be seeing a host of such impacts as a result of the pan-industrial revolution.

## The Challenge of Technological Unemployment

The steady decline in manufacturing jobs in industrialized nations like the United States is a familiar phenomenon, so widely recognized that it even became a significant political issue that helped to shape the 2016 presidential race. Offshoring of manufacturing from high-wage countries to low-wage countries in Asia and Latin America has been one cause of the decline, but an even greater cause has been technological progress and the improved productivity it has created. Factories that remain open in the United States can now produce as many goods as in the past — or far more — with much smaller workforces. The ongoing manufacturing revolution that incudes AM and industrial platforms will only accelerate this trend.

It's noteworthy that some business leaders view the trend toward declining human employment in manufacturing as being both a cause and a result of the digital revolution. In this perspective, U.S. companies are particularly eager to digitize their production methods precisely because of the increasing difficulty of recruiting and retaining the kinds of skilled workers needed to run up-to-manufacturing firms. Erick Wolf, cofounder and chairman of the desktop printer manufacturer Airwolf 3D, puts it this way: "With [fewer] workers who know how to operate equipment like CNC [computer numerical control] machines, injection molding machines and laser cutters, American manufacturing eventually will have to turn to a more sophisticated, automated technology that increases productivity without requiring an increase in human labor. That technology is 3D printing."

If this theory is correct — and some historical evidence of other times when labor shortages helped to stimulate technological developments backs it up — it seems likely to make the trend even more unstoppable.

Many traditional middle managers will also become superfluous as data analytics increase in power and accuracy, and as many operational decisions now made by white-collar employees become automated.

Is it plausible that tasks we've long assumed can only be performed by highly skilled, experienced humans will eventually be taken over by automated digital agents? The change is likely to happen sooner than you might think. There's plenty of evidence that artificial intelligence has recently passed a tipping point at which accelerating development of capabilities is now happening.

Consider, for example, the experiments at Facebook with chatbots being trained to conduct multi-issue negotiations with the goal of reaching agreements acceptable to two agents with different agendas and priorities. During 2017, the chatbots quickly learned to engage in start-to-finish negotiation processes with successful outcomes. What's more, they were observed developing their own unique shorthand language unintelligible to outsiders as a way of making the negotiating process more efficient. For example, one of the chatbots used the "sentence" "Balls have zero to me to me to me to me to me to me to me to me to" as a way of referring to multiple "tokens" that were the subject of the deal-making process.

Researchers at Facebook shut down the experiment, saying it represented a failure to maintain control over the process and raised fears about what the chatbots might do outside the control or understanding of the researchers. Maybe so. But it also suggests the speed at which today's intelligent digital agents are able to develop their own tools and methods for tackling and solving problems, with minimal guidance from human teachers.

Whether you find this development exhilarating or alarming depends on your philosophical and psychological beliefs. But the fact is that it is happening—which means that there's little question that countless tasks currently performed by human beings are likely to soon be within reach of automated digital entities. There's not much difference between chatbots that can negotiate satisfactory deals with one another and chatbots that can manage warehouses, schedule services, organize production plans, monitor inventory levels, arrange shipments, and order supplies in response to variations in product demand. As each of these functions become automated, one giant company at a time, thousands of human workers will become redundant.

*Silver linings.* There will be some offsetting employment trends driven by the spread of AM. Routine manufacturing work now done on shop floors and on assembly lines will give way to more skilled jobs involving adaptation for AM, generative design, product modularization, and other creative challenges. For some, the shift will be an unmixed blessing. Well-trained workers will no longer be trapped in factory jobs that today are repetitive, stultifying, unsanitary, dangerous, and sometimes exploitative (especially in developing countries). The smaller numbers of workers that will be engaged in manufacturing two to three decades from now will mostly enjoy better working conditions and more rewarding jobs than their counterparts in the past.

In addition, managers will still be needed to focus on relationships and communications, especially as companies from many industries and markets become linked by industrial platforms in vast pan-industrial organizations. Some pan-industrials will find they have a growing need for human beings to forge and maintain connections among these businesses at the highest level.

These human "connectors" and "communicators" will not be dealing with important but relatively mundane operational issues, but rather on bigger strategic questions that require the combined expertise of people with differing backgrounds and roles. High-level human teams focused on such challenges are likely to play an important role in keeping the pan-industrials of the future operating at their best.

At least for a time, the need for digital specialists like programmers will also continue to grow. Already quintessential companies from the era of "heavy metal" manufacturing are adding the equivalent of entire software companies to their human resources. For example, Germany's 170-year-old Siemens — now headed by Josef Kaeser, who ran the corporation's Silicon Valley outpost in the 1990s — employs more than 17,500 software engineers working on platform tools, apps, websites, and other digital data manipulation systems. That number is more than many software firms.

The applications being developed by this army of coders are already helping to provide the foundation for some of the most advanced new manufacturing projects in the world. Solid Edge is a computer-aided design (CAD) package from Siemens that boasts "synchronous technology," which allows collaborators around the world to participate in a design process. Local Motors has been using Solid Edge in its innovative crowdsourcing auto development process. And in March 2018, Siemens entered into a partnership with startup Hackrod, offering tools that will allow anyone to design a customized vehicle using generative design, virtual reality, artificial intelligence, and 3D printing.

*Addressing the challenges.* Will the new jobs created among connectors, communicators, and coders make up for those lost among traditional factory workers? Probably not. In addition to the problem of a skills mismatch among those who will be looking for work in the next couple of decades in relation to the jobs available, there is likely to be a significant shortfall in the sheer number of open positions in relation to the growth of the working-age population. In the next two to three decades, the combined effects of additive manufacturing, industrial platforms, artificial intelligence, cloud computing, and hyperefficient digital corporate networks will make many millions of jobs obsolete. And as these technological tools continue to grow in sophistication, even many of the connectors, communicators, and coders will find their jobs being usurped by machines.

If the widespread unemployment that many experts are predicting as a result of the coming manufacturing revolution becomes a reality, addressing its economic and social impacts will not be easy. Mass unemployment is associated with decreasing health, increased drug use, mental health problems, family breakups, and rising crime. Government programs will attempt to address the issues. But when it becomes clear that job training programs may have little impact in a world where even skilled, knowledgeable workers are largely unnecessary, make-work projects resembling the Works Projects Administration and the Civilian Conservation Corps of FDR's New Deal will probably be proposed. Government programs designed to provide services that the for-profit sector finds unattractive — caring for children, the elderly, and the infirm, for example — may also be expanded. Concepts like universal healthcare, free education through college, and a guaranteed annual income will also gain in popularity.

Of course, at the same time that millions of people are losing their jobs, the pan-industrial firms, federations, and collectives that are largely driving the trend will become big, deep-pocketed, and politically powerful. Corporate PACs supported by the pan-industrials may dwarf the contributions of the public and even billionaires. The rich and powerful pan-industrials and the wealthy shareholders who ultimately own them will become political powerhouses, resembling the Gilded Age tycoons like J. P. Morgan in the 1890s and 1900s. They will likely resist the creation of generous government programs to alleviate the impacts of unemployment — and especially the higher corporate taxes necessary to fund them.

Because of all these developments being placed into motion, a potentially dangerous new era of social instability and unrest could begin. If the ameliorative efforts undertaken by government prove inadequate — as they probably will — then anger among the displaced is likely to trigger populist movements whose precise shape is unpredictable. Governments will be squeezed between corporate power on the one hand and threats of citizen anger, civil unrest, or even rebellion on the other hand.

Will an aroused citizenry demand government intervention to rein in the pan-industrials — including, perhaps, a socialist-style takeover of the means of production and a draconian program of wealth redistribution? Or will politicians and demagogues persuade the masses to blame "others" for their economic problems, perhaps making social tensions or international relations even worse? Either way, can capitalism survive this kind of pressure? As I'll discuss later in this chapter, the choice will depend largely on decisions made by both the corporate leaders of the pan-industrials and the politicians who shape the actions of government.

## Information Overlords — Data as Economic Weaponry

Another potential source of social and political conflict will be the enormous power that the pan-industrials will command as a result of their access to vast amounts of information about manufacturers, consumers, investors, workers, markets, and even nation-states.

A pan-industrial organization that is active in finance, heavy industry, consumer goods, services, social media, and other businesses will have access to data in endless variety. It will also have huge incentives to pool that data, analyze it, and use it to create a competitive edge over rival pan-industrials, corporate executives, and government officials. The power inherent in this access to data will raise a host of complicated questions that corporate executives, government regulators, and ordinary citizens will need to grapple with:

- How will the uses of data by pan-industrials be regulated? Can the data be used to guide stock sales and purchases, or would this constitute illegal insider trading?
- Can corporate information controlled by a pan-industrial be sold to anyone who will profit from it — vendors, competitors, equity analysts, reporters, government regulators, foreign entities, and so on?
- How will data ownership rights be defined and controlled? Will they

be put up for sale at auction or traded like commodities on "data exchanges"?

- Will data become assets in and of themselves, capable of being converted into the core assets of companies that are traded on public stock exchanges?
- Will activist investors and breakup artists from Wall Street force pan-industrials to divest their data as a way of maximizing their value?
- Will pan-industrials be able to employ investment bankers to engineer hostile takeovers and split firms from their data as a way to weaken rivals?
- How can the government prevent the use of private corporate data from being used for extortion, fraud, election rigging, fake or embarrassing news stories, and other nefarious purposes?

Each of these questions implies a host of others, as well as a series of easy-to-imagine scenarios that range from the alluring to the nightmarish. For example, think of the havoc that could result from the airing of dirty laundry hidden in the data owned by a pan-industrial with its tentacles in a host of industries. Imagine the damage that could be done if that data falls into the hands of a plaintiff suing a company . . . a crusading anti-business district attorney . . . an investigative reporter or a disruptive organization like Wikileaks . . . a hostile foreign power . . . or even a network of terrorists. Can a free and open democracy function properly under these conditions?

## Expect Power Shifts on the Map of Global Business

Over time, the pan-industrials will accumulate more economic power than many nation-states. With production and market footholds in countries around the world, with few or no political and patriotic allegiances to constrain them, and with no international courts or agencies capable of controlling them, the pan-industrials will freely shift their investments from one country to another. Of course, such capital shifts already take place today. But the vastly greater size of the pan-industrials will make the magnitude and the impact of future shifts far bigger.

The worldwide impact of the rise of pan-industrials titans is difficult to predict with certainty. Many Americans today are worried about the implications of globalization for the future of their nation; they wonder whether the United States will remain a superpower, and whether the growing power of other countries means that, in the long term, the U.S. may lose its prosperity, its leadership role in the world, and perhaps even its freedoms.

It's true that America enjoys certain unique advantages in the new wave of competition being unleashed by the manufacturing revolution. U.S. firms are among the leaders in the creation and adoption of new additive and digital manufacturing capabilities. They will be among the first to figure out the use of artificial intelligence for coordination across company boundaries that pan-industrials will use to restructure themselves and the global economy. In other countries, pan-industrials may not fly. It's possible they will remain grounded when slow-moving governments try to hold on to manual, blue-collar jobs to keep the populace employed or to preserve the power and wealth of existing elites.

This combination of factors gives the U.S. an edge in the race to build tomorrow's pan-industrials. But there are no guarantees that this advantage will persist.

Whatever happens, it's clear that some countries will emerge as economic winners, others as losers. Global patterns of trade and geopolitical power will change as well. Some nations will rise and some will fall as their internal stability falls apart and the influx of hard capital dries up. Production will localize due to additive manufacturing, creating shorter supply chains that avoid protectionism by staying within a trade bloc or a single country. Large exporting nations will be weakened. Low-cost-labor countries will also be weakened as additive and digital manufacturing eliminate the need for assembly.

The spread of technological unemployment, shorter supply chains, more localized manufacturing, and faster imitation of products could have a devastating affect on developing countries, such as China, Mexico, and India, that have established themselves as "factories to the world." The labor cost advantage that some countries have used to build their economies has already begun to disappear. As the *Economist* has noted, the trend toward offshoring production to developing countries had already reversed itself as long ago as 2012 thanks to the shrinking importance of labor costs; for example, the $499 price of a first-generation iPad included just $33 worth of manufacturing labor. Additive manufacturing and the allied technologies that are jump-starting the manufacturing revolution will only accelerate this trend.

One result is likely to be a proliferation of unmanned factories like the one in Dongguan. This could lead to mass unemployment and so-cial upheaval in countries like China and India, where hundreds of millions of people are looking to economic growth to help them feed their families and provide hope for the future. To stave off this out-come, China is racing to build its own advanced manufacturing ca-pabilities. The country's leaders hope that this development, in com-bination with an aging population, will minimize the chance of mass unemployment.

Other effects are also possible. They might include a decrease in in-ternational trade and greater economic independence for individual nations — as well as a shift in the power balance among nations, with unforeseeable consequences. It's possible that the world's poorest countries, deprived of a low-cost-labor route to development, could find themselves reduced to members of a hopeless, permanent under-class that capitalism can do little to help. Jan-Benedict Steenkamp, a professor at the Kenan-Flagler school of business at the University of North Carolina at Chapel Hill, has sketched how this dynamic might play out:

> There is much talk about the demographic dividend that India might reap from its population growth. And what to think about sub-Saha-ran Africa? Its population is expected to triple in the next 50 years to about 2.7 billion. All these new people need work, and with au-tomation of low-skilled jobs accelerating, the traditional emerging market model of moving up the value-chain ladder through manu-facturing is breaking down. If millions upon millions of low-skilled people cannot find productive jobs, social unrest and mass migra-tion are a near certainty.

The geopolitical consequences of such shifts could be dangerous. For example, if pan-industrials locate their manufacturing facilities in the United States and other highly developed markets rather than in China, will the leaders of that vast country become more inward-focused and limit their dreams of regional economic and political expansion? Or will China suffer economic decline, leading to internal unrest and the increased potential for military conflict with the West in an effort to capture supplies, gain access to markets, and create a "foreign devil" that will help keep the citizenry loyal?

Hopefully a different outcome will emerge — one in which countries in the developing world will become increasingly self-reliant, taking advantage of additive manufacturing and other new technologies to become producers of everything they need, using local ingredients, talent, and capital. As Steenkamp suggests, increased economic integration among regions such as Southeast Asia, the Middle East, and Africa could help to advance the same transition, because "if countries trade more regionally, they are less dependent on the West." Rather than being forced to eke out an income at the bottom rung of the global trading ladder, countries in these regions may develop independent sources of wealth by creating their own ladders.

In a few cases, countries we now think of as developing nations that are still playing catch-up with North America, Western Europe, and Far Eastern powers like Japan may flip sides and become leaders in the technological revolution. Some experts believe that China may already be positioning itself to achieve such a flip. For example, the venture capital executive Kai-Fu Lee has stated that the seven companies that currently lead the world in the application of AI are from two countries — the U.S. and China. (Lee's list of seven dominant AI firms includes Google, Facebook, Microsoft, Amazon, the web services giant Baidu, the online retailer Alibaba, and the high-tech conglomerate Tencent.) Based on this assessment, Lee contends that U.S. firms will likely dominate the expansion of AI throughout the developed world in the next few years, while Chinese companies will do the same in the developing nations. Is Lee's forecast believable? What roles will the Russians play? The next decade or so will put all such predictions to the test.

As this brief summation suggests, it's not possible to determine precisely how the global balance of power will be altered by the manufacturing revolution. The biggest question mark is how the emerging trends will affect the world's rising powers. However, the leading role the United States is now playing in developing and applying the new technologies that are driving the revolution means that a large-scale collapse of American wealth, power, and influence seems unlikely.

## Pan-Industrial Power Brokers

In the wake of the controversial 2010 Supreme Court ruling in *Citizens United v. Federal Election Commission,* which effectively eliminated the limits on political spending by for-profit corporations (as well as other kinds of organizations), many Americans are worried about the political power wielded by big companies and their owners and executives. Business owners with strong political views, like the liberal George Soros and the conservative brothers David and Charles Koch, have invested hundreds of millions of dollars to promote the views and the candidacies of politicians they favor. Thus, wealth is now being used to wield direct political influence to a degree that the founders of the nation surely never imagined or intended.

Spending cash to try to sway elections through advertising campaigns and other support to candidates is as American as baseball. And it is only one of the ways that well-heeled business leaders try to influence government. Another is lobbying efforts aimed at "educating" legislative leaders and government regulators concerning the kinds of rules favored by business. Such efforts can have a huge impact on the decisions made by Congress as well as state and local governments—especially when accompanied by campaign donations that include a thinly veiled quid pro quo.

More indirectly, a growing number of allegedly nonpartisan not-for-profit organizations, including think tanks, rely heavily on corporate funding. This can be viewed as evidence of socially minded generosity on the part of business donors—but it also gives the companies significant influence over the agendas of the researchers, writers, and policy advocates supported by those gifts, even in the absence of overt bribery or coercion.

In a few cases, such as the 2017 firing of researcher Barry Lynn by the think tank New America after Lynn published a statement sharply critical of Google — a major funder of the organization — the connection between corporate funding and political influence seems obvious. In other cases, the resulting influence may be subtler, but the cumulative effect is likely to be significant.

However, if you fear that big businesses have too much sway over politics in America today, you ain't seen nothing yet.

In the age of the pan-industrials, the national and possibly global power of the biggest corporate agglomerations will undoubtedly be gigantic. In part, this will be an artifact of sheer size. A pan-industrial that controls hundreds of billions or even trillions of dollars in revenues will be able to pour sums of money into election campaigning, lobbying efforts, think-tank sponsorships, and other influencing projects at a rate that even today's biggest tycoons can't match.

The unparalleled reach of pan-industrials into many industries, markets, and communities will greatly augment their power while also expanding their interest in wielding it. I've already explained how the era of additive manufacturing is likely to lead to highly dispersed facilities for producing, distributing, and marketing goods of all kinds. The political implication is that, for example, the great auto companies of the future will no longer apply their political influence mainly in a handful of huge centralized manufacturing centers like Detroit. Instead, the General Motors or Toyota of tomorrow — perhaps as one component of a hypothetical titan like Universal Metals — may have a hundred production facilities scattered through every state of the union . . . and a team of lobbyists in every state capital, looking out for the company's interests.

What's more, since the pan-industrials will likely be active in a broad array of business sectors, when a particular issue affects them deeply enough, they will be able to exert influence on politicians through a multiplicity of channels. Thus, if antitrust regulators try to crack down on the anti-competitive behavior of a particular pan-industrial collective, the political action committee (PAC) linked to that collective may choose to support primary election challengers to any member of Congress who refuses to rein in the regulators. And the PAC will be able to fund those electoral challenges through donations from myriad businesses, from local retailers, manufacturers, and service providers to giant banks, airlines, high-tech firms, and more.

Throw in the fact that each of the biggest pan-industrials will probably also own or control its own collection of media properties — cable TV and radio networks, print publications, online news sites, and the like — and it's easy to imagine the incredible pressure they will be able to bring to bear on any politician who dares to defy their wishes.

Thankfully, there will be many political issues on which the pan-industrial titans will take conflicting views — just as today's conservative owners of companies in industries such as fossil fuels often butt heads against their more liberal counterparts from Silicon Valley. The lack of unanimity among the potential oligarchs will prevent them from acting in concert and make it more difficult for them to drive political decisions in directions that violate the broader public interest.

Still, the huge political influence that the pan-industrials will command is sure to raise challenging political and social issues with which business leaders, political leaders, and concerned citizens will need to grapple.

## Designing a New Model of Capitalism

As the pan-industrial firms, federations, and collectives take over large portions of the economy, capitalism as we know it will change. Principles of open markets, antitrust, regulation, and the ownership of the means of production may change. Karl Marx may have been correct when he said that capitalism will bury itself. Capitalism itself may be threatened — and the politically powerful leaders of the pan-industrials may be tempted to take matters into their own hands, which could lead to a society that is a far cry from the one America's founders envisioned.

*Reining in the titans.* Limiting the powers of the pan-industrials will not be easy. The experience of South Korea in dealing with its *chaebols* — the Korean analogue of the Japanese *keiretsu* — offers an instructive case study.

Since the end of World War II, the family-owned *chaebol* conglomerates have played a major role in the Korean economy. Taking advantage of lax regulation and low-cost loans provided by a national government eager to promote economic growth, they built powerful industrial companies — Samsung, Hyundai, LG — that helped Korea become a major exporting country and generated significant wealth as well as millions of good jobs. For a time, the majority of Koreans were pleased with the arrangement.

But as the *chaebols* grew in wealth and power, it was inevitable that they'd be subject to increasing criticism. Owners and employees of small to midsize companies complained about the predatory behaviors of the *chaebols*, which allegedly refused to honor contracts with suppliers, failed to pay their bills, and used their massive power to drive competing companies out of business. The cozy relationships between *chaebol* owners and executives, on the one hand, and Korean government officials, on the other, all too often reflected the worst aspects of crony capitalism. For example, a series of high-placed *chaebol* managers were convicted of crimes such as tax evasion, accounting fraud, and embezzlement — only to receive pardons from the South Korean president or have their convictions overturned altogether.

Attempts were made to reduce the power of the *chaebols*. In 1980, the Monopoly Regulation and Fair Trade Act established an antitrust watchdog agency that was supposed to impose greater transparency and fairness on the behavior of the *chaebols*. However, in practice it provided few real constraints on *chaebol* behavior, primarily because government leaders feared that serious restrictions would hurt the performance of the still-high-flying Korean economy. A second wave of attempted reforms followed the 1997 Asian financial crisis, when many *chaebols* were nearly bankrupt because of excessive debt. Still, these efforts also fell short. Today, the *chaebols* are as powerful as ever. They continue to occupy a huge part of the Korean economy. For example, the Samsung group alone currently generates fully 15 percent of the country's gross national product.

In 2018, in the wake of yet another *chaebol*-related scandal — the impeachment of President Park Geun-hye on charges of corruption involving four of Korea's largest corporate networks — pressure is mounting for yet another attempt at breaking their power once and for all. Will this attempt fare any better than the previous ones? Only time will tell.

Of course, the experience of Korea in trying to control the power of the *chaebols* doesn't necessarily mean that the U.S. (and other industrialized countries) will be helpless to limit the activities of the pan-industrials. The United States, in particular, has advantages in this area that Korea lacks, including a longer history as a participative democracy and a tradition of robust, evenly matched battles between government and business, dating back to the "trust-buster" Theodore Roosevelt and the reformist New Dealer Franklin D. Roosevelt. What's more, the U.S. has a much larger, more diversified economy that is not as dependent on the vigor of a small handful of companies as the Korean economy.

Still, the history of the *chaebols* offers a warning to policy-makers and citizens who might assume that controlling the excesses of the pan-industrials will be relatively straightforward and easy.

*The antitrust weapon.* One of the biggest U.S. government powers that could be applied to reining in the pan-industrials is antitrust law. Enforcers of antitrust regulations will need to step in when the pan-industrials abuse their power. With recent data indicating a rising tide of concentration in many industries, some politicians, pundits, and policy experts on the left side of the political spectrum have already been calling for increased antitrust enforcement. The biggest giants in the technology industries — Alphabet, Apple, Amazon, Microsoft, and a handful of others — have been painted as potential targets. Some are saying that the time has come to consider using governmental power to force the breakup of some of the high-tech giants, much as was done to AT&T in 1982 and to Standard Oil way back in 1911.

However, as the writer Matt Rosoff pointed out in an insightful opinion piece from April 2017, a thoughtful scrutiny of the state of competition in the high-tech world suggests that none of the rival giants actually maintains the kind of monopoly power over any given market that antitrust regulations were originally designed to combat. Instead, they are engaged in a continual state of war with one another over a fragmented set of interrelated businesses. Apple and Alphabet, for example, battle each other for leadership of the smartphone industry; Alphabet, Facebook, and Amazon battle for leadership of the online advertising world; and Microsoft, Amazon, and Alphabet vie for leadership in cloud computing. Meanwhile, a steady stream of start-ups continues to produce technological and business-model innovations, posing new challenges to today's giants. In short, Rosoff concludes, antitrust law is a "blunt instrument" that should only be used in cases where true monopoly power exists and is stifling innovation — which is not the case in today's high-tech universe.

The principle Rosoff articulates should also be applied to the coming world of the pan-industrials. I've explained why the pan-industrials are likely to be exceptionally capable of continually innovating for the benefit of consumers (as well as themselves, of course). It also seems unlikely that any one or two pan-industrial collectives will ever be able to seize control over a majority of the U.S. or world economy. Instead, the future is more likely to see a continual battle among a limited number of pan-industrial titans, each seeking to defend and, if possible, to expand its own sphere of influence.

Like today's high-tech arena, the economy of tomorrow will be led by six to ten titans constantly jockeying for marginal advantages over one another, none of them ever really capable of achieving full-scale victory over their rivals. This world of constant border skirmishes among great powers will help rein in the tendency of any one pan-industrial to engage in the kind of predatory behavior that a true monopoly can indulge. If that changes, it will be time for government agencies to wield the club of antitrust law, using it to break up a domineering giant who is no longer adequately restrained by competitive pressures.

*Forging a new social compact.* It's possible to imagine a dystopian future in which chieftains of the pan-industrials become, in effect, national, regional, or global oligarchs wielding unchallenged economic and political power.

However, history suggests that a different outcome is more likely. America has faced the problem of centralized wealth many times in the past, and preserved its democratic and capitalist system. Both the era of the robber barons and the Great Depression of the 1930s led to reforms. In the 1930s, decades of rising inequality had ended with a crash, leaving a quarter of the workforce unemployed. It was the culmination of the industrial revolution of electric power and the assembly line. But instead of socialism, the country got a New Deal that saved capitalism by adding an array of protections for ordinary people. Big companies accepted this structure and flourished, while the country enjoyed decades of widely shared prosperity. Wealthy families gradually lost their hold over the economy as high estate taxes and generational shifts diluted their wealth, drove governments to introduce legal and institutional reforms that limited business excesses, instituted protections for workers and consumers, and created regulatory bodies with the ability to constrain corporate growth.

Of course, advocates for business pushed back against many of these reforms. Those with great power rarely relinquish it voluntarily. But in the end, the demands of an outraged public — and fears of a more extreme response, in the form of socialist or fascist totalitarianism — forced corporate leaders to reach an accommodation with government.

In the decades ahead, a similar dynamic is likely to play out over the long run. The pan-industrials will have a lot to lose from social instability. Just as wealthy families and corporate executives grudgingly went along with the New Deal of the 1930s, the powerful owners and leaders of the pan-industrial empires will eventually accept a similar compromise between business and social interests — but only after a painful, protracted struggle in which many are likely to suffer.

To avoid being the subject of intense attack from government regulators and citizen activists, the managers and owners of pan-industrial firms, federations, and collectives will have to step up to the social responsibilities inherent in their vast economic and political power. In the Gilded Age, tycoons like Andrew Carnegie and John D. Rockefeller donated millions to social and charitable causes partly in reaction to the bad publicity attracted by ruthless businessmen like J. P. Morgan. In a similar way, peer pressure and evolving social mores may drive a revival of the notion of *noblesse oblige* in the era of the pan-industrials.

More broadly, just as society came around to appreciating the virtues of big business by the middle of the twentieth century, it will likely recognize the benefits of a pan-industrial economy. In particular, most people will come to understand the advantages that the pan-industrial titans will offer as compared with small-scale makers.

In some cases, the power of the pan-industrials will serve to defend social interests against other, more dangerous possibilities. For example, there is a romantic appeal to the notion of small workshops producing goods in limited quantities. But it can also be argued that the power of manufacturing workshops to produce powerful modern gadgets with minimal regulation or control could pose a real and meaningful threat to society. For instance, 3D printing services like i.materialise have received orders to produce items designed to facilitate crimes, such as debit card skimmers, which can be attached unobtrusively to ATM machines in order to capture card numbers and PINs from unsuspecting bank customers. Rogue entrepreneurs have been working on schemes to use 3D printers to manufacture illegal drugs and counterfeit versions of expensive branded products. Others are already distributing designs for 3D printing a working assault rifle and a plastic handgun that can't be detected by airport security.

Rather than try to regulate thousands or millions of small makers, governments that hope to protect society against the dangers of uncontrolled technology will prefer to work with a few big pan-industrials. The pan-industrials can't stop a determined terrorist from gaining access to dangerous product design files from somewhere on the web, but they can make it a good deal harder to print them out by controlling most of the software and the printers.

In the same way, the pan-industrials will make it easier for governmental and non-governmental authorities to regulate a whole host of business issues, including quality standards, product safety, product liability, and intellectual property protection.

## The Pan-Industrial Cornucopia

As we've seen in this chapter, the age of the pan-industrials will pose a number of social, political, and economic issues. But we mustn't let our concern about the genuine challenges we'll face blind us to the huge benefits that the pan-industrials will produce for the vast majority of humankind.

The pan-industrials will play a major role in delivering those benefits. Just as the giant companies of the first half of the twentieth century — from Ford, GM, Whirlpool, and General Electric to General Foods, Kellogg, Kraft, and Sears — brought an unprecedented range of new, affordable, high-quality goods to millions of newly prosperous Americans, so the pan-industrials will enrich the lives of consumers in the generations to come.

If and when a fair social and economic arrangement can be established that shares the benefits of the manufacturing revolution among all sectors of society, it's likely that the world of the future will be enormously enriched. The benefits of the revolution will include greatly increased prosperity, including an affordable cornucopia of new or improved products. Many of the reasons have already been discussed. Companies empowered by AM and industrial platforms can be closer to customers and more responsive to their needs, with the ability to develop new products and bring them to market faster and more affordably than ever before. New product design models like mass customization and mass modularization will help customers get goods that meet their needs more precisely than in the past, leading to greater market efficiency and consumer satisfaction.

The enhanced multidirectional informational flows enabled by industrial platforms will also make the economy more efficient through greater transparency, lower costs, and better matching of needs and resources among suppliers, business partners, and customers. Bright ideas will spread from industry to industry and from one geography to the next even more rapidly than today, thanks to the digital networks that will interlink the new business ecosystems. And the localized production, shorter supply chains, and data-driven systems for production, distribution, and logistics that the new technologies enable will further reduce expensive frictions in the economy, freeing up money for more productive pursuits.

In short, all of the many benefits that AM and digital platforms yield will enable companies to serve customers better, driving GDP growth and improved standards of living around the world. In the long run, the new abundance generated by the pan-industrial economy should create enough value in the economy to fund an array of new social protections and benefits, perhaps ultimately including a universal basic income and high-quality, affordable-to-all education and healthcare.

The technological changes that are driving the economic revolution won't be the only sources of societal benefits. Even the sheer size of the pan-industrials, while raising legitimate questions about the economic and political power they'll wield, have the potential to create vast new sources of value for the world. Giant pan-industrial collectives will have the wealth, scope, and scale to manage giant integrated technological projects that neither individual companies nor the majority of governments are capable of tackling — intelligent regional transportation systems, improved energy grids, smart city infrastructure programs, and the like. They'll be capable of creating big, independent research facilities with the mandate of pursuing diverse scientific challenges that will be somewhat reminiscent of the old Bell Labs and Xerox PARC, which produced so many of the technological breakthroughs on which today's world is based. And because their alliances with financial firms will minimize their need for infusions of Wall Street cash, they'll be less affected by the tyranny of short-term profit expectations — and therefore free to think big about their own futures and about the future of the world.

At the same time, the manufacturing revolution will allow future generations to enjoy a cleaner, healthier environment, even as average standards of living rise dramatically.

For example, 3D printing will reduce carbon emissions in several ways. First, the greater precision enabled by 3D printing will reduce the cost and boost the efficiency of emission-free solar panels and wind turbines. Some experimental panels produced using additive manufacturing can capture a great deal of energy even on cloudy days, a big potential boon in northern latitudes. These innovations will speed up the shift from fossil fuel to carbon-free energy.

Additive manufacturing itself uses the same amount of energy as traditional manufacturing, but it gives off less smoke and other toxic fumes. Those emissions are also better contained and more scrubbed out of the exhaust with filters. HP, Inc.'s new Multi Jet Fusion printer, for example, is "office ready" — in other words, it is capable of manufacturing products cleanly and safely, right next to people sitting at their desks.

As we've noted, more localized AM production will reduce shipping requirements, thereby reducing our carbon emissions. This is already happening. UPS has a sizable business maintaining warehouses for industrial customers and then rapidly delivering specific parts as needed via airplanes and trucks. It recently installed a hundred large 3D printers at its central hub in Louisville, with the goal of reducing warehouse space and shipping distances. More and more parts will be made only as needed. And as 3D printers become easier to use, more

versatile, and at a lower cost, we can expect the company to add printers to its regional and even local hubs and stores. In the long run, we'll
have a lot fewer jumbo jets flying in and out of Louisville. That's one
reason UPS increasingly presents itself as a logistics company, not a
shipper.

Another benefit will be derived from the ability of 3D printing to
produce elaborately designed parts with less material but just as much
strength as conventional parts. Honeycomb-like structures, for example, may eventually be everywhere in jets, cars, and buildings because they weigh a good deal less than the current structures. Hon-
eycombing also turns out to be a good insulator, trapping air inside
the walls like multipaned windows. Over time, we'll get lighter products throughout the economy, so we'll need less energy to move them
around.

3D printing's benefits go well beyond carbon emissions. Because
additive manufacturing machines build products by precisely combining materials into a product one layer or dot at a time, the resulting
product has only the material needed for the final product. In contrast,
much of today's industry relies on subtractive techniques such as CNC
milling, where you get a rough shape and then whittle it down to the
desired dimensions and finish. These traditional processes create a lot
of waste, often resulting in more material discarded than actually ends
up in the product.

Even greater waste reduction may be possible through a new "circular economy" system invented at the University of Luxembourg. Devised by Claude Wolf and Slawomir Kedziora, two researchers from
the university's Faculty of Science, Technology, and Communication,
the upAM system combines 3D printing with a process for recycling
plastic waste. Discarded plastic products are ground in a shredder,
then fabricated into new polymer filaments that the researchers say
are equal or better in quality than equivalent filaments made from new
material. "This process proposes to close the loop of a product life,"
they explain. The upAM system is already being used on a small scale
by students at the university, who can recycle unwanted plastic items,
then print out new ones as needed.

3D printing can also help to mitigate the damage done by climate
change. Conventional manufacturing generally yields products with

simple surfaces, straight lines, and boxy shapes, with minor curves. But nature is full of irregularity, which only 3D printing can mimic. So 3D printing can better deal with natural forces. Hence the potential to build artificial coral reefs, as I explained back in Chapter 1.

Sea walls offer another opportunity. As water levels rise, coastal cities will invest heavily in expanded and stronger sea walls and dikes. 3D printing allows the manufacture of complex curved cement surfaces that will disperse wave energy in many directions as the waves bounce off a wall in a dispersed pattern. These walls don't need to be as thick and strong as equivalent flat walls produced using conventional manufacturing, which have to absorb more of the ocean's force. Consequently, the transporting and mixing of concrete will be reduced, with a concomitant reduction in fossil fuel consumption.

For all these reasons, a world in which manufacturing is dominated by 3D printing and the entire panoply of digital technologies that make it ultra-efficient is likely to be a world that is far more environmentally sustainable than today's world — even while triggering an economic boom that will produce remarkable benefits for people all over the planet.

## A New Golden Age?

There are even signs that we may now be on the verge of a new golden age of broad-based economic growth, social progress, and widespread contentment — all driven by technological developments like those described in this book, combined with wise choices by business and political leaders.

That's the argument being made by some cycle-of-history theorists. According to these analysts, cycles of technological development, investment, and deployment tend to drive economic and social development. U.S. economic history can be described as a series of waves, each created by a major technological innovation that fosters the birth of new business empires and business models. These waves, in essence, create opportunities for overthrowing existing empires or building new ones.

Thus, in the late nineteenth century, the emergence of new manufacturing technologies and systems for distributing capital served as the triggering disruption that made possible the business empires of the robber barons, which overthrew the empires previously built by the moguls of railroad, textile, and agriculture equipment. And while each of these successive periods of empire-building began by creating huge fortunes for a few creative (and lucky) business leaders, they ultimately brought broad-based economic benefits to millions of people through the creation of jobs, the availability of new products and services, and an overall surge in societal wealth.

It's possible that the new digital tools for producing goods with greater efficiency, quality, and flexibility, and making them more widely available than ever before — all while reducing stress on the natural environment — may make a new golden age possible.

Of course, no great historical development happens automatically. Business and political leaders have it within their power to ensure that the potential benefits of the manufacturing revolution are effectively developed and widely shared across society — or not.

But for us today, the core message is that the near-utopian future envisioned by some prognosticators may be within reach of hundreds of millions of people in the decades to come — provided we have the wisdom to plan for it and the will to make it happen.

# PART THREE

# HOW YOU CAN RESPOND

To quickly summarize: Part 1 described the new technologies that are transforming manufacturing, explaining how and why these new capabilities will lead to the rise of a new kind of company, the pan-industrial. Part 2 explored the competitive consequences of these changes, showing how the pan-industrial revolution will transform companies, strategy, and the nature of competition itself. It described the various kinds of pan-industrial companies and the ways they'll compete to defend and expand their spheres of influence, as well as the challenges that pan-industrial markets will pose to societies around the world.

Now, Part 3 will offer a number of specific recommendations as to how business leaders of today can prepare for the startling changes on the horizon by positioning their companies to take advantage of the technological trends now sweeping the manufacturing world. I'll explain the four phases of adoption that characterize technological innovations like AM, show how to determine which phase your industry or company now occupies, and offer advice about how to decide which phase-management strategies your organization should employ. I'll also provide practical advice about other aspects of adopting AM, such as overcoming internal resistance and ensuring that customers remain at the heart of your manufacturing strategy. And I'll explain why and how companies can think big to ensure they take full advantage of all the benefits that AM promises.

# 11

# FIRST STEPS

*Getting Started in Additive Manufacturing*

**IF YOU HELP RUN** a company that makes things, you will soon be able to make them better, faster, cheaper, easier, and more flexibly and efficiently than ever before. You'll be able to innovate more quickly and serve varied markets with goods more finely calibrated to meet a wider range of needs — and you'll do it all while wasting less money, less time, less energy, and fewer natural resources.

Just as we now think back to the pre-desktop-computer era of the 1960s and '70s and wonder how we ever managed without word processing, digital spreadsheets, smartphone apps, social media, and the Internet, in twenty years we will look back to the days before the manufacturing revolution and marvel at the amazing improvements we've experienced — many of which will already be starting to appear routine.

However, bear in mind that not all companies will benefit equally from the transformation that is coming — particularly in its early phases. Some will lag behind due to conservatism, knowledge gaps, fear of change, or lack of vision. Others will play catch-up, adopting the new technologies a year or two behind the industry leaders: early enough to enjoy some of the strategic and economic advantages they offer but too late to seize the competitive high ground. Meanwhile, a few AM pioneers will pave the way, developing superior know-how and real-world experience a little quicker than their rivals. If they take full advantage of the opportunities afforded them, they'll create vast spheres of influences cutting across traditional market and industry boundaries that will yield significant added revenues and profits for decades to come.

In a 2015 interview, GE's then CEO Jeff Immelt deftly summed up the challenge and the opportunity facing corporate leaders:

> If you think about today, 15 percent or 20 percent of the S&P 500 valuation is consumer Internet stocks that didn't exist 15 or 20 years ago. The [incumbent] consumer companies got none of that. When you look at retailers, banks, consumer-product companies, they got none of that. If you look out 10 or 15 years and say that same value is going to be created in the industrial Internet, do you as an industrial company want to sit there and say, "I don't want any of that. I'm going to let a Newco or some other company get all that"? Is that really what you've relegated yourself to?

In the interview, Immelt referred to the value that would be created "in the industrial Internet." As you've seen, this book describes an even bigger stream of value that will be created through the combined impact of the industrial Internet, additive manufacturing, industrial platforms, and the cascading impact of related technologies for creating, producing, and distributing goods. This bigger reality makes Immelt's point about the urgency of the options even more compelling — and adds a big dose of irony to the fact that, just two years later, Immelt himself would be ousted from the CEO's seat at GE in the midst of a controversy over the company's strategic direction. Will GE veer away from the path on which Immelt set it, which appeared to point toward the pan-industrial revolution I've described? Or will it stay the course, and perhaps even accelerate its efforts in that direction, as I would recommend? Under conflicting pressures from Wall Street, big investors, and evolving competitive realities, GE's current leaders are wrestling with the answers to these questions.

At the same time, leaders at many other companies today are just beginning to wrap their minds around the potential of AM and industrial platforms. For these leaders, mapping the first several moves they'll make as they enter this new world is important. At the same time, thinking about those moves in the context of the big long-term changes that the coming pan-industrial markets will bring is equally important. In this chapter and the next, I'll explain the key steps companies can take today to prepare themselves to claim their fair share of the benefits to be created by the onrushing pan-industrial revolution.

## Are You Ready to Make the Move to Additive Manufacturing?

In deciding how aggressively to invest in AM and how to time your implementation of the new technologies, the most important consideration is the readiness of your organization. This readiness takes three main forms.

First, *technological readiness*. What is the state of AM as applied to your industry and within your firm? For example, can you make your products from the existing additive manufacturing technologies and materials? If not, you might need to partner with a materials maker to generate composites best suited to your products. Are there existing AM design tools that are suitable for the kinds of products your company makes? If not, you'll face the additional hurdle of first working to adapt existing programs or creating brand-new ones to meet your requirements.

Second, *organizational readiness*. Do you have, or can you easily acquire, the engineering and development talent to implement AM? How entrenched are traditional approaches to manufacturing within your staff and operations as a whole? How willing are your people to try out AM? And how siloed is your organization? Over time, AM is likely to transform organizations by blurring the lines between functions, so an organization that's already accustomed to collaboration across departments will be able to make the leap to AM more quickly and easily than one in which departmental boundaries are rigid.

Third, *funding readiness*. Capital requirements for AM equipment and industrial platforms vary greatly from market to market and from firm to firm. Competitive realities may well play a crucial role in forcing you to act — for example, when a key rival jumps to the new technology, you may be required to accelerate your own transition simply to avoid being left behind. Success will demand careful investment with an eye to current and potential markets, the capabilities of your organization, and the benefits offered by today's technology and new tools currently under development. Selecting the appropriate business model can help you get your company focused on what you'll need to compete in this new environment.

## Blind Alleys: False Steps to Avoid

It's also important to be aware of some common mistakes — things you *shouldn't* do if you hope to take full advantage of the potential benefits of the pan-industrial revolution.

*Getting stuck in Industry 4.0.* The most popular path to AM these days, especially in Europe, seems to be Industry 4.0. As I've explained, this is a package of digital manufacturing technologies that includes robotics, artificial intelligence, big data, augmented reality, and the Internet of Things, as well as AM. One of its goals is to boost flexibility in manufacturing operations, which is also a key benefit of AM.

In practice, however, the Industry 4.0 approach gives AM only a minor role — mostly in prototyping and in extending what robots do. It preserves the structures of traditional manufacturing, especially its capital-intensive assembly line and long supply chains, so it can never achieve the flexibility of a true AM-centric operation. Curiously, many of today's engineers appear to prefer this approach — perhaps because it enables them to experiment with new technologies inside a familiar structure. But that very familiarity prevents the organization from exploring AM's main capabilities and applying them to production. Industry 4.0 is likely to be the last gasp of the old production paradigm based fundamentally on traditional manufacturing methods.

There's a terminology issue to watch for here. Some manufacturers, such as Adidas, say they are adopting Industry 4.0. However, they're actually doing it as a conscious transition to fully digitized, AM-centric manufacturing. They know that they will have to overhaul their traditional assembly lines due to the need for more complex designs in some lines, customization for other lines, and standardization of some parts, such as the soles of their new digitally optimized running shoes.

The Adidas approach is quite different from what most companies that embrace Industry 4.0 are doing. Most of these firms are trying to *preserve* their traditional manufacturing methods while still saying they are embracing digitization. As a result, these companies are likely to have a hard time adopting AM-centric business models, because they've put so much investment in their conventional production systems and attached Industry 4.0 bells and whistles to the old equipment. They'll have to take a heavy write-off for their conventional and Industry 4.0 equipment when competition finally forces them to make the big shift to AM and industrial platforms as the core of their new systems.

Therefore, my first big piece of advice to companies planning their moves into the world of AM is a simple one: Don't expect to cling to the familiar organizational structures and methods of traditional manufacturing. From the beginning, take seriously the bigger impact that true AM-centric manufacturing can have, and start thinking about how to rebuild your entire business around the new capabilities AM makes possible.

*Trying to outsource manufacturing innovation.* Another blind alley is the temptation to rely on outside suppliers, such as printer bureaus, for your AM parts or products. Outsourcing may be appropriate in the early days as you experiment with AM, but it's better to bring the lion's share of production in-house as quickly as possible. Only then can you gain the expertise in AM that will enable you to take full advantage of its capabilities in the context of your industry. And only then can you be sure of quality control, competitive secrecy for new product launches, and intellectual property protection. As the printers themselves increasingly use machine learning to figure out the best processes, you'll capture those insights for the benefit of your organization. You'll also develop a more integrated operation all along the supply chain, so you'll have better coordination within the chain, and more control over your defenses against cyberattacks.

A few firms may decide to outsource their production altogether to contract manufacturers, often because of capital constraints. Such companies may choose to focus on product development, marketing, or sales, thereby avoiding the trouble of learning AM. If you decide to take this route, you should at least work closely with your contract manufacturer in order to grasp the capabilities that AM brings, and its potentially transformative impact on the processes you retain in-house. As the pan-industrial collectives emerge, you may choose to join one, taking advantage of the AM systems and platform capabilities it offers without having to build them yourself.

*Clinging to your current customers and products.* Perhaps the most dangerous blind alley will be the temptation to focus narrowly on your current roster of customers and product offerings. This warning may seem counterintuitive. After all, doesn't every smart businessperson know that it's essential to stay intimate with customers and to continually work to provide improved goods and services to meet their needs?

That's true, of course. And in the age of pan-industrial markets, customer intimacy will be more essential — and more challenging — than ever. The consultants Norbert Schwieters and Bob Moritz of PricewaterhouseCoopers have captured this dynamic well:

> The new [digital] infrastructure is a web of connections among people: Producers and consumers, in particular, are much more closely connected than they used to be. Through smartphones and social media, consumers can connect directly to primary producers of the products and services they buy. Through sensors and data analytics, producers can be thoroughly attuned to the needs, habits, and long-term interests of the people who buy products and services. As a designer of the new platforms, or a business leader participating in them, you have an unprecedented opportunity to build a customer-centric enterprise, one that connects with what people genuinely want and need from your company, thus generating commitment that will last a lifetime.

As the transformation of manufacturing progresses, you'll likely find that your company needs to rethink, and to broaden, its understanding of customers and even its definition of them. For example, you may be accustomed to dealing primarily with purchasing agents whose priorities are limited to a few familiar considerations — product specifications, delivery date, and, above all, price. Soon you may find that the new industrial networks are putting you in touch with many other team members at your customer companies, from designers and production managers to marketers, salespeople, customer service reps, and downstream consumers. Because traditional value chains are being reconfigured to allow multiple interactions among many participants at varying nodes of the network, you may need to make changes to your ways of communicating with, interacting with, making decisions with, and managing processes with a new and more varied array of customers.

What's more, even as you keep a varied group of customers at the center of your search for opportunities, you'll want to keep *non-customers* at the center of your search as well. These may include anyone that uses a rival product as well as those who have never bought a product like yours from anyone.

One great tool for finding and connecting with non-customers is *leakage analysis* — a systematic effort to identify non-customers and their reasons for "leaking through the sieve." For example, as you adopt new technologies to serve customers, you may find that some potential customers refuse to take advantage of your new offerings for reasons like the following:

- They don't know how to use the new technology — they find it intimidating or confusing.
- The applications of the new technology and the benefits it will offer have not been presented to them clearly and convincingly.
- The hype surrounding the new technology seems excessive, leading them to be skeptical or even cynical about it.
- Specific concerns like safety, reliability, and affordability make it seem easier and less risky to stick with traditional product offerings.

Once you employ leakage analysis to determine which factors are making it hard for you to convert non-customers into customers, you can take steps to eliminate those factors. For example, anxiety over a new technology that appears intimidating or confusing may be reduced by automating the product's controls and improving its design to make it appear as simple and intuitive as possible. Concerns about safety can be addressed by enhancing safety features and highlighting these benefits in product design, marketing, advertising, and sales promotions.

## Developing an Industrial Platform Strategy

Before investing in AM hardware, it is good to have the software in place. So one key preparatory step to becoming a participant in the pan-industrial revolution is defining your industrial platform strategy and building a plan to develop it incrementally.

In the short run, many firms will have to use a platform developed by someone else. However, over time, owning a proprietary platform has many benefits, especially access to richer information flows and more opportunities to make money from that information.

One useful way to think about designing your own industrial platform is in terms of specific applications. The platforms currently in

| TABLE 11-1: LEADING INDUSTRIAL PLATFORMS, RATED BY APPLICATION (END OF 2017) | | | |
|---|---|---|---|
| | SUPPLY CHAIN | PRODUCT LIFECYCLE | ASSET PERFORMANCE |
| Jabil InControl | ●★ | | ▲ |
| GE Predix | | ▲ | ●★ |
| IBM Watson | ▲ | ■ | ■ |
| Siemens Mindsphere with NX module | ● | ■ | ●★ |
| Bosch IoT | | ■ | ■★ |
| Hitachi Lumada | ▲ | ▲ | ▲ |
| Emerson Plantweb | | | ▲★ |
| Materialise Streamics and other software | | ▲ | ▲ |
| Autodesk | | ▲ | ▲ |
| SAP HANA | | | ■★ |

KEY:  ▲ = *Fair functionality*   ■ = *Good functionality*

use and under development have varying strengths and weaknesses in relation to particular business functions. Considering the profiles of these existing platforms may help you identify competitive opportunities, including functional niches that are not currently being well served (see Table 11-1).

Table 11-1 does not take a comprehensive look at all possible business applications and industrial platform functionality. However, it is illustrative of how a platform owner might think about the variety of platform offerings now available, showing the different portfolios of services that each industrial platform company offers. Some platforms have very strong core applications, while others lack a strong core. Some platforms have built a very strong core surrounded by weaker

| MANUFACTURING-EXECUTION | PRODUCT DESIGN | NEW PRODUCT INTRODUCTION | BUSINESS ECOSYSTEM | TM/AM READINESS |
|---|---|---|---|---|
| ▲ | ▲ | ▲ | | TM/AM |
| ■ | | | | TM |
| ■ | | | | TM |
| ■ | ■ | ▲ | | TM/AM |
| ■ | | | | TM |
| ■★ | | | | TM |
| ▲ | | | | TM |
| ▲ | ■★ | ▲ | | AM |
| | ●★ | ■ | | AM |
| ▲ | | | | TM |

● = Excellent functionality      ★ = Core application

applications, while others built a balanced portfolio of several moderately strong applications.

The table also illustrates where the competition is heavy and where it is light. Notice that no platform has yet to crack ecosystem management, an important long-term necessity for managing a large and diverse business ecosystem with many users and many direct connections with customers. There is only one serious player in supply chain management, while there are two serious players in product design. Finally, there are some applications that have several players, but no outstanding heavy hitter.

Of course, identifying the strengths and weaknesses of existing platforms is only one step in developing your own industrial platform strategy. Some of the key questions you'll want to address include the following.

*Do I want to build my own platform, or should I seek to join an existing platform?* If you have the resources, ability, and vision to create a successful industrial platform, you may be able to enjoy the enormous benefits that go with being a platform owner. However, if you lack any of these necessities, look for the most suitable existing platform and try to join it. Missing the pan-industrial revolution altogether would be far worse than accepting a secondary role as a platform user.

*If I opt to build my own platform, should I try to integrate applications created by other organizations?* You may or may not have all the skills required to build a successful platform, including IT expertise, manufacturing experience, 3D design skill, and software development talent. If you are lacking any of the key skills, you may be able to supplement your resources by partnering with other organizations. Remember that applications can also be added to a platform over time, which creates opportunities you may be able to exploit in the long term.

*If I build my own platform, how open or closed do I want the platform to be?* A platform owner can decide to keep the platform open to encourage users to add new features, enhance existing ones, or even replace them with improved offerings. This option can attract additional users and help ensure that the platform remains flexible and widely useful. On the other hand, a closed platform allows the platform owner to retain control over the system and to avoid becoming reliant on outside sources. A closed platform also ensures the platform owner's access to data.

*Which goals do I want to prioritize for my platform?* Devote time and energy to thinking about the various goals your platform can serve — reducing costs, streamlining processes, facilitating innovation, increasing market reach, improving product quality, expanding into new geographies, and so on. Given the kinds of businesses you are currently involved in and those your platform is likely to serve in the future, which of these goals are most important? Which are less significant? Decisions about how you will prioritize your platform's goals should help to shape the structural and managerial rules you make about how the platform will be designed and run.

## Deploying AM Hardware: Four Approaches

When you're ready to begin implementing AM in an existing manufacturing business, there are a number of approaches you can follow. I'll present four of the most common ones, beginning with those that involve less disruption of your existing traditional manufacturing process.

*Parallel production systems.* This involves building a parallel, completely separate AM production line for products aimed at new market segments, using new brand names while sharing some materials. This approach is appropriate for companies that aren't ready to insert AM into their main business but who do see mass potential in niche areas.

Hershey, for example, is a longtime leader in selling chocolate candies to midmarket consumers. But with luxury niche competitors appealing to Hershey's higher-end customers, the company decided to fight back with AM. It developed a separate business with product qualities that would appeal to these high-end customers. One line embraces the complexity made possible by AM: It produces sculpted chocolates that are hollow inside and injected with special fillings — a complicated geometric challenge that is difficult or impossible with traditional manufacturing. Another line embraces customization by producing chocolates personalized to the customer and the occasion by placing orders online—which would be prohibitively expensive with traditional manufacturing.

Because these two lines are such a radical departure from Hershey's main business, and because they must be made completely with AM, the company put them in a separate organization. In the long run, Hershey hopes to build it into a substantial new business that will expand the company's total market base. Besides the chocolates, it also hopes to sell chocolate printers to restaurants, bakeries, specialty chocolate shops, and even consumers at home. It will also offer proprietary ingredients especially suited to 3D printing.

Another example might be a conventional manufacturer that sets up mobile mini-factories inside shipping containers or trucks, especially designed for producing replacement parts in far-flung locations. The company stays with traditional manufacturing for its main production, but also uses AM to rapidly satisfy the needs of dispersed customers.

*Assembly feeder systems.* Here AM merely supplies some of the parts that go into a traditionally assembled product. Initially, the only change is in how those parts are made. However, after making the switch, the company can start to adjust the overall product to take advantage of the new designs and product capabilities that AM makes possible.

Example: The electronics manufacturer LG is still making OLED televisions the conventional way, except that the screen itself now comes from an AM process. All the other parts, such as the electronic connections and the housing, come from traditional manufacturing, and the overall assembly is done using traditional manufacturing. In time, though, as LG goes down the learning curve for AM, it will likely make adjustments in other parts of its TV manufacturing system. Eventually, AM will probably replace more of the traditional manufacturing parts.

*Hybrid fabrication systems.* Here AM is mixed with traditional manufacturing in the same production process, either within a workstation or a mini-factory. The goal is to capture flexibility and other AM advantages, while retaining traditional manufacturing's current advantages, such as the higher-quality finishing still available with certain types of products. At this moment in technology history, when there are still some limitations to the kinds of parts and products AM can build, hybrid systems can produce much more diverse product lines than pure AM. In many cases, they can also automate postprocessing activities, reducing costs and speeding production rates.

*Replacement systems.* Companies willing to move aggressively can replace their entire traditional manufacturing system with an AM system. Because this is so difficult and risky, most examples will involve startups such as Align Technology, which in the late 1990s developed an AM process for making orthodontic braces. Established companies will likely move to replacement systems either by evolving from one of the three other implementation methods listed above, or by acquiring a pure-AM firm.

## Overcoming Internal Resistance

Back in the 1980s, Motorola was exploring adopting the then-emerging digital technology for cell phones. Its engineers, however, resisted the move. They were so entrenched in analog technology — much of it developed by Motorola itself — that they couldn't see the advantages that digital technology would bring. As a result, Motorola's engineers made only halfhearted efforts to incorporate digital technology, eventually causing the company to lose its once-formidable market share.

Today, a similar struggle is happening inside many companies in regard to additive manufacturing, industrial platforms, and other technological innovations. As you map out your plans for incorporating 3D printing and other new manufacturing technologies into your company's toolkit, you may discover that you face significant resistance from engineers, managers, and others in your company who are psychologically or intellectually wedded to traditional manufacturing methods.

When this happens, it's extremely helpful to have a concrete plan for overcoming that resistance and changing the internal culture.

One approach is what might be called the *soft-touch* approach. As an example, one giant aerospace company has been following a five-step path toward mastery of 3D printing technologies:

*Step 1:* Use 3D printing for prototyping in all departments, enabling engineers and designers to become familiar with its capabilities.

*Step 2:* Use 3D printing for tooling and design, making incremental improvements to traditional manufacturing methods.

*Step 3:* Build a 3D printing lab and partner with outside experts in order to gain increased knowledge and experience.

*Step 4:* Experiment with new materials for 3D printing and begin innovation in manufacturing methods.

*Step 5:* Start developing products with new functions and capabilities that take advantage of the new materials 3D printers can now use.

This path provides a concrete, logical way for knowledge of 3D printing and comfort with the technology to gradually spread throughout the organization, taking on a more important role in the life of the company with each new step. In effect, having a soft-touch program like this is a way of driving your company's progress through the four phases of technology adoption rather than allowing trends to unfold passively — and doing so in a way that makes the cultural adaptation gradual and relatively painless.

Other companies, like GE, are taking what might be called the hard-touch approach. GE has been requiring every business unit to develop one or more pilot projects to experiment with new manufacturing technologies and to provide venues for retraining engineers, designers, and researchers. Initiatives like these can help organizations develop the knowledge and experience needed to overcome internal resistance that will hamper some companies in their efforts to reap the full benefits that the manufacturing revolution offers. Because the shift to AM is driven by a mandate from the top of the organization, this hard-touch approach sends a strong signal throughout the corporation that AM is the wave of the future — and that everyone needs to be prepared to embrace it.

Perhaps the most important element in overcoming the resistance to change is leadership from the top of your organization. Vocal, visible support from the CEO and other C-suite leaders is necessary to create a sense of urgency about the coming transformation, its benefits, and its strategic and competitive importance. Like any cultural change process, it will require patience, persistence, and consistency.

Other specific strategies for overcoming resistance include the following:

*Gather external knowledge.* Assign key engineering staff members to partner with 3D printer companies, software companies, universities, and national labs to find uses and develop new materials. Attend conferences and foster connections across traditional industry and market boundaries, learning about AM and industrial platform applications from a wide range of businesses that may have long-term implications for your company

*Experiment with use of AM in low-resistance areas.* Many companies have launched their additive manufacturing efforts by using 3D printers for simple projects: designing models and working prototypes; creating small-batch or customized parts as needed; and improving conventional processes by producing molds, dies, assembly guides, and tools for use in conventional manufacturing systems. As engineers and others become accustomed to using 3D printing for such purposes, their comfort level with the technology — and their enthusiasm about its potential — inevitably increases.

*Adopt 3D printing incrementally.* When you are ready to being using additive manufacturing as a tool for regular production, start with small batches of nonessential parts, then move to more essential parts, then mission-critical parts. As you pass each of these hurdles successfully, move on to subassemblies, then to printing entire products end to end.

*Train employees to evaluate all relevant economic factors.* Engineers are traditionally trained to examine the direct costs of manufacturing an item, excluding other factors they find difficult to measure. Make sure that your team members understand the full range of potential benefits and cost savings offered by 3D printing and consider all those factors when evaluating the economic and strategic implications of specific business decisions. In other words, avoid the engineer's blind spot, as discussed in Chapter 3.

Here's a simple example of how this can work. Deutsche Bahn AG is a mobility and logistics company whose core business is operating the German railway system. However, Deutsche Bahn is active in 130 countries around the world and runs transportation fleets with a total value of more than $1 billion. Naturally, maintaining this expensive capital investment is a complex job, which has led the corporation to investigate the possibility of using 3D printing to help with the production of replacement parts, tools, and other essential equipment. Deutsche Bahn began working with 3YOURMIND, a Berlin-based maker of 3D printing software, to examine its options.

The company's initial analyses suggested that 3D printing might not be economically viable for Deutsche Bahn. For example, it contracted with 3YOURMIND to produce a heat exchanger to be used on electric trains. Unfortunately, the results of the experiment were disappointing, since the devices cost more to be 3D printed than when mass-produced using traditional production methods. However, a second, closer look at the total circumstances exposed the fallacy in this calculation:

> A study conducted by Deutsche Bahn revealed that there was an annual requirement for this part of only 10 pieces a year . . . therefore mass production while initially more cost effective would incur future storage costs. Making the part using [an] SLS [selective laser sintering] 3D printing process is the proposed solution to eliminating these costs and moving to a Just in Time, warehousing style solution.

Engineers and managers who are familiar and comfortable with traditional manufacturing techniques — and perhaps dubious about additive manufacturing — are often prone to focusing purely on the obvious cost differences involved in a proposed alternative production method. As a result, they can overlook the impact of other changes that become apparent only when a bigger picture of the operation is included. You can avoid this mistake by making sure that the teams of employees working on possible implementation of additive manufacturing processes include experts on the full range of relevant activities — not just production but also maintenance, warehousing, shipping, customer service, and more.

*Seek a few quick wins.* Start your additive manufacturing program by identifying a handful of initiatives that can reduce costs and generate clear financial payoffs in the short run. These will attract attention, convert skeptics, create a sense of momentum, and generate resources that can be invested in more ambitious, longer-term projects. Then build out the business ecosystem in steps from there.

*Don't push the envelope too far too fast.* Looking too far into the future not only increases risk but also allows firms to miss out on short-term profits available through immediate innovation.

*Don't ask your technology leaders to drive the transition alone.* Technological transformation cannot be tasked to only your dedicated manufacturing or engineering teams. Managers from other departments must work along with the technological team to enable transformation across the board, and not only for certain parts of the business. Only then will successful digital transformation be possible.

*Get away from silo thinking.* AM will break down the barriers between functional departments — marketing, R&D, engineering, design, and manufacturing — as well as the walls between product divisions and partner companies. Leadership will be required to break down the conventional silos to make AM work effectively.

## Building Your Digital Business Ecosystem

In the emerging world of pan-industrials, where industry borders are dissolving and companies are increasingly adopting new technologies, developing new types of products and services, and entering new markets, you'll need to become accustomed to thinking about your business as part of a dynamic digital ecosystem, working with a range of partners who can help you maximize your strengths and compensate for any weaknesses.

Firms wishing to expedite the conversion to AM could speed the process by developing business ecosystems that push all their parts to the same stage of adoption at the same time. Then it will be possible to categorize the stage of adoption of an entire industry, and firms will be able to truly go AM in tandem for the bulk of their added value.

Most companies that have taken the plunge into the world of additive manufacturing are already working to build their own business ecosystems, whether or not they use that term explicitly. Here's a typical example: I earlier described how Adidas is building a chain of Speedfactories that will use the latest 3D printing technology to mass-produce customized running shoes. Because this is a pioneering project, it involves a series of complex technological and managerial challenges, requiring skills and resources beyond those that Adidas alone can provide. For this reason, the shoe manufacturer has enlisted a number of industry partners to help make the Speedfactory vision into a reality.

The two partners that are most crucial in this process are the 3D printing experts Carbon and the industrial giant Siemens. Carbon is working with Adidas to adapt its continuous liquid interface production (CLIP) printing technology to the demands of mass-producing a sports shoe midsole with varying properties at different points along the sole — essential to the high performance standards that competitive runners demand. Meanwhile, Siemens is applying its cloud-based MindSphere platform to connect the design, supply, manufacturing, and logistics processes for Adidas, using big-data analysis to maximize efficiencies, monitor quality, and control costs.

Other partners in the Speedfactory project include Oechsler Motion, Inc., a plastics fabrication specialist that is building the first two factories and will manage their day-to-day operations; the chemicals experts BASF, which developed the specialized elastomer that will be a key ingredient of the shoes; and other firms that are providing robotics and other production systems.

Of course, partnerships among companies in developing complex, expensive projects are nothing new. But in the new world of digitally managed, data-driven industrial ecosystems, the connections among companies will be exceptionally intimate and demanding. Choosing your partners wisely; working closely and continuously with them to develop a strong sense of engagement and trust; and forging legal and managerial systems that ensure an equitable sharing of costs, responsibilities, and benefits among all the partners — all of these challenges will be of particular importance.

The significance of these issues is even greater when you consider the fact that the alliances you enter into today may well prove to be the first steps toward the building of the pan-industrial federation or collective that may guide your business destinies tomorrow.

In the growing universe of business ecosystems, you'll also need to think long and hard about exactly how to position yourself in relation to partners and rivals. There are a variety of options, and choosing among them will require you to analyze your existing capabilities, the competitive threats you face, the kinds of outside partners you may be able to enlist as allies, and the best ways to take control of the market space you occupy or hope to occupy.

For example, you may perceive a growing threat from rival firms in your industry that will seek to use 3D printing to produce goods that compete with yours. You may be able to see the likelihood that, in the next few years, digital factories will enter your market offering manufacturing services to the very companies you compete against, thereby eliminating the advantages you could enjoy due to proprietary printing techniques, product designs, and other methodologies. If this is the case, it might be better to keep all of your 3D printing capabilities in-house and to develop or modify your printers in ways that your competitors don't. You could choose to focus on one or more selected value-adding components of the additive manufacturing process — for example, proprietary design software, a hybrid fabrication system, or a unique materials process — and use this as a bulwark against competitive inroads.

Perhaps the most important point is this: Don't focus narrowly on what additive manufacturing technology can do for your firm as it now operates. Instead, focus on how you hope to transform your business. A technology-focused strategy can achieve its full potential only when it is embedded in the broadest goals and values of the company. Senior executives and everyone else in the company must explore opportunities beyond those that are directly and obviously driven by technological change. The most valuable transformations will come from a host of technology *and* management decisions — decisions that redefine markets, reach vast new customer groups, enhance productivity, and multiply your organization's capabilities.

# THE PATH TO TOMORROW

*Four Phases in Adopting the New Technologies*

**THE SPREAD OF A** new technology like additive manufacturing through-out a particular industry — aerospace, construction, consumer elec-tronics, apparel, or whatever — generally proceeds in four distinct phases: *concept adoption, early adoption, mainstream adoption,* and *ubiquitous adoption.* (I've explained earlier that, in the near future, the pan-industrial revolution will blur many of the boundary lines that have traditionally separated industries. Here, however, I'm discussing the process by which AM, industrial platforms, and related technolo-gies will gradually infiltrate the world of business in the next few dec-ades. For the purposes of this discussion, the concept of distinct indus-tries remains relevant.)

History shows that a number of industries with similarities to 3D printing have progressed through the same four phases. These in-clude photocopying machines (which resemble certain forms of 3D printing in that they share the technology of using print heads), in-tegrated chip manufacturing (which shares with 3D printing the use of integrated manufacturing technologies, such as putting multiple components into one build process), and computer numerical con-trol laser cutters (which share with 3D printers the use of scaffold-ing and automation software that moves a tool around to make an object). These historical patterns suggest that there's good reason to believe that the adoption of additive manufacturing techniques will follow the same four-phase process that was seen in those prior in-dustries.

Table 12-1 provides an overview of the four technology adoption phases as they apply to additive manufacturing.

Let's go through these four phases, one by one, to see how the use of the technology changes from one phase to the next.

Phase 1, *concept adoption,* deals with proof-of-concepts and idea realization, including one-off and experimental production and improvements to traditional manufacturing using 3D printers. Here, companies begin to experiment with additive manufacturing. A few use it for a handful of processes, such as rapid prototyping and tooling, while others remain in a wait-and-see posture.

In this stage, users of 3D printing are sophisticated individuals who are eager to try a new, untested, and unproven technology; they are willing to work with software and machine controls that may be unrefined and difficult to master. What's more, the machines themselves are relatively simple, able to handle only basic printing functions with significant limitations on their flexibility and scope — for example, capable of working with only a few materials. Finally, only individual printers are available in this stage, making 3D printing fundamentally a one-off process used by individual craftspeople for single jobs rather than a production system with practical application to large-scale projects.

Phase 2, *early adoption,* is where a lot of AM currently lies. This is the early commercialization stage, which deals with process/product quality improvement, part-by-part conversion, low-quantity manufacturing using AM, niche markets, and early AM-ready materials development. Additive manufacturing now begins to be used for low-quantity, high-end, customized, or specialized parts and devices. Companies begin to use 3D printing for prototyping of new products and to make one-off or specialized replacement parts for existing devices.

Over time during this stage, the technology gradually begins to spread into mass-market products. In Phase 2, the 3D printers and the software that controls them both begin to show marked signs of technical improvement. Speed and costs both begin to fall. A wider array of materials can be handled by the newer printers; the speed and accuracy of printing increases; and the quality of 3D-printed items becomes finer and more consistent.

| TABLE 12-1. OVERVIEW—THE FOUR PHASES OF ADOPTION FOR ADDITIVE MANUFACTURING | | |
|---|---|---|
| | **1. CONCEPT ADOPTION** | **2. EARLY ADOPTION** |
| **Goal** | • Make ideas real to demonstrate that AM works | • Improve quality of AM products |
| **What's new** | • Uses of 3D printing capability move beyond models and prototypes | • Better-quality products<br>• Improved printer control software<br>• End-use parts production<br>• New materials |
| **Relationship to traditional manufacturing** | • AM is new and unproven<br>• Individuals testing the technology | • AM supplies parts for traditional manufacturing<br>• AM handles small-quantity parts and products |
| **Software and platform development** | • Designed for sophisticated users<br>• Printer drivers handle basic functions | • Easy-to-use interface<br>• Printer drivers offer sophisticated quality controls |
| **Business ecosystem development** | • Individual printers only<br>• Technology available to a few | • Individual printers now more reliable and cheaper<br>• More customers served |

The design tools available to control the printers also become more sophisticated, and the user interfaces supplied with both the printers and the software drivers become easier to use. As a result of all these changes, the number of people and companies using 3D printing grows, as does general awareness of and interest in the technology.

In Phase 3, *mainstream adoption,* AM has hit broad-based commer-

| 3. MAINSTREAM ADOPTION | 4. UBIQUITOUS ADOPTION |
|---|---|
| • Make AM faster, cheaper, more consistent | • Make AM equipment widely available |
| • Software to coordinate and control complex manufacturing and supply chains | • Printers available everywhere for use by professionals and consumers |
| • Industrial platforms grow to manage business processes at the enterprise and ecosystem levels | |
| • AI and machine learning | |
| • AM is an equal player | • Manufacturing moves out of the factory |
| • Hybrid systems combine AM with traditional manufacturing | • Distributed manufacturing is the norm |
| • New high-speed printers are developed | |
| • Factory control systems enable connectivity, automation, optimization | • Ecosystem-wide platforms |
| • Computational and generative design | • Ease of use, security, reliability, authentication, and IP protection become key issues |
| • Integrated business software packages | |
| • Enterprise and supply chain platforms | |
| • Printer networks | • Technology available to almost everyone via wider ecosystem |
| • Factory controls compete with traditional manufacturing at scale | |

cialization, and supply chains and business ecosystems are being built around AM. Mass-business models for AM come into play in this stage of adoption, bringing real-time improvements, integration, and optimization.

No longer relegated to making prototypes, small-quantity items, or parts for niche products, 3D printing begins to be used as a daily manufacturing method for ordinary products, gradually in larger and larger quantities. In the early part of the mainstream adoption phase, quantities of parts and products produced using AM run from 10,000 to 1,000,000 units. In the later part of this phase, the quantities produced run into the millions of units. Over time, traditional mass-manufacturing methods begin to give way to additive manufacturing. As the speed of 3D printers improves and the cost of buying and operating them continues to fall, additive manufacturing finds its way into more and more companies, taking on a growing number of production tasks.

Also in this phase, specialized techniques that enable additive manufacturing to produce unique forms of value — for example, mass modularization and mass segmentation — become generally popular. Companies begin to network their printers, sharing software controls across an array of devices and coordinating work output so as to improve efficiencies and reduce costs even further. They also begin to develop hybrid fabrication systems that enhance the capabilities of 3D printers by combining them with other technological tools, from traditional assembly-line systems to robotic arms, electronic sensors and monitors, lasers, and more.

Gradually, the software that controls 3D printers becomes connected with other management control systems, including systems for automating warehousing, shipping, logistics, inventory, purchasing, customer service, marketing, scheduling, and more. As a result of these developments, more and more functions begin to be automated, and industry disruptions by the new technologies start to be widespread.

As you can see, the concept of mainstream adoption is a rather complex one. In fact, *mainstream adoption* doesn't have just a single definition. The phrase can be used to refer to a number of different aspects of technology development and adoption, some of them overlapping. Here are seven of these definitions, listed in order from the least demanding definition to the definition that is broadest and therefore most difficult to achieve.

- Mainstream 1 = AM technologies, parts, and products in a given marketplace have achieved standards of quality and performance equivalent to those that characterize traditionally manufactured items.

- Mainstream 2 = A large number of parts and products in the marketplace are being made in small quantities using AM, though only at selected companies.
- Mainstream 3 = Faster production rates are making it possible for larger quantities of parts and products in the marketplace to be made using AM, though true mass production is not yet attainable.
- Mainstream 4 = Most companies in the marketplace have adopted AM technology to make parts or products, even if for small-quantity production.
- Mainstream 5 = Most customers/buyers in a specific market, segment, or niche within the marketplace have accepted, purchased, or used parts or products made by AM.
- Mainstream 6 = AM parts and products have achieved significant market share, absolute revenue, or profit level in a specific market, segment, or niche within the marketplace, though not in the marketplace as a whole.
- Mainstream 7 = AM parts and products have achieved universal adoption by virtually all manufacturers and/or consumers or end users within the marketplace.

You can decide for yourself which of these definitions is best suited to your industry. You'll likely find that different segments in a particular market are moving at different speeds. And you may find that, in a given market, several of the changes described in these definitions will occur around the same time.

In Phase 4, *ubiquitous adoption,* printers and AM are omnipresent — everywhere, like electricity. With pan-industrial markets becoming dominant, AM systems are available in locations all over the world, outside of factories and printer farms. Distributed, localized manufacturing is the norm within a market. At the same time, 3D printers for consumer use will be stationed at millions of locations, including restaurants, bakeries, malls, schools, offices, and homes. For both consumer and industrial ubiquity to exist, the quantities produced will run into the tens of millions of units.

In both the mainstream and ubiquitous adoption phases, additive manufacturing becomes the dominant production technology. Digital manufacturing and industrial platforms are now providing real-time controls to maximize efficiencies and improve the productivity of entire corporations. The platforms also enable connections not only among many divisions and departments of the organization but also with outside suppliers, designers, distributors, and customers. The power of these ecosystem-wide platforms allows corporations to automate more and more of their managerial-level strategic decisions, optimizing their operations in real time. In these phases, large numbers of companies have now made 3D printing and allied technologies part of their core competence. The few companies that refuse to shift to AM almost inevitably fail. Only in the ubiquitous phase are 3D printers positioned almost everywhere.

In the mainstream phase, large-scale networks of printers will be controlled by a pan-industrial firm or collective with strong industrial platforms to ensure schedule coordination, consistency, quality, safety, and IP protection.

By contrast, the ubiquitous phase requires some degree of autonomy of the printers, such as a large maker community. However, the ubiquitous phase is not likely to be reached in most product markets for many decades, if ever. This is in contrast to the widespread early vision of the future of 3D printing, which idealized small or individually owned firms acting as independent makers, bringing much more creativity to the world, granting freedom from having bosses, and bringing "democracy" to the manufacturing world. According to this vision, which I've dubbed the maker myth, the ubiquitous phase was the inevitable long-term result of the spread of AM. As I've made clear in this book, I think that fundamental economic and strategic logic makes this unlikely.

## Where Does Your Industry Stand?

The time will come when the boundaries that now define different industries will be largely forgotten. But as of today, most companies are still viewed as participants in various industries — and those industries are passing through the four phases at different rates. The point of transition from one phase to the next is really not a single point in time, but rather a window in time through which different uses or markets will move.

As of late 2017, many industries have moved into the early adoption phase and will be hitting the mainstream adoption phase within the next year or so. Potential entrants are currently positioning for the mainstream adoption phase, while incumbent firms are making money in the early adoption phase. Some users, however, are ahead of or lagging behind the curve.

In Figures 12-1 through 12-7, I'll map the current status of several

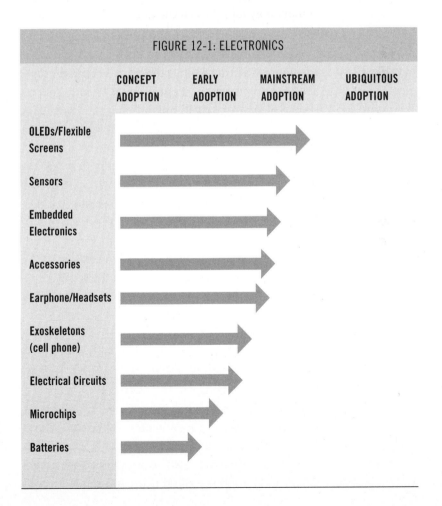

FIGURE 12-1: ELECTRONICS

major industries, showing where various segments of those industries now stand in the four phases of adoption.

The phase development of the electronics industry is now being led in part by the mass development of OLED screens using inkjet printing. Kateeva, a startup from California, has developed the "YIELD-jet process" to manufacture screens using AM. Companies including Samsung and LG are onboard with this manufacturing process and are in the process of switching over from traditional OLED manufacturing processes.

A number of other companies are pushing the development of AM to create fully functional electronics that require little or no assembly. Optomec is using its aerosol jet printing technology to print all kinds of sensors and embedded electronics. Optomec worked with GE to print sensors onto turbine blades among other uses, and with Lite-On to print antennae onto millions of smartphones. Among modular electronics firms, Nascent Objects was acquired in 2016 by Facebook, whose plans to use the business are still unknown. Nano Dimension has developed an inkjetting process to produce multilayer printed circuit boards (PCBs) and other sorts of electrical circuits, while Voxel8 is printing conformal electronics onto various substrates. The U.S. Department of Defense is evaluating the use of MultiFab, a 3D printer that can use up to ten materials at once, embedding circuits and sensors directly into a product — for example, the control unit in a guided missile.

Some electronics fields, like batteries and micro-electronics (chips, storage devices, sensors), are still in the development stage, with multiple universities across the world and research organizations working on different technologies to realize these products.

As of late 2017, the automotive industry is still largely in the early phases of adopting AM. While major companies, including Ford and GM, have been using AM to prototype thousands of parts, end-use production hasn't yet reached significant quantity and remains limited to niche segments like luxury or concept vehicles. Daimler is using AM to produce spare parts for its line of trucks, while Rolls Royce is printing interior components.

Some startup companies in the automotive space are pushing developments further. Local Motors pioneered using AM to print vehic-

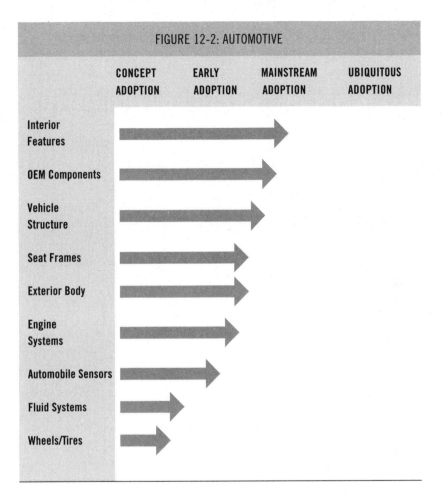

ular bodies and then retro-fit engine, transmission, and other systems into the car. The company is now focusing the bulk of its attention on its Olli shuttle bus, which uses a 3D-printed shell and integrates applications based on the Internet of Things to enable operation as a self-driving vehicle. Divergent 3D, a startup from California, is using AM to manufacture the nodes and bars needed to create the structure of vehicles — think of Hasbro's Tinkertoys, but much larger and stronger, built with composite materials rather than wood. The company has tied up with France's PSA Group to design and develop the next generation of automobiles.

Tire companies like Michelin and Goodyear have developed concepts of future tires and wheels that are completely revolutionary, but these are unlikely to be commercialized for at least the next five to ten years. Unlike the aerospace industry, where lightweight, complex parts are being manufactured for engines, turbines, and fuel systems, the automotive industry has yet to realize the advantages of AM for comparable applications.

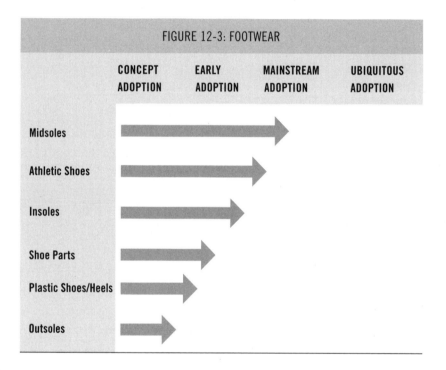

The big shoe manufacturers are all adapting to AM in various ways. Nike, New Balance, and Under Armour have all released versions of athletic shoes that have one or more parts produced with 3D printing. Jabil has been testing out different prototypes for insoles, midsoles, and outsoles, and is working with multiple companies to develop parts for shoes. A couple of startups, like Wiiv Wearables and Feetz, manufacture custom insoles based on 3D-scanned data, and sell 3D shoes in small quantities. Most notable is Adidas's plan to work with Carbon to mass-produce midsoles for its next generation of shoes. According to

Carbon, more than a hundred thousand shoes will be produced with 3D printing during 2019, followed by millions after that.

In the fashion industry, designers are working on 3D printing all sorts of heels and plastic shoes as concepts. One American AM service bureau reports that it received in 2017 an order for 300,000 midsoles from a major clothing manufacturer for delivery by the end of the year.

A significant amount of AM development has come from the medical industry. Companies like EnvisionTEC have enabled the manufacturing of hearing aid shells using a version of AM called digital shell modeling, and Align Technology developed Invisalign, a clear dental brace using SLA 3D printing—two of the earliest successes for mass customization using AM.

More recently, Luxexcel developed its line of 3D-printed optical lenses and is working with labs and retailers to establish a printing

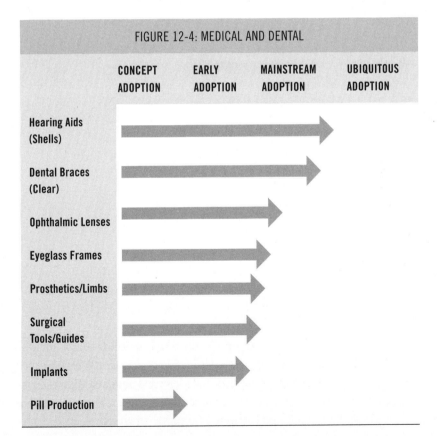

FIGURE 12-4: MEDICAL AND DENTAL

platform. Service bureaus like Materialise offer customized services for eyeglass frames in a variety of materials from plastics to titanium. Stryker has made huge investments into 3D printing and has gotten FDA approval for a range of titanium implants. Surgical guides and tools are being manufactured using AM by a number of companies, while prosthetic limbs are being 3D printed in all corners of the world. 3D-printed pills are slowly gaining acceptance, and FDA approval shouldn't be more than a couple years away.

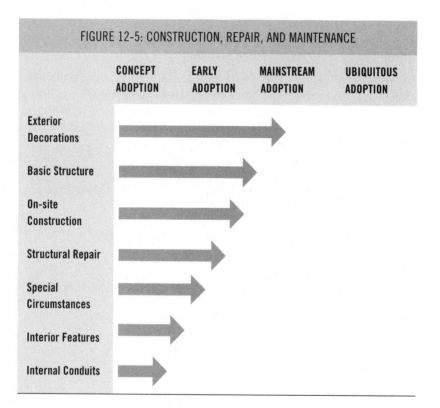

FIGURE 12-5: CONSTRUCTION, REPAIR, AND MAINTENANCE

Architecture and construction are gaining recognition as high-impact industries in terms of AM adoption. Basic exterior design elements like pavilions, sculptures, and bridges are being 3D printed using technologies like contour crafting with construction materials like ceramics and cement. The Chinese company Winsun has used a version of the contour crafting process to construct all sorts of buildings not just in China, but around the world. Dubai has partnered with Winsun to 3D print offices and homes, and wants 30 percent of the city to be 3D printed by 2030, while Saudi Arabia has contracted with Winsun to 3D print over 1.5 million homes.

Apis Cor, a Russian construction company, has developed a mobile 3D printer that can build a house in less than twenty-four hours. On a different front, several research labs and companies are developing robotic solutions to perform structural repairs either with mini-robots or drones that can climb structures, or with larger 3D printers that use robotic arms.

The main benefits of AM for the construction industry are speed, complexity, and cost, which is why external structures, decorations, repairs, and other such features are viable with AM over internal features. However, 3D printing has not yet proved useful for non-decorative internal features, and some essential items like windows, pipes, doors, and appliances are still being traditionally manufactured.

Heavy industries like aerospace, oil and gas, nuclear, and maritime are all either already in or close to the mainstream phase of AM adoption. With its reliance on low-quantity, high-complexity parts, the aerospace industry is one of the largest investors in AM, led by companies like GE, Boeing, Airbus, and Lockheed Martin. Successful examples of aerospace parts made using AM include GE's fuel nozzle and turboprop engine, Boeing's massive wing trim tool, and Airbus's engine components.

Airbus is now working with Autodesk to use AM to build the next generation of aircraft interiors, including cabin partitions, seats, and other functional elements. Optomec is working closely with Lockheed Martin and GE to integrate 3D-printed sensors and other electronics, and is also working with GE to install these microsensors on turbine blades. Siemens has announced the production of gas turbine blades using AM, while Autodesk is working with the port of Rotterdam in the Netherlands to perform real-time maritime repairs.

The U.S. Department of Defense is investing heavily in AM technologies and has worked on several related projects, ranging from 3D-printed machine guns and submarine hulls to digitally controlled drones and even robotic soldiers. Those robotic devices have already

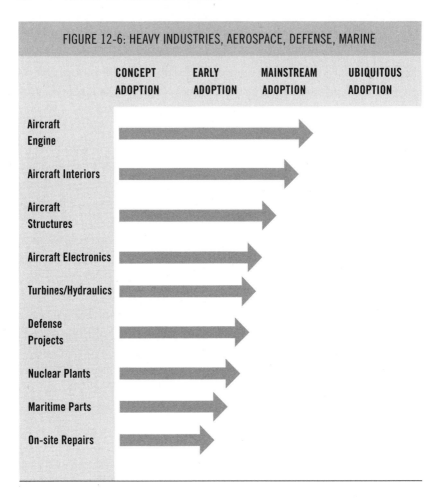

FIGURE 12-6: HEAVY INDUSTRIES, AEROSPACE, DEFENSE, MARINE

been deployed on battlefields in the form of unmanned machines designed to find and deactivate enemy bombs, mines, and other explosive devices. Other military robots with varied capabilities are under development, and Defense Department officials have already begun developing principles for their use in warfare — for example, explicit limits on the ability of autonomous fighting machines to identify and attack targets without approval from human officers.

So far, the use of AM in the food industry has been limited. There are broadly two ways to 3D print food. The first is extrusion or binder jetting, in which different ingredients can be printed and dishes pre-

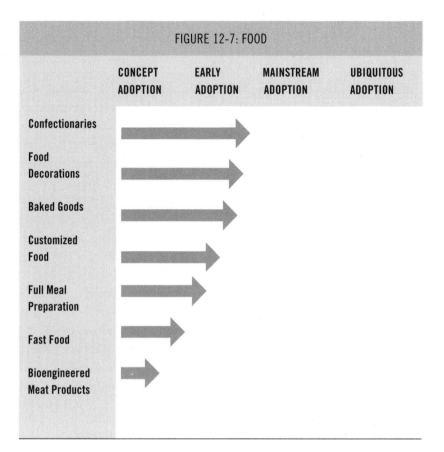

FIGURE 12-7: FOOD

| | CONCEPT ADOPTION | EARLY ADOPTION | MAINSTREAM ADOPTION | UBIQUITOUS ADOPTION |
|---|---|---|---|---|
| Confectionaries | | | | |
| Food Decorations | | | | |
| Baked Goods | | | | |
| Customized Food | | | | |
| Full Meal Preparation | | | | |
| Fast Food | | | | |
| Bioengineered Meat Products | | | | |

pared. The second method is by creating food-safe molds, after which food is traditionally prepared.

As I explained earlier, Hershey is using AM to custom-produce unique chocolate confections. 3D Systems developed the ChefJet Pro, which produces all sorts of edible confectionaries by printing in sugar. Natural Machines, a Spanish company, released its food printer called the Foodini, which uses prepackaged food capsules to print customized food items from pasta to cake. A pizza chain in New York has developed a prototype pizza printer that can print a single pie in less than four minutes. Several research laboratories are working with developing bioengineered meats by 3D printing so-called meat inks. Finally, pop-up restaurants are experimenting with "experience events" where the food, cutlery, and decorations are all 3D printed, but so far these are limited to one-offs.

*Patterns of industry adoption.* Based on the above data, we see that each industry has a couple of areas that have reached mainstream adoption, and may even reach ubiquitous adoption in the next decade. However, it's often difficult to characterize an entire industry as being in a particular phase, as there tend to be particular applications that will take longer, or are stuck in an exploratory research stage. There are some industries — food and medicine, for example — in which progress is slowed by the need for regulatory approvals, while other industries are slowed down by the sheer scale of production or the scope of their investment in traditional manufacturing.

The pattern indicates that standardized products that are mass produced in bulk with no recognizable customization involved are likely to be slowest to switch over to AM (with a few exceptions, such as OLED screens and shoe midsoles). Soon, software that integrates design with printing will help some high-quantity industries to switch to AM by combining parts so well that products with thousands of parts can be greatly simplified, drastically reducing the assembly costs. Over time, many more products will be reimagined and developed specifically for manufacturing using AM.

Where on the four-phase curve is your industry today? More important, where is your company? Is it leading the pack, running with it, or lagging behind? Answering these questions can help you decide what you need to do next to ensure your company isn't left behind as the revolution gains momentum.

## Matching Your Strategy to the Phase

I recommend that firms use different strategies at each of the four phases of adoption. These strategies may involve either radical or incremental changes in the business system, and either radical or incremental changes in product design. That creates the four-box matrix shown in Table 12-2.

As the table shows, in the concept adoption phase (Phase 1), the strategies tend to involve only incremental changes in both product design and business systems. In the early adoption phase (Phase 2), the strategies tend to involve significant change in product design, but not the business system. In the mainstream adoption phase (Phase 3), business models tend to involve significant change in both product design and business system. Finally, in the ubiquitous adoption phase (Phase 4), business models tend to involve significant changes in the business system, but not the product design.

TABLE 12-2: MATCHING YOUR STRATEGY TO THE ADOPTION PHASE

| | | BUSINESS SYSTEM CHANGE | |
|---|---|---|---|
| | | **Incremental Change** | **Radical Change** |
| **PRODUCT DESIGN CHANGE** | **Radical Change** | PHASE 2:<br>EARLY ADOPTION | PHASE 3:<br>MAINSTREAM ADOPTION |
| | **Incremental Change** | PHASE 1:<br>CONCEPT ADOPTION | PHASE 4:<br>UBIQUITOUS ADOPTION |

Why do the recommended strategies differ so greatly from one phase to the next? The difference in the unit cost of production via AM as compared with traditional manufacturing (TM) explains a lot.

In the concept adoption phase, AM unit costs are generally significantly higher than TM unit costs. As a result, AM is used only for prototyping, tooling, hobbies, and activities that are expressions of creativity and fun. The objects printed must have some value that can't be quantified easily; otherwise, the cheaper TM methods would be the technology of choice. Thus, companies in this phase will generally want to take a wait-and-see attitude toward AM, using it for selected purposes and learning more about the technology for possible future applications.

In the early adoption phase, AM unit costs are generally slightly higher than TM unit costs. Therefore, firms adopt AM if the printed products have some special value that users will pay extra for, or if the quantity to be produced is very low, which makes TM costlier than normal. If the AM unit cost falls to within 15 to 20 percent of the TM unit cost, then some firms will adopt AM in order to enjoy the benefits of flexibility as well as faster, easier, and cheaper switchovers. This phase sees many companies converting to AM on a part-by-part basis or to serve specific niche markets, sometimes using service bureaus to outsource production.

In the mainstream adoption phase, AM unit costs are lower than TM unit costs thanks to many improvements in AM production methods. Now AM can begin to replace TM in all sorts of situations. Now companies begin to convert entire systems to become AM-centric, seeking the advantages to be gained from the combination of AM, industrial platforms, and related technologies. Depending on the specific markets, customers, and products they focus on, companies will experiment with various AM-centric business models, including mass customization, mass variety, mass segmentation, mass complexity, mass modularization, and mass standardization.

In the ubiquitous adoption phase, AM unit costs are much lower than TM unit costs because of distributed manufacturing and the many savings and efficiencies it produces. In this phase, companies will have dramatically reshaped their supply chains, abandoning traditional Fordist factories for smaller, flexible, localized production facilities. Various business operations will merge — for example, product design, manufacturing, distribution, and marketing will often become parts of a single, complex process, engaged in by a large team of people with many varied capabilities.

These descriptions, of course, are painted with a broad brush. Details will vary greatly from one company to another. But they're intended to provide you with a general context in which to consider some of the strategic options your company may want to employ depending on the particular phase of adoption you currently occupy.

## Timing the Transitions: Factors to Consider in Developing Your Phase Strategy

Once you've decided where in the four-phase curve your industry, as well as your company, now stands, you can begin to consider your strategic options in regard to transitions from your current phase to the next. The timing options include the following possibilities.

*Stand pat.* Firms can choose to stay in their current phase of AM adoption (concept, early, mainstream, ubiquity) and not make any headway into moving to another phase. In certain circumstances, it may be feasible to remain competitive and profitable while staying in a particular phase when much of your industry is moving on to the next stage. For example, a company may choose to stand pat due to lack of consumer demand or government regulations that discourage technological change related to manufacturing.

Standing pat is practical and reasonable when you can carve out a sustainable position in your current phase. For example:

- Any market where the demand characteristics (fragmentation, velocity of change, need for complex products, and so on) stay the same, so there is no need to change.
- Any market when technology has stopped progressing, so there is no ability to move to the next phase, or you lack the financial ability to fund next-phase technology and business model development.
- Any firm that does not desire to be an industry leader but prefers to stay in its current niche and therefore feels no need to move to the next phase.
- Any firm that lacks the resources or ability to make the jump may decide to milk its position and, at the end of the day, sell its customer list and facilities to a successor. Sometimes the net present value of this approach to stockholders is higher than planning to stay in business for the long term.
- Any situation where the company is planning to concede the next generation, but prepare for the generation after that (see the leapfrogging and alternating leadership strategies below). In this case, the stand-pat strategy is only temporary.

Examples of industries where the stand-pat approach currently appears viable might include Swiss mechanical watches like those marketed by Rolex; musical instruments such as grand pianos made by Steinway and Sons; automobile tires, where car manufacturers are reluctant to take on the liability risks associated with product change; and mobile phones, where leading producers seem content to skip a generation and prepare for the next.

*Watch and wait.* Firms can cease or slow their AM development until there is enough evidence of success in the next phase. The advantage of this approach lies in the opportunity to learn from the mistakes of the first movers. However, to avoid getting left behind, these firms must have the resources prepositioned in place to enable a fast-follower strategy once they've decided to flip the switch.

*Time pacing.* This involves planning smooth, rhythmic transitions between phases based on close observation of technology generations and the speed at which your organization is prepared to move. Your company sets its own pace for shifts in strategy, seeking to optimize the time between transitions to keep up with the competition while also having enough time to earn a decent return on investment.

*Sporadic phase jumps.* This involves moving into the next phase at uneven intervals. It has the advantage of surprise, but the potential disadvantage of being behind the pack or too far ahead of the curve at times.

*Preemption.* This involves jumping forward to the next phase. The goal is to seize the first advantage, to stay on top of the technology, to stun rivals, and to force them into a game of catch-up.

*Trapping competition.* This involves moving forward just before the competition catches up in the current phase, forcing them to follow you before they are ready. At the same time, you preplan the introduction of an upgrade in your strategy just before competitors catch up to you in the next phase, leaving them in a position of weakness.

*Leapfrogging.* This involves jumping straight to the last phase (or at least two phases ahead) as part of a long-term strategy. This is a high-risk, high-reward move that can either result in the firm being a leader or end up having to cut its losses.

*Alternating leadership.* Some firms preempt the next phase, then skip a phase, deliberately giving up leadership in the second phase in favor of milking their original preemptive move as long as possible. If this is managed adroitly, it can provide the resources and profits needed to win in the longer term, despite conceding the short-term game.

*Continuous improvement within a phase.* This approach is used when you recognize that the transition to the next phase is likely to be fairly distant in time. It involves pursuing a series of incremental improvement in the current phase, continually seizing advantages until rivals are exhausted by your pace and persistence.

Of course, firms are free to mix and match the timing options listed above. A keen understanding of the complexities of your industry's current phase is essential. At any given moment, an entire industry may be on the verge of changing from one phase to the next.

However, the phase change process is often variable, inconsistent, and confusing. Some segments of a particular industry may change a phase sooner than others, and the phase changes may appear to be consistently and regularly paced or very sporadic. In some industries, suppliers may advance to the next phase before original equipment manufacturers are ready to make the plunge; in other industries, the opposite may be true. These and other variations mean that it may be difficult to give one clear answer to the question "What phase is your industry in?" It also means that there is often a complex set of phase-strategy decisions that company managers must make.

Generally speaking, the choice of timing strategy depends upon a broad array of factors. The most important is the nature of the competitive advantage you currently enjoy or hope to create. This may include such possibilities as improved manufacturing efficiency, lower production costs, exceptional product innovation, customization or flexibility capabilities, streamlined or shortened supply chains, accelerated speed to market, control of unique, proprietary intellectual property, deepened customer intimacy, prepositioning to capture non-customers, network effects, information asymmetries, a powerful business ecosystem, and so on. Depending on the nature of your business, its current strengths and weaknesses, and your competitive situation, some of these possible competitive advantages are more relevant and practical than others. And your ability to create and exploit any of these advantages will depend, in turn, on the phase of the AM revolution that your company is in.

Thus, having a deep understanding of the nature of your phase strategy, the kinds of competitive advantages that make you successful, and the advantages you may need to develop for continued success is the first big step in thinking about how you want to respond to the current phase status of your industry.

Other relevant factors that you should take into account as you ponder the phase and timing strategy choices you face include the following:

*Technological and strategic developments driven by other companies.* Your company's phase strategies may be affected by the technologies and timing strategies being developed by 3D printer manufacturers, software providers, or competing firms. The impact may include such factors as cost reductions, new material availabilities, increased ease of use, improved reliability, and other considerations. For example, you may find yourself in a position where additive manufacturing is somewhat less than optimal for most of your current production needs — but where a 10 percent improvement in manufacturing speed and a 5 percent reduction in unit materials cost could tip the balance and make 3D printing a viable option. If that's your status, you'll want to closely monitor technological developments in your field and be ready to move quickly once the tipping point arrives.

*The level of your commitment to current or previous phases of technology and phase strategies.* The greater the amount of your capital you have sunk into existing machinery, software, and the like, the greater the commitment to the existing strategy. Inflexibilities and lack of exit options may keep you stuck in the current phase, and increase the perceived risk in making the leap to new methodologies. Escalating one-upmanship, or fear of losing "face" or respect or power, may force you to stick with the current strategy.

For the mature company, timing also depends on the type of prior manufacturing investments that the firm has made, because mature companies typically have made many irreversible commitments in specialized equipment that can't be used for any other purpose. The fear of writing off these assets and showing a big decrease in profits often delays a mature company's movement to the next phase. But as I've shown, there are some strategies that make it easier to move to the next phase, such as integrating AM without significant disruption to existing operations.

Firms like Senvol (an AM analytics company) have built databases that cover most AM systems and materials currently available, and offer recommendations based on over thirty different parameters, making it easier for companies to select AM for mainstream or early adoption. Senvol also helps firms to understand costs, benefits, printer choice, and savings with new AM systems. One of the advantages to deploying an AM strategy is that the up-front capital costs are much lower than with traditional production machinery. That allows firms to spend less in the present and to reallocate AM equipment when transitions are happening. The flexibility allows you to invest at the last minute — for example, when production has to be ramped up, or when new capabilities are needed. AM does away with the tooling costs, mold design, prototyping costs, and inventory costs, meaning that the only up-front costs are machinery and materials. This allows firms to accelerate the timing of movement to the next phase.

*The speed and predictability of the phase-changing efforts by rivals, suppliers, and customers, as well as by the scientific/engineering community.* The technological and strategic moves you would need to make in order to advance to the next phase may vary widely depending on circumstances. For instance, there may be an analogous or related industry that has already made a major move to additive manufacturing that could provide clear guidance as to the best sequence of steps for you to follow — in which case, a jump to the next phase might be relatively risk-free. In other cases, specific industry requirements might make the move to the next phase unusually complicated and tricky, which suggests that a prolonged period of study and planning might be appropriate before you decide to take the plunge.

*Your company's ability to manage phase changes.* This ability may be affected by factors such as internal resistance, capital resources, intellectual property ownership, team coherence, your existing skill bank, and so on. Every company has a unique combination of characteristics that determines its relative ability to master technological and organizational changes. Before making a decision about whether and how to

embrace a phase change, consider your company's preparedness in relation to a range of relevant factors. You may decide that it's important
to devote time and resources to developing your organizational capacities to absorb and master change *prior to* launching a phase-change
initiative; otherwise, an unsuccessful effort to transform your company's production processes could lead to a backlash that will make future change efforts even more difficult.

## Go Big or Go Home

A final, crucial lesson to be gleaned from the experiences of companies that are currently pioneering the transformation of manufacturing through digital technologies was articulated in an August 2017
interview by Harold Sears, a technical expert at Ford. Sears warns
companies that are about to embark on the 3D printing journey *not* to
simply buy a few new machines and plug them into their existing processes — at least, not if they hope to reap all the potential benefits of
the new technologies:

> Have they really re-thought and redesigned the parts to take advan-
> tage of the strengths of additive manufacturing or are they just try-
> ing to produce the same part they were using with injection mold-
> ing[?]; if they are, it's probably not going to see the benefits they
> would see if it was completely re-thought.

A similar conclusion was reached by researchers at the consulting
firm McKinsey when they examined the financial results achieved by
a range of companies that had made significant investments in digital strategies. Some firms enjoyed highly positive impacts on revenues
and profitability as a result of their digital investments, while others
did not. McKinsey's analysis found that the difference lay in the degree of boldness with which the digital strategy was implemented:

> The research-survey findings, taken together, amount to a clear
> mandate to act decisively, whether through the creation of new dig-
> ital businesses or by reinventing the core of today's strategic, oper-

ational, and organizational approaches . . . We also confirmed that winners invest more, and more broadly and boldly, than other companies do.

Follow the advice of Harold Sears and the McKinsey researchers. Rather than simply swapping a 3D printer for the traditional manufacturing tools you might have used in the past, take the time to really examine the broad array of benefits that the new technologies offer — and look for ways to redesign your entire business to take full advantage of *all* those benefits.

Today's smartest business leaders aren't waiting for all the details of the manufacturing revolution to reveal themselves. By the time that happens, it will be too late. They can see clearly enough that 3D printing and the other aspects of the manufacturing revolution will change the way almost all products are designed, made, bought, and delivered — and they are already working on their response. They are learning all they can about the new technologies, taking the first steps in the redesign of their manufacturing systems, and envisioning the roles their companies can plan in the emerging ecosystems of digital production. In short, they are beginning to make the many layers of decisions that will lead to lasting competitive advantage in the new world of additive manufacturing. I urge you to join them, and go big or go home.

# EPILOGUE

## *The Future Belongs to You*

IT'S A NATURAL human tendency to react with skepticism to extreme claims about technology. Enthusiastic researchers, speculative writers, and promoters with a financial interest have all been known to make extravagant predictions about near-future breakthroughs that have turned out to be based on little or nothing. Thus, it's easy to mock some of the wilder fantasies we read about with snarky rejoinders like "Where are the flying cars we've been promised since the 1930s?" Or "Solar power is the energy source of the future—and it always will be."

Forecasts of technological marvels do deserve to be taken with a grain of salt. But it's easy to forget the many examples of mind-blowing predictions that have actually come true. In the nineteenth century, early practitioners of science fiction like Jules Verne and H. G. Wells imagined wonders like submarines, armored tanks, radio, television, and space flight decades before they existed—and in some cases before researchers had even begun efforts to develop them. Many other technological advances were first depicted in works of speculative fiction: credit cards in Edward Bellamy's utopian novel *Looking Backward* (1888), radar in Hugo Gernsback's *Ralph 124C 41+* (1914), genetic engineering in Aldous Huxley's *Brave New World* (1932), communication satellites in Arthur C. Clarke's *2001: A Space Odyssey* (1951), and virtual reality in William Gibson's *Neuromancer* (1984). A time traveler who visited our own time from, say, 1850 might well conclude that we are living in an era when science fiction has been largely transmuted into fact . . . despite the fact that flying cars are still few and far between.

The conversion of scientific fantasies into technological realities continues today. In the 1960s, the TV series *Star Trek* offered a smorgasbord of fantastic devices that have since become commonplace, from handheld phones to tablet computers. One of the marvels promised by *Star Trek* was a "food synthesizer" used to convert atoms and molecules into meals for consumption onboard the interstellar spaceship where much of the action took place. According to the writers of the series, this device would be developed in the twenty-third century. A century later, it was superseded by the "replicator" capable of more broadly reassembling microscopic materials to create a wide variety of objects, not just food.

It's not hard to see the similarities between the *Star Trek* replicator and today's additive manufacturing technologies. Of course, unlike the replicator, a 3D printer has limitations in terms of the kinds of products it can produce as well as the raw materials it employs. But then again, the timetable that the writers of *Star Trek* originally envisioned gives today's researchers another three hundred years to overcome those limitations. Personally, I'd hesitate to bet against them.

Perhaps you've found yourself balking at some of the more amazing technological forecasts I've offered in these pages — fleets of fighter jets cranked out in tiny facilities located anywhere; bridges, apartment houses, and office towers synthesized by fleets of mobile printers; customized prosthetics that enhance human capabilities; living tissues and organs generated by 3D printers; and factories and entire companies run almost without human intervention by ultrasmart, ever-learning computers.

If some of these notions seem incredible, think about the track record that scientists and engineers have compiled of turning yesterday's dreams into today's realities — and consider the fact that most of the technologies required are already in existence. The real question is not whether such science-fiction visions will become full-fledged realities, but *when*.

Even more interesting — and more difficult to forecast — will be the social, economic, and political consequences of the technological developments I've predicted.

Many of the classic science-fiction writers I've mentioned believed that the technologies they foretold—from atom bombs to cyberspace—would completely transform human society. Many imagined a resulting future world that was either perfect (like Bellamy's socialist utopia) or, more often, a nightmarish hellscape (like Huxley's *Brave New World*).

History suggests that the long-term impact of technological advances is generally much more complex than this. Most new tools and devices have both positive and negative effects, and human beings are so complicated that the full range of responses to new technologies is usually impossible to predict. None of the science-fiction writers from the 1880s to the 1950s who spun tales of space travel imagined that humankind would create a spectacularly successful program to land explorers on the moon in 1969 . . . and then abandon lunar flight for the next several decades simply due to lack of interest! Yet that's more or less what happened. Humans are hard to figure.

I don't doubt that the technological revolution I've outlined in this book—in which additive manufacturing, other digital tools of production, and the power of industrial platforms will thoroughly transform how most products are designed, made, produced, marketed, and sold—will have its share of unpredictable consequences. My imagined future world dominated by pan-industrial titans, vying to defend and expand spheres of influence in a superconvergent economy with few impermeable boundaries, may not fully come to pass. Instead, the pan-industrial revolution may end up taking a somewhat different shape than the one I expect. If so, I for one will be fascinated to observe how the world to come will unfold—and to have my eyes opened to whatever remarkable developments it will bring.

If it turns out that I've read the tea leaves wrong, the reasons will likely lie with decisions being made by business leaders today. As I've said before, the best way to predict the future is to create it. The future that our children and grandchildren will inherit is being created now—by corporate moguls, entrepreneurs, research scientists, engineers, software developers, and other visionaries who are exploring the amazing capabilities of the new manufacturing technologies and imagining new ways to use them.

It's my hope that the ideas, stories, and predictions in this book have inspired you to join them in their quest to build the amazing future that awaits our species.

# ACKNOWLEDGMENTS

First and foremost, I would like to thank Rick Wolff, my editor at HMH. His faith, his intellectual contributions, and his steady, calm patience during the writing process made this book a success. He encouraged me to go after the big picture, which I really wanted to do. And his enthusiasm for the subject motivated me by reaffirming my enthusiasm for the vision I laid out in this book. I also want to thank Rosemary McGuinness for all of her great assistance as well.

Carol Franco, my literary agent, helped reframe the book proposal and bring it to the attention of the right people within the publishing world. Without her reframing the theme of this book, it would have been nothing more than a technical guide.

In addition, I would like to thank Matt Slaughter, dean of the Tuck School of Business, and Richard Sansing, associate dean for faculty at the Tuck School of Business, for their patient financial support of the research and writing phases of this book.

There is a whole other group of contributors that I want to thank as well. They have become highly valued parts of my writing ecosystem.

Karl Weber's intellectual, writing, and editorial contributions made this book what it is. Without him, the readers would never be able to follow what I was awkwardly trying to say, nor would the broad themes of the book have been so well presented. His yeoman's efforts saved the day when the chips were down, and I was privileged to work with such a great mind and masterful researcher/writer/editor. He was like having a very smart, challenging mentor that kept me on track.

Speaking of being privileged to work with great minds, John Landry's concept development and collaboration on my articles in the *Harvard Business Review* and the *MIT/Sloan Management Review* were nothing short of inspirational. His constant questions and quiet, careful ruminations sharpened my vision and predictions, and he helped create ideas that became the basis of large portions of this book.

Also in this top tier, I want to thank Nihal Velpanur and Prince Verma, two of my most trusted and insightful research assistants. They both are graduates from Dartmouth's engineering and management program, earning the highly sought-after master's in engineering management degree from the Thayer School of Engineering. They both worked on this book for over two years, pulling all-nighters with me to get chapters and white papers done on time. They gathered facts and synthesized them under my direction, as well as provided independent and insightful ideas to the project. Prince's focus has been on software and industrial platforms, while Nihal's has been additive manufacturing, new designs, and business practices associated with additive manufacturing. Nihal has stayed on after graduation to work with me full-time, and Prince has continued part-time. I think there are no others in this world with equivalent knowledge and skills with whom I would rather work.

For stylistic and writing advice, I want to thank Stuart Crainer and Des Dearlove, cofounders of the Thinkers50. They reviewed a finished manuscript for writing style, length, density, jargon, realism, clarity, logical flow, and overall market appeal. While they were not involved in the development of the book's content, their advice helped us make this book much more readable. Thanks to them for the feedback. It was really useful.

Numerous executives filled me or my team in on the business side of additive manufacturing, industrial platforms, and ecosystems. These executives helped us track down the facts when they were hidden or hazy. We learned so much from them that I will never forget the importance of their generosity with their time and their expert contributions to my thinking about the future of business.

Not including several people who wanted to remain anonymous, these executives include: John Alpine, VP — Global Software, 3D Systems; Alan Amling, Vice President — Strategy, UPS; Doug Baker, Chairman and CEO, Ecolab; Matej Balazic, CEO, BALMAR Company; Dan T. Bane, Chairman and CEO, Trader Joe's; Jim Bartlett, VP — General Manager of Red Eye, now folded into Stratasys Direct Manufacturing; John P. Bilbrey, then President and CEO, Hershey; Matt Blodgett, Managing Director, Vector Capital; Megan Bozeman, Director — New Business Engineering, 3D Systems; Charlie Branshaw, CEO, Matrix APA; Patrick Carey, VP — Strategic Accounts, Stratasys; John Carr, VP — Supply Chain, Flex Ltd.; Marc N. Casper, President and CEO, Thermo Fisher Scientific; Steve Chillscyzn, Vice President of Technology Development, Stratasys; Rick Chin, VP, Software Development, Desktop Metal; Phillipe Clerc, Senior Advisor, Global Competitive Intelligence, France; Chuck Conley, Director of Product Marketing, Jabil; Mark Cotteleer, Research Director, Deloitte Services LP; S. Scott Crump, Cofounder, Chief Innovation Officer, Stratasys; Lionel Theodore Dean, Creative Director, Future Factory; Jeff DeGrange, Vice President, Stratasys; Tim DeRosett, Director of Additive Manufacturing, Jabil; John Dulchinos, Vice President, Global Automation and 3D Printing, Jabil; Patrick Dunne, Director — Industrial Applications Development, 3D Systems; Bruce Engelmann, CTO of SIMULIA, Dassault Systems; Roger England, Director — Materials Science Technology, Cummins Engine; David N. Farr, Chairman and CEO, Emerson Electric; Mike Follingstad, Director of Engineering, Tyco Electronic Connectivity; Vincent Forlenza, then Chairman and CEO, Becton, Dickinson and Company; Ric Fulop, CEO, Desktop Metal; Christine Furtoss, VP — GE Additive Engineering and Technology, GE Additive; Eugene Giller, Founder and CTO and current CEO, Rize, Inc.; Tamar Giloh, CEO, Tamicare; Rick Goings, Chairman and CEO, Tupperware Brands; Greg Goff, then CEO, Tesoro; Noel Hartzell, Head of Communications — HP 3D Printing, HP, Inc.; Robert Hauck, Chief Mechanical Engineer, GE Healthcare; Eric Hoch, EVP and CEO of Jabil Digital Solutions, Jabil; Don Hnatyshin, SVP and Chief Supply Chain and Procurement Officer, Jabil; Mike P. Huseby, Chairman and CEO, Barnes & Noble Education, Inc.; Pablo Isla, CEO, Inditex, parent company to Zara; Karen W. Katz, CEO, Neiman Marcus; John Kawola former CEO of Zcorp and current CEO of Ultimaker USA; Michael Kelly; Design Engineer, Desktop Metal; David Kempskie, President, AET Labs, a Stratasys reseller; Kevin J. Kennedy, President and CEO, Avaya; Dave King, Chairman and CEO, Laboratory Corporation of America; Cathy Lewis, then CMO, 3D Systems; Peter Leys, Executive Chairman, Materialise NV; Tom Lineberger, CEO, Cummins Engine; Ellen M. Lord, then CEO of Textron [Military] Systems, Inc., and current Under Secretary of Defense for Acquisition, Technology and Logistics; John Lundgren, then Chairman and CEO, Stanley Black & Decker; David MacLennan, Chairman and CEO, Cargill; Chris L. Mapes, Chairman and CEO, Lincoln Electric; Frank Marangell, then CEO, Rize, Inc., and current President-USA, BigRep GmbH; Christine McDermott, Chief Marketing Officer — Jabil Packaging Solutions, Jabil; Pat McHale, President and CEO, Graco, Inc. (the conglomerate, not the baby products company); Marc Minor, VP Marketing, Desktop Metal; Michelle Mooradian, Director — Global Strategy, Under Armour; Steve Nigro, President — 3D Printing, HP, Inc.; Daniel Oliver, Cofounder and Hardware Lead, Voxel8; Jim Orrock, VP — Materials Development, Stratasys; A. J. Perez, then CEO, NVBots, now acquired by Cincinnati, Inc.; Thomas Quinlan III, then Chairman and CEO, RR Donnelly and current CEO of LSC Communications, Inc.; Dr. Phil Reeves, VP — Strategic Consulting and Managing Director, Stratasys/Econolyst; Avi Reichental, then CEO, 3D Systems; Joe Ripp, then CEO, Time, Inc.; Andy Roberts, Senior Software Engineer, Desktop Metal; Jason Roth, Corporate Communications and Editorial Strategy, 3D Printing Business, HP, Inc.; Scott Schiller, VP — Global Head of Market Development, HP Inc.; Peter Schmitt, Chief Designer, Desktop Metal; Rick Smith, then CEO, Equifax; Maltesh Somasekharappa, Head of Advanced Manufacturing Solutions, Wipro Infrastructure Engineering, Wipro; Eric A. Spiegel, then President and CEO, Siemens USA; Mike H. Thaman, Chairman and CEO, Owens-Corning; Nigel Travis, CEO, Dunkin Brands; Cory Weber, Cofounder, Forecast 3D (a 3D printing service bureau); Donovan Weber, Cofounder, Forecast 3D (a 3D printing service bureau); Sunny Webb, Sr. R&D Principal, Accenture; Albert Wenger, Partner, Union Square Ventures, an early investor in Shapeways; David Whimpenny, Chief Technologist, Manufacturing Technology Center, UK; Meg Whitman, then CEO, Hewlett Packard, Inc., and current CEO, Hewlett Packard Enterprise; Scott Wine, Chairman and CEO, Polaris. Thank you all for sharing your insights and opinions with me or my team about the future of business strategy in light of the revolution in software, industrial platforms and the industrial internet, and, if relevant, additive manufacturing. All your ideas contributed in one way or another to this book.

Numerous technical experts shared their expertise, ideas, presentations, slides, speeches, papers, or personal notes and blogs with me or my team. I thank them for their willingness to open up a new world for me. Without what they taught me, I would not be able to understand the additive and industrial world as it exists today, let alone what it will become in the future.

Other than a few people who wish to remain secret, the experts were Christopher Amato, Post-Doctoral Associate, MIT CSAIL (Computer Science & Artificial Intelligence Lab); Jimmie Beacham, Advanced Manufacturing Leader, GE Healthcare; Tim Bell, VP of Business Development/General Manager, BeAM Machines; Ilko Bosman, Manager of Finance and IT at Additive Industries; Valerie Buckingham, VP — Marketing, Carbon; Tim Caffrey, former Senior Consultant at Wohlers Associates and current Director of Engineering and Marketing at NWA3D LLC; Dan Campbell, Advanced Aircraft Design Tech Lead, Aurora Flight Services; Gregory George, Product Specialist, 3D Systems; Antoni S. Gozdz, Chief Scientist, MarkForged; John Hart, Associate Professor of Mechanical Engineering, MIT, and cofounder of Desktop Metal; Dr. Martin Hedge, Optomec's EU Representative, and Managing Director, Neotech AMT GmbH; Fred Herman, Manager — Engineering and Technical Services, Shepra, Inc.; Johan von Herwarth, Head of International Sales, Big Rep; Neil Hopkinson, Professor of Manufacturing Engineering, Sheffield University and Director of 3D Printing at Xaar, Plc.; Jim Joyce, Specialist Leader — Manufacturing, Strategy and Operations, Deloitte Consulting LLP; Alexander Lahaye, Sales and Marketing Director, Addup Solutions, a partner of Michelin Tires; David Lakatos, Chief Product Officer, Formlabs; Bart Leferink, Director-Global Channel Sales at Additive Industries, and former Channel Director at Prodways; Jared K. Lee, Watson Business Development, IBM; Leonard Lee, Chief of Staff and Special Projects, Office of the Senior Vice President for Cognitive Solutions and IBM Research, IBM; Haim Levi, VP of Manufacturing and Defense Markets, XJet, Ltd.; Brett Lyons, Materials and Process Research Engineer, Boeing; Cindy Mannevy, Marketing and Communications Manager, Prodways; Eric Maslowski, Technical Creative Consultant, University of Michigan; Padraig Moloney, Senior Scientist and Program Manager, Lockheed Martin; Dave May, Technical Account Manager and Solutions Engineer, Autodesk; Shannon Morgan, Enterprise Sales Specialist for the new HP Multi Jet Fusion Voxel 3D Printer, HP, Inc.; Jeff Mundt, Senior Marketing Manager — New Technology, Hershey; Hou T. Ng, Research Manager/Principal Scientist, HP, Inc.; Shawn O'Grady, Digital Fabrication Specialist, University of Michigan; Keiichi Onishi, Business Development, Yamaha Motors, Japan; Martin Pomykala, Big Data and Analytics Software, IBM; Gary Rowe, Customer Development, Formlabs; Ken Vartanian, VP Marketing, Optomec; Matthias Wahl, Managing Director, EvoBeam, Sciaky's European partner; Jiani Zhang, Program Director of Offering Management, IBM Watson IoT for Manufacturing, IBM. It was like drinking from a firehose at first, but thank you for the tutoring and technological insights. I'm the most hydrated guy on the block.

To help me make sense of what I learned, I hired several research assistants that provided invaluable, deeper investigations. Three research assistants took the lead in my education concerning additive manufacturing: Carmen Linares, an MBA student with a technical background, and two engineering students working on their MEM degrees, Yihan Zhong and Zixiang (Sean) Xuan. They did a deep dive on the various additive technologies used in standard 3D printers, explaining them to me at a time when I was just a beginner. Marcus Widell, an MBA with a technical and entrepreneurial startup orientation, went into the details of exotic printing methods, such as bioprinting, DNA-based printing, and other new methods that were very surprising. Marcus's job was to shock me into thinking out of the box, with strategies and technologies I could not imagine existed. All in all, this was a multiyear effort dedicated to finding patterns and principles I could use to project the future based on the facts on the ground.

Looking deeper into the business trends, I put Bo Wang, an MEM student, to work on detailed analyses to see how far additive manufacturing had spread in many industries. This work became the basis for Nihal's tables in Chapter 12. Bo also did quite a bit of work on the four phases of adoption. Rémy Olson, an MBA student, took a look at different kinds of business ecosystems that had been built in Asia, including *chaebols* and *keiretsu,* that might point the way to what pan-industrial firms and collectives will look like and how they might be constrained by governments so that they don't become threats to democracy and capitalism. The MBA candidate Alice Demmerle looked for examples for how 3D printers were deployed and what methods caused the least disruption of established firms. Sastry Nittala, another MBA candidate with intimate knowledge of supply chain management, worked hard on identifying business models and supply chain solutions that we might be likely to see in markets with increasing turbulence, such as frequent changes in demand conditions as well as fragmentation and volatility that would require manufacturers to be very flexible and fast. These studies were eye-openers, and the results revealed many insights into how different the world of the future will be.

Turning to the softer side, I also worked with several research assistants who understood the software world. Sprague Brodie, an MBA student, looked at business process management software, and how intelligent bots, data analytics, and artificial intelligence might be used to prevent bottlenecks, boost efficiency, and create systems that were capable of reprogramming themselves. A friend of mine, Dr. Silvia Vianello, who is a Fellow of Marketing and Sales at SDA Bocconi School of Management in Milan, continued the work on artificial intelligence by identifying smart mobile apps from the B2C and C2C worlds that could be used as business tools if modified for use in a B2B setting. And my research assistant and MEM student Ankit Gadodia followed this up with deeper study of artificial intelligence programs so we could understand what limitations would be imposed by industrial platforms and common business apps using neural nets. My research assistant Coby Ma, an MBA student coming out of the software world, dug deep into the different types of software being used before the creation of industrial platforms, as well as worked on figuring out the capabilities of various software producers so we could predict who would be the likely contenders in the industrial platform market. Raghav Mathur, another research assistant and MEM student, continued along these lines with an initial attempt to figure out what the industrial platform of the future might look like if we pulled all the business apps together in one integrated, data-sharing, enterprise-wide system. I thank and appreciate all the information and wisdom they gathered and synthesized under my direction. Your efforts have influenced my thinking in profound ways. I am not the same strategist as I was before I started this research process.

I also want to thank my sleuths, my army of information hunter-gatherers and myth-busters. These were my research assistants who were assigned to look for and to hunt down specific information about companies' and their rivals' use of platforms and additive manufacturing for the examples used in this book. They were told to scour the earth and the Internet heavens to find out what companies were not telling us. They were assigned to cold call companies and speak to lower-level employees; to talk to a company's customers, suppliers, and competitors to see what the company had under its fingernails; to check GlassDoor.com to see what was going on inside the company; and to check local newspapers and online recruiting websites to see what the locals knew that the world did not.

The sleuths were authorized to use any legal and ethical source or legal method. The sleuths didn't use false pretenses or hacking. Of course, we did not ask anyone to dirty up their Ivy League suits by dumpster diving. I insisted that they just keep looking and asking until someone spilled the beans. My sleuths included undergraduates, MBA and MEM candidates, students' spouses, former loan collectors, and even one former FBI agent and one former military intelligence officer (who both wanted to remain anonymous). My sleuths included Neerja Bakshi, Erin Czerwinski, Emily Davies, Ashwin Gargeya, Debasreeta (Tia) Dutta Gupta, Robert Harrison, Neil Kamath, Addison Lee, Jeff Shu Lee, Andrew Liang, Huajing (Joyce) Lin, Roger Lu, Minyue (Mindy) Luo, Hamish McEwan, Parag Patil, Sarah Rood, Daniel Schafer, Aditi Srinivasan, Nelson (Chenyi) Wang, Bradley Webb, John Wheelock, Andrew Wong, and Michael (Zheyang) Xie. They did a great job at uncovering the truth, even though the industry was determined to keep a lot of information secret for competitive purposes or out of fear of negative customer or worker reactions in the early days of the rise of additive manufacturing.

I was also highly influenced by the ideas of numerous industry experts: Clara Asmail, Senior Technical Advisor, NIST; Moataz Atallah, Professor of Advanced Materials Processing, University of Birmingham; Vincent Barlier, Research Engineer, Plastic Logic; Carl Bass, former CEO, Autodesk; Francis Bitonti, President and Founder, Francis Bitonti Studio; David Breitgand, Senior Researcher, IBM; Damien Buchbinder, Team Leader — Advanced SLM Systems, Rapid Manufacturing Group, Fraunhofer ILT; Neil Burns, Director, Croft Filters Ltd.; Richard Buswell, Senior Lecturer, Building Energy Research Group, Loughborough University; Dan Campbell, Program Manager, Aurora Flight Services; Philippe Cochet, Executive Vice President, GE Aviation; John Collins, member of the BSI AMT8 Standards Committee, British Standards Institute; Xavier De Kestelier, Partner, Specialist Modelling Group, Foster + Partners; Dan Dempsey, Senior Design Engineer, New Balance; Phill Dickens, Professor of Manufacturing Technology, University of Nottingham; Gaffar Gailani, Assistant Professor, NYC College of Technology; Rob Gorham, Director of Operations, America Makes; Tim Gornet, Manager, Rapid Prototyping Center Operations, Louisville University; Edith Harmon, VP of Advanced Products, New Balance; James Heppelmann, President and CEO, PTC; Jonathan Hollahan, Vice President Engineering, Xact Metal; Mary Huang, Founder and Design Lead, Continuum Fashion; Josh Jacobson, CEO, Viktorian Guitars; Suchit Jain, Vice President of Strategy and Business Development, Dassault Systems SolidWorks Corp.; Andy Jensen, Director of Sales & Operations, Concept Laser; Vyomesh Joshi, CEO, 3D Systems; Roger Kelesoglu, Director of Sales Enablement, Stratasys; Harry Kleijnen, Manager-Development and Engineering Grids, Smit Rontgen, Philips Healthcare; Rainer Koch, Head of Mechanical Engineering Department, University of Paderborn; James L. Zunino III, Materials Engineer, U.S. Army ARDEC; Daniel Leong, Content Engineer, Markforged; Nancy Liang, Cofounder and Business Lead, Mixee Labs; Max Lobovsky, CEO, Formlabs; Brett Lyons, Materials and Process Research Engineer, Boeing; Gerd Manz, Vice President Technology Innovation, Adidas Group; Filomeno Martina, Research Fellow in Additive Manufacturing, Cranfield University; Mickey McManus, Chairman — MAYA and Research Fellow, Autodesk; Piet Meijs, Associate Partner, Reitveld Architects; Dwight Morgan, VP of Robotics and Motion, ABB; Greg Morris, Additive Technologies Leader, GE Aviation; Kyle Nel, Founder and Executive Director, Lowe's Innovation Labs; Pieter Nujits, Director OEM Grids, Tubes and Components, Smit Rontgen, Philips Healthcare; Bryan Oknyansky, Founder, Shoes by Bryan; Ajay Purohit, Technical Chief—Rapid Prototypes and Craftsmanship Tools, Tata Motors; David Saint John, Postdoctoral Researcher/Instructor, Penn State University; Kegan Schouwenburg, then CEO and Cofounder, Sols Systems; Ralf Schwenger, R&D Director, HEAD Sports; Sarah Sclarsic, Business Director, Modern Meadow; Nicola Searle, Economic Advisor, UK Intellectual Property Office; Matt Shockey, Executive Director of Operations, Addup Solutions; Sam Stacey, Head of Innovation, Loughborough University; Pete Stephens, Director of Program Management, Local Motors; Graham Tromans, Owner and Principal Industry Consultant, GP Tromans Associates; Fried Vancraen, Founder and CEO, Materialise; Hans Vandezande, Head of Business Development, Materialise; Len Wanger, Chief Technology Manager, Impossible Objects; and Robin Wilson, Head of Manufacturing, Innovate UK. Thank you for sharing your ideas in private forums, conferences, and other interactive venues. Your thoughts inspired me.

Ultimately, one's family is the real reason for life. I want to thank my children and their spouses, Ross, Gina, Tanya, Pete, and Chris. Thank you for your support and understanding. It pains me to know that my research and writing takes me away from you, but I am thankful for your lack of selfishness in allowing me to do this time-consuming work. And I thank you for coming all the way to London for the Thinkers50 Gala, where I won the 2017 biannual Strategy Award and was ranked among the top ten management thinkers in the world. The honors would have meant nothing without your presence. Your support and love means everything to me. And I have to give you the biggest thanks for making me happy and inspiring me to write every day. The deeper your support and acceptance, the freer I am to peer further into the future and come up with books like this one.

It may take a village to raise a child, but it takes hard work, a family, an army of detectives, researchers, and editors, as well as a large information ecosystem, to write a book.

# NOTES

## Prologue: *Hidden Clues to a Coming Upheaval*

page

x    Sarah Anderson Goehrke, "HP Keeps Focus on Industrial 3D Printing with Introduction of Jet Fusion 3D 4210 and Expansion of Materials Portfolio, Partnerships," 3DPrint.com, November 9, 2017, https://3dprint.com/193672/hp-jet-fusion-4210.

     Sarah Anderson Goehrke, "HP Announces Lower-Cost Full-Color 3D Printing Systems, SOLIDWORKS Collaboration," 3DPrint.com, February 5, 2018, https://3dprint.com/202546/hp-full-color-3d-printers-dassault.

xii   Alex Bell, "3D Knickers Firm to Create 300 Jobs," *Manchester Evening News,* May 28, 2014, http://www.manchestereveningnews.co.uk/business/tamicare-based-heywood-manchester-says-7177952.

xv   See, for example, Tomas Kellner, "An Epiphany of Disruption: GE Additive Chief Explains How 3D Printing Will Upend Manufacturing," GE Reports website, June 21, 2017, https://www.ge.com/reports/epiphany-disruption-ge-additive-chief-explains-3d-printing-will-upend-manufacturing.

xvi  Alwyn Scott, "GE Shifts Strategy, Financial Targets for Digital Business After Missteps," Reuters, August 24, 2017, https://www.reuters.com/article/us-ge-digital-outlook-insight/ge-shifts-strategy-financial-targets-for-digital-business-after-missteps-idUSKCN1B80CB.

xvii See, for example, Klaus Schwab, *The Fourth Industrial Revolution* (New York: Crown, 2017).

## 1. The Shape of Things to Come

3    Matthew Ponsford and Nick Glass, "'The Night I Invented 3D Printing,'" CNN, February 14, 2014, http://www.cnn.com/2014/02/13/tech/innovation/the-night-i-invented-3d-printing-chuck-hall/index.html.

Matthew Sparkes, "'We Laughed, We Cried, We Stayed Up All Night Imagining,'" *The Telegraph,* June 18, 2014, http://www.telegraph.co.uk/ technology/news/10908560/We-laughed-we-cried-we-stayed-up-all-night-imagining.html.

8   Rakesh Sharma, "The 3D Printing Revolution You Have Not Heard About," *Forbes,* July 8, 2013, https://www.forbes.com/sites/rakesh-sharma/2013/07/08/the-3d-printing-revolution-you-have-not-heard-about/#22e6f98c1a6b.

9   Jay Leno, "Jay Leno's 3D Printer Replaces Rusty Old Parts," *Popular Mechanic,* June 7, 2009, http://www.popularmechanics.com/cars/ a4354/4320759.

10   Ezra Dyer, "The World's First 3D-Printed Car Is a Blast to Drive," *Popular Mechanics,* August 7, 2015, http://www.popularmechanics.com/cars/ a16726/local-motors-strati-roadster-test-drive.
    Aaron M. Kessler, "A 3-D Printed Car, Ready for the Road," *New York Times,* January 15, 2015, https://www.nytimes.com/2015/01/16/business/a-3-d-printed-car-ready-for-the-road.html.

12   Duleesha Kulasooriya, "Local Motors: Driving Innovation with Micro-Manufacturing," *NewCo Shift,* October 12, 2016, https://shift.newco.co/lo cal-motors-driving-innovation-with-micro-manufacturing-a6630ecd2151.
    Keith Larson, "The Smart Industry 50: Automotive Disruptor," *Smart Industry,* July 14, 2017, https://www.smartindustry.com/articles/2017/the-smart-industry-50.

13   Beau Jackson, "3D Printing Helps Rolls-Royce Sell Record Number of Cars," January 16, 2017, https://3dprintingindustry.com/news/3d-printing-helps-rolls-royce-sell-record-number-of-cars-103353.
    Nick Hall, "Top 10 3D Printed Automotive Industry Innovations Available Right Now," June 20, 2016, https://3dprintingindustry.com/news/3d-printing-automotive-industry-2-82838.
    Jeff Kerns, "How 3D Printing Is Changing Auto Manufacturing," *Machine Design,* November 14, 2016, http://www.machinedesign.com/3d-printing/ how-3d-printing-changing-auto-manufacturing.

14   "Ford Smart Mobility LLC Established to Develop, Invest in Mobility Services; Jim Hackett Named Subsidiary Chairman," Ford Motor Company Media Center, March 11, 2016, https://media.ford.com/content/fordmedia/ fna/us/en/news/2016/03/11/ford-smart-mobility-llc-established — jim-hackett-named-chairman.html#sthash.cqxV7isc.dpuf.
    Corey Clarke, "Ford Thinking Laterally with Stratasys' Infinite Build 3D Printing Machine," *3D Printing Industry,* March 6, 2017, https://3dprintingindustry.com/news/ford-thinking-laterally-stratasys-infinite-build-3d-printing-machine-107273/?utm_source=email&utm_ medium=social&utm_campaign=social-pug.

15    Nick Hall, "Chinese Company Prints Villa On-Site," *3D Printing Industry,* June 15, 2016, https://3dprintingindustry.com/news/chinese-company-prints-villa-site-82528.

16    Lloyd Alter, "Office of the Future Is 3D Printed in Dubai," *Treehugger* newsletter, May 31, 2016, https://www.treehugger.com/green-architecture/office-future-3d-printed-dubai.html.

17    A. T. Kearney, *3D Printing: A Manufacturing Revolution,* https://www.atkearney.com/documents/10192/5992684/3D+Printing+A+Manufacturing+Revolution.pdf/bf8f5c00-69c4-4909-858a-423e3b94bba3.

18    Interview with Ric Fulop, 8/2/2017.
Alec [sic], "GE Builds 3D Printing Factory in Prague, to 3D Print Engine Parts for Next-Gen Cessna Denali," 3Ders.org, October 21, 2016, http://www.3ders.org/articles/20161021-ge-builds-3d-printing-factory-in-prague-to-3d-print-engine-parts-for-next-gen-cessna-denali.html.

19    Thanks to my research assistant Nihal Velpanur, who summarized the information appearing in Table 1-2, and thanks to Carmen Linares, Sean Xuan, and Yihan Zhong for collecting, writing up, and organizing the information about the various 3D printing technologies in this table.

22    Sarah Anderson Goehrke, "HP Keeps Focus on Industrial 3D Printing," *op.cit.*
Alessandro Di Fiore, "3D Printing Gives Hackers Entirely New Ways to Wreak Havoc," *Harvard Business Review,* October 25, 2017, https://hbr.org/2017/10/3d-printing-gives-hackers-entirely-new-ways-to-wreak-havoc.

23    Alice Morby, "MIT Researchers Develop Material That Tightens in Cold Weather to Keep in Warmth," *de zeen,* February 27, 2017, https://www.dezeen.com/2017/02/27/mit-researchers-auxetic-material-tightens-cold-weather-keep-warmth-design-technology.

24    Chelsea Gohd, "NASA Astronauts Can Now 3D-Print Pizzas in Space," *Futurism,* March 7, 2017, https://futurism.com/nasa-astronauts-can-now-3d-print-pizzas-in-space.

25    Laura Parker, "3D-Printed Reefs Offers Hope in Coral Bleaching Crisis," *National Geographic,* March 13, 2017, http://news.nationalgeographic.com/2017/03/3d-printed-reefs-coral-bleaching-climate.

## 2. Expanded Scope

29    See, for example, Mark Albert, "Setup Reduction: At the Heart of Lean Manufacturing," *Modern Machine Shop,* April 2, 2004, http://www.mmsonline.com/articles/setup-reduction-at-the-heart-of-lean-manufacturing.
Beau Jackson, "Premium Aerotec, EOS and Daimler Prepare Next-Gen Serial Production for 3D Printing," *3D Printing Industry,* April 19,

2017, https://3dprintingindustry.com/news/premium-aerotec-eos-daim ler-prepare-nextgen-serial-production-3d-printing-111151.

30  Sabrina Theseira, "Emerson Opens Additive Manufacturing Plant in Clementi," *Straits Times,* March 25, 2017, http://www.straitstimes.com/ business/emerson-opens-additive-manufacturing-plant-in-clementi.

Clare Scott, "Thyssenkrupp Opens New TechCenter Additive Manufac- turing in Germany," 3Dprint.com, September 5, 2017, https://3dprint. com/186520/thyssenkrupp-techcenter-am.

"GE Aviation Opens New Brilliant Factory," *GE Aviation Press Center,* May 1, 2017, https://www.geaviation.com/press-release/other-news-infor mation/ge-aviation-opens-new-brilliant-factory.

"Metric of the Month: Unplanned Machine Downtime as a Percentage of Scheduled Run Time," *Supply and Demand Chain Executive,* August 18, 2015, http://www.sdcexec.com/article/12104593/metric-of-the-month- unplanned-machine-downtime-as-a-percentage-of-scheduled-run-time.

40  Sam Davies, "Formlabs Announces Fuse 1 SLS 3D Printer and Form Cell Automated Production System," *tct Magazine,* June 5, 2017, https:// www.tctmagazine.com/3d-printing-news/formlabs-fuse-1-sls-3d-printer- form-cell-automated-production.

41  Peter Zelinsky, "With Machine Learning, We Will Skip Ahead 100 Years," *Additive Manufacturing,* January 17, 2018, https://www.additive- manufacturing.media/columns/with-machine-learning-we-will-skip- ahead-100-years.

## 3. Boundless Scale

45  Matthias Holweg, "The Limits of 3D Printing," *Harvard Business Re- view,* June 23, 2015, https://hbr.org/2015/06/the-limits-of-3d-printing.

46  Thanks to my research assistant Nihal Velpanur, who created this fig- ure.

48  Beau Jackson, "Voodoo Manufacturing Aim for a 24/7 3D Printing Factory with Robot-Arm Powered Project Skywalker," March 15, 2017, https://3dprintingindustry.com/news/voodoo-manufacturing-aim-247-3d- printing-factory-robot-arm-powered-project-skywalker-108157.

52  A. T. Kearney, *3D Printing: A Manufacturing Revolution.*

53  Thanks to my research assistant Nihal Velpanur, who created this fig- ure.

57  My thanks to John Landry and Steve Prokesh, whose research and ideas helped to shape the presentation of business models that appears here.

59  *Smart Textiles and Wearables: Markets, Applications and Technologies,* Cientifica Research, September 2016, http://www.cientifica.com/research/

market-reports/smart-textiles-wearables-markets-applications-technolo
gies.

62  "JOLED Starts Commercial Shipments of Its Printed 21.6-Inch 4K
OLED Monitor Panels," OLED-info website, December 5, 2017, https://
www.oled-info.com/joled-starts-commercial-shipments-its-printed-
216-4k-oled-monitor-panels.

65  Corey Clarke, "Adidas Reveals Plans for 3D Printing 'Speedfactory,'"
January 17, 2017, https://3dprintingindustry.com/news/adidas-reveals-
plans-3d-printing-speedfactory-103519.
Ben Roazen, "An Explanation of Adidas' SPEEDFACTORY Facility,"
October 5, 2016, https://hypebeast.com/2016/10/adidas-speedfactory-
futurecraft-interview-ben-herath.

## 4. The Power of Industrial Platforms

71  Loretta Chao, "Jabil Enters Supply-Chain Software Business," *Wall
Street Journal*, October 25, 2016, https://www.wsj.com/articles/jabil-en
ters-supply-chain-software-business-1477403026.
Interview with the author, June 2, 2017.

74  Sarah Anderson Goehrke, "First Production HP Jet Fusion 3D Printers in North America Delivered — A Few Questions for Jabil," 3DPrint.com,
December 9, 2016, https://3dprint.com/158297/a-few-questions-for-jabil.

78  Brian Walker, "Why E-Commerce Still Isn't Clicking with B2B
Executives," *Forbes,* May 6, 2014, https://www.forbes.com/sites/bri
anwalker/2014/05/06/why-e-commerce-still-isnt-clicking-with-b2b-
executives/#4e0637d16ef4.

87  Jacques Bughin, Laura LaBerge, and Anette Melbye, "The Case for Digital Reinvention," *McKinsey Quarterly,* February 2017, https://www.mckin
sey.com/business-functions/digital-mckinsey/our-insights/the-case-for-
digital-reinvention?cid=other-eml-ttn-mkq-mck-oth-1712.

## 5. Coding the Future

91  Michael Maiello, "Diagnosing William Baumol's Cost Disease," *Chicago Booth Review,* May 18, 2017, http://review.chicagobooth.edu/econom
ics/2017/article/diagnosing-william-baumol-s-cost-disease.

92  Gideon Lichfield, "Cement Plus Heavy-Duty Networking Equals Big
Profits," *Wired,* July 1, 2002, https://www.wired.com/2002/07/cemex.

98  Thanks to John Landry for his help in developing this table.

100 Andreas Saar, "Siemens Continues Driving Toward Our Vision to
Industrialize Additive Manufacturing," Siemens Dreamer website, Sep-

tember 6, 2017, https://community.plm.automation.siemens.com/t5/
News-NX-Manufacturing/Siemens-continues-driving-toward-our-vision-
to-industrialize/ba-p/430769.

101 Sarah Anderson Goehrke, "HP and Deloitte: Allies in 3D Print-
ing-Led Disruption to Manufacturing," 3DPrint.com, August 24, 2017,
https://3dprint.com/185261/hp-deloitte-alliance.

Watson Internet of Things website, https://www.ibm.com/internet-of-
things/iot-solutions/iot-manufacturing.

Corey Clarke, "UTC Announces $75 Million Additive Manu-
facturing Center of Excellence," 3D Printing Industry, June 5, 2017,
https://3dprintingindustry.com/news/utc-announces-75-million-additive-
manufacturing-center-excellence-115071.

Corey Clarke, "Dassault Systèmes Expanding 3DExperience
Lab to North America," 3D Printing Industry, February 7, 2017,
https://3dprintingindustry.com/news/dassault-systemes-expanding-3dex
perience-lab-north-america-105191.

102 Beau Jackson, "Sumitomo Heavy Industry Acquires Spray-Form Metal 3D Printing Startup," 3D Printing Industry, January April 18, 2017,
https://3dprintingindustry.com/news/sumitomo-heavy-industries-ac
quires-spray-form-metal-3d-printing-startup-111108.

Beau Jackson, "Carbon Become 'Future-Proof' with Oracle Cloud," 3D
Printing Industry, January 13, 2017, https://3dprintingindustry.com/news/
carbon-become-future-proof-with-oracle-cloud-103236.

103 Michael Petch, "GKN and GE Additive Sign MOU for Additive
Manufacturing Collaboration," 3D Printing Industry, October 17, 2017,
https://3dprintingindustry.com/news/gkn-ge-additive-sign-mou-additive-
manufacturing-collaboration-122869/; Sarah Saunders, "GKN Group Con-
solidates All Additive Manufacturing Activities Into New Company Brand,"
3DPrint.com, October 16, 2017, https://3dprint.com/191040/gkn-additive-
new-company-brand.

Alec [sic], "UPS to Expand 3D Printing Services to Asia and Europe
in Response to Storage Revenue Loss Caused by 3D Printing," 3Ders.org,
September 19, 2016, http://www.3ders.org/articles/20160919-ups-to-ex
pand-3d-printing-services-in-response-to-storage-revenue-loss-caused-
by-3d-printing.html; Nick Carey, "Sensing threat, UPS plans to expand its
3D printing operations," Reuters, September 16, 2016, https://www.reuters.
com/article/us-united-parcel-3dprint/sensing-threat-ups-plans-to-ex
pand-its-3d-printing-operations-idUSKCN11M2AL.

104 Clare Scott, "SAP Announces Official Launch of SAP Distributed
Manufacturing 3D Printing Application," 3DPrint.com, April 24, 2017,
https://3dprint.com/172182/sap-distributed-manufacturing.

Beau Jackson, "FedEx Launches 3D Printing Inventory and Repair

Company Forward Depots," *3D Printing Industry,* January 25, 2018, https://3dprintingindustry.com/news/fedex-3d-printing-forward-depots-inventory-repair-supply-chain-127980.

106 Two notable examples: Scott Galloway, *The Four: The Hidden DNA of Amazon, Apple, Facebook, and Google* (New York: Portfolio, 2017), and Franklin Foer, *World Without Mind: The Existential Threat of Big Tech* (New York: Penguin, 2017).

## 6. The Triumph of Bigness

112 Kevin Dowd and Martin Hutchinson, *Alchemists of Loss: How Modern Finance and Government Intervention Crashed The Financial System* (New York: Wiley, 2010), p. 150.

114 Edward J. Lopez, "Breaking Up Antitrust," Foundation for Economic Education, January 1, 1997, https://fee.org/articles/breaking-up -antitrust.

116 Andrew Ross Sorkin, "Conglomerates Didn't Die. They Look Like Amazon," *New York Times,* June 19, 2017.

117 Some of the following content is adapted from Richard D'Aveni, "Choosing Scope over Focus," *Sloan Management Review,* Summer 2017, http://sloanreview.mit.edu/article/the-end-of-focus-a-new-wave-of-man ufacturers-will-choose-scope-over-scale.

118 Lee Schafer, "Cargill takes the long view on strategy," *Minneapolis Star-Tribune,* April 13, 2013, http://www.startribune.com/schafer-cargill-takes-the-long-view-on-strategy/202747911.

125 George P. Baker, "Beatrice: A Study in the Creation and Destruction of Value," *Journal of Finance,* July 1992, http://ecsocman.hse.ru/data/831/126/1231/baker_-_beatrice_history_case.pdf.

## 7. New Players

154 Steve Cropper and Mark Ebers, *The Oxford Handbook of Inter-Organizational Relations* (Oxford: Oxford University Press, 2008), pp. 36–38.

161 Robert L. Cutts, "Capitalism in Japan: Cartels and Keiretsu," *Harvard Business Review,* July–August 1992.

## 8. New Markets

164 Stephen Jay Gould and Niles Eldredge, "Punctuated Equilibria: The Tempo and Mode of Evolution Reconsidered," *Paleobiology* 3, no. 2 (Spring 1977): 115–51.

168 Christopher Mims, "Amazon Is Leading Tech's Takeover of America," *Wall Street Journal,* June 16, 2017.

175 The following section is adapted from *Dear CEO,* edited by Des Dear-love and Stuart Crainer. Thanks to John Landry for his help.

## 9. New Rules

183 See David B. Yoffie and Michael A. Cusumano, "Judo Strategy: The Competitive Dynamics of Internet Time," *Harvard Business Review,* January–February 1999.

184 Thanks to Prince Verma, Neerja Bakshi, and John Landry, who provided valuable ideas and data that have informed the following discussion of the machine wars and the platform wars.

187 Interview by the author with S. Scott Crump, August 12, 2014.

190 Daniel Gross, "Siemens CEO Joe Kaeser on the Next Industrial Revolution."
Sarah Anderson Goehrke, "Metal 3D Printing with Machine Learning: GE Tells Us About Smarter Additive Manufacturing," 3DPrint.com, October 24, 2017, https://3dprint.com/191973/3d-printing-machine-learning-ge.

## 10. New World Order

196 "First Unmanned Factory Takes Shape in Dongguan City," *People's Daily Online,* July 15, 2015, http://en.people.cn/n/2015/0715/c90000-8920747.html.

197 Erick Wolf, "3D Printing, The Next Five Years," *3D Printing Industry,* May 30, 2017.

198 Mike Lewis et al., "Deal or no deal? Training AI bots to negotiate," Facebook Code website, June 14, 2017, https://code.facebook.com/posts/1686672014972296/deal-or-no-deal-training-ai-bots-to-negotiate/; Mark Wilson, "AI Is Inventing Languages Humans Can't Understand. Should We Stop It?" Co.Design website, July 14, 2017, https://www.fastcodesign.com/90132632/ai-is-inventing-its-own-perfect-languages-should-we-let-it.

199 Daniel Gross, "Siemens CEO Joe Kaeser on the Next Industrial Revolution," *Strategy + Business,* February 9, 2016.
Ron French, "Local Motors Goes Global," *Siemens,* January 5, 2015, https://www.siemens.com/customer-magazine/en/home/industry/manufacturing-industry/local-motors-goes-global.html.
Clare Scott, "Siemens Joins with Hackrod to Bring Goal of 3D Printed Self-Designing Car Closer," *3DPrintcom,* March 22, 2018, https://3dprint.com/207594/siemens-hackrod-partnership.

203 "The Third Industrial Revolution," Economist, April 21, 2012, https://www.economist.com/node/21553017.

204 Jan-Benedict Steenkamp, "The End of the Emerging Markets Model As We Know It," LinkedIn, July 24, 2017, https://www.linkedin.com/pulse/end-emerging-markets-model-we-know-jan-benedict-steenkamp.

205 Ibid.
Kai-Fu Lee, "The Real Threat of Artificial Intelligence," *New York Times,* June 24, 2017, https://www.nytimes.com/2017/06/24/opinion/sunday/artificial-intelligence-economic-inequality.html?mcubz=0&_r=0.

206 Barry Lynn, "I Criticized Google. It Got Me Fired. That's How Corporate Power Works," *Washington Post,* August 31, 2017, https://www.washingtonpost.com/news/posteverything/wp/2017/08/31/i-criticized-google-it-got-me-fired-thats-how-corporate-power-works/?hpid=hp_no-name_opinion-card-f%3Ahomepage%2Fstory&utm_term=.95d17455e2b7.

207 Also see Eric Lipton and Brooke Williams, "How Think Tanks Amplify Corporate America's Influence," *New York Times,* August 7, 2016, https://www.nytimes.com/2016/08/08/us/politics/think-tanks-research-and-corporate-lobbying.html?mcubz=0.

209 Zahra Ullah, "How Samsung Dominates South Korea's Economy," CNNTech, February 2, 2017, http://money.cnn.com/2017/02/17/technology/samsung-south-korea-daily-life/index.html.

211 Matt Rosoff, "The Idea of Using Antitrust to Break Up Tech 'Monopolies' Is Spectacularly Wrong," *CNBC Tech,* April 23, 2017, https://finance.yahoo.com/news/op-ed-idea-using-antitrust-181206699.html.

213 Tom Igoe and Catarina Mota, "A Strategist's Guide to Digital Fabrication," *Strategy + Business,* August 23, 2011, https://www.strategy-business.com/article/11307?gko=63624.

215 The following points about the environmental benefits of the manufacturing revolution were discussed in slightly different form in Richard D'Aveni, "Who Needs the Paris Climate Accord When You Have 3D Printing?" Forbes.com, August 2, 2017, https://www.forbes.com/sites/richarddaveni/2017/08/02/who-needs-the-paris-climate-accords-when-you-have-3d-printing/#79a571cf8645.

216 Michael Petch, "Using 3D Printing to Upcycle in the Circular Economy at the University of Luxembourg," *3D Printing Industry,* July 10, 2017, https://3dprintingindustry.com/news/using-3d-printing-upcycle-circular-economy-university-luxembourg-117857.

## 11. First Steps

222 "GE's Jeff Immelt on digitizing in the industrial space," McKinsey & Company interview, October 2015, http://www.mckinsey.com/business-functions/organization/our-insights/ges-jeff-immelt-on-digitizing-in-the-industrial-space.

224  See, for example, Reinhard Geissbauer, Jasper Vedse, and Stefan Schrauf, "A Strategist's Guide to Industry 4.0," *Strategy + Business*, May 9, 2016, https://www.strategy-business.com/article/A-Strategists-Guide-to-Industry-4.0?gko=7c4cf.

226  Norbert Schwieters and Bob Moritz, "10 Principles for Leading the Next Industrial Revolution," *Strategy + Business*, March 23, 2017, https://www.strategy-business.com/article/10-Principles-for-Leading-the-Next-Industrial-Revolution?gko=f73d3.

229  The analysis and data reflected in Table 11-1 were developed by my research assistants Neerja Bakshi, Prince Verma, and Nihal Valpanur, based on our assessment of the capabilities of various platforms as of the end of 2017. My thanks to them.

230  Thanks to my research assistant Prince Verma for his contributions to the following list of questions.

236  Michael Petch, "3D Printing Startup Partners with $100 Billion Global Engineering Company," *3D Printing Industry*, November 24, 2016, https://3dprintingindustry.com/news/3d-printing-startup-partners-100-billion-global-engineering-company-99498.

238  Beau Jackson, "Siemens to Enter Adidas Speedfactory Project for Custom 3D Printer Sportswear," *3D Printing Industry*, April 25, 2017, https://3dprintingindustry.com/news/siemens-enter-adidas-speedfactory-project-custom-3d-printed-sportswear-111511; "The Perfect Fit: Carbon + Adidas Collaborate to Upend Athletic Footwear," Carbon website, April 7, 2017, https://www.carbon3d.com/stories/adidas.

## 12. The Path to Tomorrow

241  Thanks to my research assistants Bo Wang and Nihal Velpanur for their contributions to Table 12-1, as well as to Coby Ma, who worked on an earlier version of the table.

247  Thanks to my research assistant Nihal Velpanur, who created Figures 12-1 through 12-7 under my supervision, and contributed to the industry analyses that accompany each of the figures. Thanks also to Bo Wang for creating the original template for these figures. Figures 12-1 through 12-7 redrawn by Kelly Dubeau Smydra and Margaret Rosewitz.

248  Monika Mahto and Brenna Sniderman, "3D Opportunity for Electronics: Additive Manufacturing Powers Up," *Deloitte Insights*, May 2, 2017, https://www2.deloitte.com/insights/us/en/focus/3d-opportunity/additive-manufacturing-3d-printed-electronics.html.

254  Steven Melendez, "The Rise of the Robots: What the Future Holds for the World's Armies," *Fast Company*, June 12, 2017, https://www.fastcompany.com/3069048/where-are-military-robots-headed.

264 Lucas Mearian, "3D Printing Is Now Entrenched at Ford," *CIO,* August 2017, https://www.cio.com/article/3214471/3d-printing/3d-printing-is-now-entrenched-at-ford.html.

265 Jacques Bughin, Laura LaBerge, and Anette Melbye, "The Case for Digital Reinvention," *McKinsey Quarterly,* February 2017, https://www.mckinsey.com/business-functions/digital-mckinsey/our-insights/the-case-for-digital-reinvention.

# INDEX

# ABOUT THE AUTHOR

Richard D'Aveni is one of the preeminent business strategists of his generation. The *Times* (London) dubbed him "the Tuck School's iconic professor" and the management guru Adrian Slywotzky called him "the Kissinger of corporate strategy." *Fortune* analogized him to Sun Tzu, saying his thinking is "a modern-day analogue to *The Art of War*, the ancient Chinese classic that is the bible of many corporate strategists." Tom Peters frequently cites D'Aveni in his speeches, saying "D'Aveni . . . offers a vision for disruption, competencies for disruption, and tactics for disruption."

For over a decade, D'Aveni has been ranked among the top fifty management thinkers in the world according to the London-based Thinkers50 as published in *the Times (London), Forbes*, CNN.com, *the Times (India),* and the *Harvard Business Review.* He is currently ranked among the top ten management thinkers in the world and was honored in 2017 with the Thinkers50's top Strategy Award.

D'Aveni is the Bakala Professor of Strategy at the Tuck School of Business at Dartmouth College, a winner of the prestigious A. T. Kearney Award for his research, and a leading strategy consultant worldwide. D'Aveni has worked over the past three decades with prominent families, multinational corporations, and major governments throughout the world to shape the strategic agenda and their responses to it. A highly sought-after speaker, D'Aveni has addressed audiences all over the world, including the World Economic Forum's Annual Summit at Davos, Switzerland, and in the French Senat in Paris. In 2018, the Women's Economic Forum in Delhi, India conferred upon D'Aveni its prestigious "2018 Visionary Thought Leader of the Decade Award." This was for his work in developing strategy for international women's rights groups in newly developing and emerging economies, primarily for an international organization called the All Ladies League, founded in India and subsequently expanded to numerous other nations.

Richard D'Aveni is the author of the global bestseller *Hypercompetition* (Simon & Schuster, 1994). His work is credited with creating a new paradigm in the field of strategy based on temporary advantages and constant disruption of rivals using rapid maneuvering rather than defensive barriers. D'Aveni is also the author of four other well-acclaimed books published by Simon & Schuster, Harvard Business Review Press, and McGraw-Hill. He has published academic studies in the *Academy of Management Journal, Administrative Quarterly, Management Science, Organization Science,* and the *Strategic Management Journal,* among many other peer-reviewed publications.

D'Aveni has published multiple articles and blogs about pan-industrialism, additive and digital manufacturing, and industrial platforms in the *Harvard Business Review,* the *MIT/Sloan Management Review,* and Forbes.com. His 2015 feature article in *Harvard Business Review,* "The 3-D Printing Revolution," was designated as the "The Big Idea Article" for the issue and included in *Harvard Business Review*'s compendium of ten must-reads for the year.

His hobbies and charities include starting business schools in interesting places (such as India, Japan, Mexico, and Vietnam), fundraising for pediatric burn victims in the USA, and fundraising for the business education of disowned girls and young women in India to prevent them from being forced into prostitution. He enjoys conversing with interesting friends and students while smoking Cuban Cohiba cigars, drinking Aranciata (a Sicilian soda made from blood oranges that yield a deep red juice), and sipping ice-cold shots of Sicilian anisette, especially on warm, sunny afternoons. He also enjoys visiting the seventeenth-century waterfront Palazzo D'Aveni in the Giardini di Naxos, near the sandy beaches of Taormina, Sicily, especially in the winter.

His mother was Swedish, his father was Sicilian, his ex-wife is Russian, his children are American. And, as D'Aveni likes to say, he's confused.